Sight Unseen

How Frémont's First Expedition
Changed the American Landscape

ANDREW MENARD

University of Nebraska Press / Lincoln and London

An adaptation of the "Eastern Kansas" section
appeared as "Striking a Line through the Great
American Desert" in *Journal of American Studies*
45, no. 2 (2011): 267–80. Copyright Cambridge
University Press, reproduced with permission.

Library of Congress
Cataloging-in-Publication Data
Menard, Andrew, 1948–
Sight unseen: how Frémont's first
expedition changed the American landscape / Andrew Menard.   p. cm.
Includes bibliographical references and index.
ISBN 978-0-8032-3807-7 (cloth: alk. paper)
1. West (U.S.)—Discovery and exploration.
2. West (U.S.)—Description and travel.
3. Land settlement—West (U.S.)—History—
19th century. 4. Frontier and pioneer
life—West (U.S.) 5. Frémont, John Charles,
1813–1890—Travel—West (U.S.) I. Title.
F592.M46 2012
978 — dc23   2012008722

Set in Garamond Premier by Kim Essman.
Designed by Nathan Putens.

To Ruth

Contents

Illustrations

Introduction

{ THE GOLDEN MEANE }

EVEN THE MOST INDIFFERENT GLANCE AT A MAP OF THE
United States ought to make it clear that our landscape has been ruled
by a compelling horizon. A nation so eager to advance was too impatient
to locate the rivers and mountains that might act as natural boundaries.
Instead, it chose to send out long lines of latitude and longitude that
would define an entity as enormous as Kansas or Wyoming and as small
as the forty-acre farm—a vast and rigorous cartographic grid that the
artist Robert Smithson once called a landscape of "interchangeable distances." To look down at this landscape from thirty-five thousand feet,
or drive mile after mile on roads that cleave straight to the horizon, is
to experience firsthand a country that was often conquered or claimed
only on maps.[1]

John Smith's *A Map of Virginia* (1612) can be seen as the prototype:
"Virginia is a Country in America that lyeth betweene the degrees of 34
and 44 of the north latitude. The bounds thereof on the East side are the
great Ocean. On the South lyeth Florida: on the North *nova Francia*.
As for the West thereof, the limits are unknowne." The "unknowne"
would be a guiding principle of American landscape, provoking endless
outbursts of fear, curiosity, and deceit and embodying the "providential"
or "manifest" destiny of one of history's great land grabs. It would be a
principle of blindness as much as ignorance, just as the landscape itself
would represent an act of expulsion as well as enclosure. Such a landscape
could be seen as anything from barren to fertile, vacant to void, pristine
to wasted.[2]

From the first landfalls, Europeans saw little more than they wanted
to see. Columbus writes of finding honey in Hispaniola, even though
honeybees are not native to the New World and there is no record of

xi

them before 1530. A map of the settlements near what is now Kittery, Maine, declares "(by Mapp) how England's strength doth lye Unseen in the *Rivers* of the New Plantations" — exactly the kind of "Mapp" that would figure so prominently in the fictions of Jorge Luis Borges and Smithson's aptly named "non-sites." Daniel Denton's *Brief Description of New-York* (1670) is only marginally less imaginary: it refers to the territory of the Hudson Valley as "a known unknown part of America" — a view that extended horizontally to those "places lying to the Northward yet undiscovered by any English" as well as vertically to the "Bowels of the earth not yet opened" to gold and silver mines. Denton's claims later foundered on the facts — just as Puritans who repeatedly invoked the image of a "land of milk and honey" had to send to England for cattle as well as bees, since they weren't native to the new land, either.[3]

A blind respect for maps was matched by an enduring faith in latitude for its own sake. It was here that those who sought to occupy the New World first showed a weakness for the idea of "geographical predestination." One of the earliest eyewitness accounts of New England, Thomas Morton's *New English Canaan* (1637), describes the supposedly benign landscape as "a golden meane betwixt two extreames." Ignoring widespread crop failure and near starvation among the first immigrants, Morton writes that God, "Creator of the universall Globe," has planted the colony in a "Zona temperata" that "doth beginne her boundes at 40. Degrees of Northern latitude, and endes at 45. Degrees of the same latitude" — where it "doth participate of heate and cold indifferently, but is oppressed with neither" and is therefore "most apt and fit for habitation and generation." Such a "golden meane" also passes through Spain, southern France, and most of Italy, but it was not yet clear that the expansive land mass of America made comparisons to European climate moot. A similar optimism led the early settlers of Carolina to believe they could duplicate the silk and olive industries of the Mediterranean and a traveler of the mid-1800s to declare that the valley of the upper Guadalupe River in Texas "has been continually reminding me of Greece, though I never saw Greece." Still more fanciful was Richard

Hakluyt's *Divers Voyages Touching the Discouerie of America* (1582), an atlas of sorts, which cast a shadow at least as long as the Lewis and Clark expedition and the first transcontinental railroad. Hakluyt never left his native England, except to serve as a chaplain in Paris for five years, yet he managed to convince generations of geographers and explorers that a waterborne passage to Asia had to bisect the continent somewhere near the fortieth parallel.[4]

• • •

IT IS A COMMONPLACE OF AMERICAN LANDSCAPE THAT the abstract and unseen loom larger than the seen. Among other things, the relentless reach of maps made it almost inevitable that the royal charters of the early 1600s would reemerge as the republican land acts of the late 1700s. It was then that the United States Congress, exercising its federal jurisdiction for the first time, began to authorize the geometric grid of sections and townships that would eventually make everything north of the Ohio and west of the Mississippi the most regular and rigidly proportioned landscape in the world. Much like the old charters, the land acts assumed an absolute identity between map and territory. As the surveyor general of the United States put it in 1819, "a few geographical positions on the map of the public surveys, being accurately determined by astronomical observations, it is obvious that, with very little difficulty, the longitude and latitude of every *farm*, and of every *log-hut* and *court house*, may be ascertained." Whether settlers followed the grid west or the grid followed them west, the grid itself could expand as needed, forming the universal and abstract *space* of the grid — a space Gertrude Stein once described as looking the same "from above from below and from custom and from habit." To quote a character in James Fenimore Cooper's *The Pioneers* (1823): "We must run our streets by the compass, coz, and disregard trees, hills, ponds, stumps, or, in fact, anything but posterity."[5]

Even with something as abstract as the grid, however, latitude outweighed longitude for many decades. Indeed, it could be argued that the nation began as a self-conscious expression of latitude since, as one

historian has observed, the signatures on the Constitution "appear neither in alphabetical order, nor by presumed importance or seniority,
nor in a haphazard fashion" but "grouped, instead, by state with the
states themselves appearing in *geographic* order from north to south."
Not surprisingly, until the early 1840s or so, Americans almost always
emigrated due westward, adhering to the latitude of their birth and
taking with them the relatively fixed separation between North and
South that signified the nexus of regionalism and sectionalism. Thomas
Jefferson elected to see this as an expression of character — of like seeking
like. Like many others at the time, he believed that climate separated
northerners and southerners. In 1785 he went so far as to say that these
sectional traits "grow weaker and weaker by gradation from North to
South and South to North" and that "an observing traveler, without the
aid of the quadrant may always know his latitude by the character of the
people among whom he finds himself. It is in Pennsylvania that the two
characters seem to meet and blend." However, the southern boundary
of Pennsylvania would soon separate, not blend, North and South — as
the Mason-Dixon Line became a typically invisible or abstract form
of partition. That the Mason-Dixon Line was also the first accurately
surveyed line of latitude in North America is only fitting. One way or
another, the nation was ruled by latitude. In a version of Blaise Pascal's
observation that a shift of three degrees of latitude is enough to usurp
jurisprudence, Jefferson himself later wrote, arguing against the Missouri
Compromise and the dividing line of 36°30' North that would etch
slavery west of the Mississippi: "A geographical line, coinciding with a
fixed principle, . . . will never be obliterated; and every new irritation
will mark it deeper and deeper." Over three decades after the Missouri
Compromise, latitude was still so influential that when Jefferson Davis,
secretary of the army, was ordered to pick the best route for a transcontinental railroad, he had to commission four separate surveys to appease
sectional interests — a survey between the forty-seventh and forty-ninth
parallels (referred to as the "New England" route), a survey of the thirty-
eighth parallel (Thomas Hart Benton's chosen route), a survey of the
thirty-fifth parallel, and a survey of the thirty-second parallel (the route

favored by the South and by Davis himself). No route at all was chosen until the Civil War eliminated Southern opposition to anything but a Southern route, allowing Congress to pick a central route along the forty-first parallel.[6]

. . .

CONFRONTED WITH A MYSTERIOUS NEW CONTINENT, EURO-peans commonly called it "a land of milk and honey" or "an howling wilderness." Of the two, wilderness seemed to exert the greater force. As early as 1651 Thomas Hobbes had equated America with the so-called state of nature—a theoretical stage of human history where there was no civil law or government and where, as he put it, humans lived in a state of perpetual "warre, as of every man, against every man." For Hobbes, this implied a world in which there was "no place for Industry"; "no Culture of the Earth"; "no commodious Building"; "no Knowledge of the face of the Earth; no account of Time; no Arts; no Letters; no Society." Laments of this sort would be customary among European visitors to America for the next two centuries—and would be acknowledged, and often adopted, by Americans themselves through the nineteenth century. Clergyman Timothy Flint, in his early history of the Mississippi valley, wrote: "The English, when they sneer at our country, speak of it as sterile in moral interest. It has, say they, no monuments, no ruins, none of the massive remains of former ages; no castles, no mouldering abbeys, no baronial towers and dungeons, nothing to connect the imagination and the heart with the past, no recollections of former ages to associate the past with the future." Equally negative lists would be compiled by Washington Irving, Thomas Cole, Nathaniel Hawthorne, Henry James. It suggests that America may have remained "unknowne" for so long because even Americans saw it as just a negative image of Europe—what Europe *wasn't*. Apparently, they couldn't see what was before them, except by looking over their shoulders.[7]

John Filson's "Adventures of Col. Daniel Boon" and Jefferson's *Notes on the State of Virginia* began to elaborate a different version of the American landscape. Each contains a prospect that would become emblematic in the nineteenth century: Boone, "from the top of an eminence," sees "with pleasure the beautiful level of Kentucke"; Jefferson, "on a very high point" of the Blue Ridge, sees "a small catch of smooth blue horizon" which shows a "distant finishing." What's so singular about these views is that each occurs within a landscape that otherwise seems so dense, chaotic, and precarious. Boone is constantly threatened by Indians, as the very prospect which offers such "a series of wonders, and a fund of delight" suddenly morphs into a dreadful scene of captivity. Throughout his travels, Boone's "astonishing delight" in "beauteous tracts" of "inconceivable grandeur" alternates with a less elated or benign response: "The aspect of these cliffs is so wild and horrid, that it is impossible to behold them without terror. The spectator is apt to imagine that nature had formerly suffered some violent convulsion; and that these are the dismembered remains of a dreadful shock; the ruins, not of Persepolis or Palmyra, but of the world!" Jefferson finds a similar "disrupture and avulsion" in the "cloven" rocks of the Blue Ridge, where the Shenandoah and Potomac Rivers come together and, "in the moment of their junction," "rush together against the mountain, rend it asunder, and pass off to the sea."[8]

Jefferson and Filson were among the first Americans to suggest that their native landscape could be different from European landscape without being inferior. Both appear to have been influenced by Thomas Burnet's *Sacred Theory of the Earth* (1684), which argued that the globe's surface, once a smooth plain, had been fractured by a catastrophic deluge welling up from the earth's interior, leaving a series of mountain ranges composed of its shattered rubble. Burnet developed this theory after visiting the Alps. While he condemned the Alps as "the greatest Examples of Confusion that we know in Nature," he also saw their beauty: "There is something august and stately in the Air of these things, that inspires the Mind with great Thoughts and Passions; we do naturally, upon such Occasions, think of God and his Greatness." Sentiments such as this would become characteristic of the European sublime by the end of the eighteenth century. It is why the Alps themselves, nearly invisible as an aesthetic object to the Romans and the Renaissance, were a magnet for the artists and poets of the romantic period. By looking to this example, Jefferson and Filson found a way to inscribe the uniqueness of American landscape within the conventions of European aesthetics, implying that the "cloven" features of the Blue Ridge and the "wild and horrid" cliffs of Kentucky were equal to anything in the Alps. Fifty years later, Thomas Cole still sounded a little defensive when he remarked that, though the character of American scenery "may differ from the old world's, yet inferiority must not therefore be inferred." But Jefferson set things in motion when he said of Niagara Falls, the Blue Ridge, and the Natural Bridge of Virginia: "It is worth a voyage across the Atlantic to see these objects; much more to paint, and make them, and thereby ourselves, known to all ages."[9]

Ultimately, geology became a way to transform landscape itself—from a preoccupation with human history to that of natural history. The same thing could be said of botany or zoology in that the unruly richness of American nature seemed sublime in itself and offered an obvious contrast to the more shorn and noisome landscape of Europe. Jefferson filled many pages of the *Notes* proving that American mammals often outshone their less vigorous European counterparts, while Filson made it clear that America was a paradise of useful wildlife and plants. Such a strategy both separated the two continents as physical entities and implied that the new continent might be superior in certain respects—not only as a scenic prospect but as a source of natural resources. Essentially, it allowed Jefferson and Filson to invert the "state of nature" as a negative image. No longer was the American landscape to be considered sterile or void. Instead, it was to be seen as a kind of ideal plenitude that fell infinitely short of being realized, either because it remained unexplored and "unknowne" or because it remained undeveloped. The very thing that seemed to signify the backwardness of American landscape—its unimproved wilderness—was finally taken to be its most unique asset. Indeed, all those lamentations of lack—Flint's "no recollections of former ages to associate the past with the future"—would be little more than rearguard actions. At worst they would represent a fear of falling short in the midst of plenty, at best an incentive to find our past in the future use of nature's bounty. Americans were already ideologues of the future in Jefferson's and Filson's day, and they would become fanatics in the nineteenth century. In 1840 editor and poet Nathaniel P. Willis blithely observed: "Instead of looking through a valley, which has presented the same aspect for hundreds of years—in which live lords and tenants, whose hearths have been surrounded by the same names through ages of tranquil descent," an American's "first thought is of the villages that will soon sparkle on the hill-sides, the axes that will ring from the woodlands, and the mills, bridges, canals, and railroads, that will span and border the stream that now runs through sedge and wild-flowers." An American, Willis concluded, "must feed his imagination on the *future*."[10]

· · ·

IT IS HARD TO IMAGINE ANYTHING MORE UNKNOWN OR unseen than the future. Yet one of the most glaring features of American landscape is how often the "Mapp" has become the territory. Over and over again, individuals have laid their hands on a thin piece of parchment—their little finger in one ocean, their thumb in the other—and made the continent their own. In "The Great Nation of Futurity," an unsigned editorial published in the *United States Magazine and Democratic Review* in 1839, John O'Sullivan began to compile the "Mapp" that would be known as Manifest Destiny.[11]

The 1840s can be seen as that defining moment when both North and South looked to longitude as the locus of sectional and party interests. Manifest Destiny would not be a slogan until midway through the decade, but it came to symbolize an era in which the nation as a whole woke up to what Thomas Hart Benton, serving under Andrew Jackson as a military aide, had discovered during the War of 1812: that "until then his mind had been one-sided, and that there was a West as well as an East to our country." It was a national epiphany, a vast and inevitably troubled reweighting of the country westward. The nature and the limits of the republic were debated with the fervor of the Puritans after King Philip's War and the framers of the Constitution after the Revolutionary War. In articles entitled "Oregon" and "Texas" and "California," the *Democratic*

Review, a Jacksonian journal, argued in favor of expansion, while the *American Review*, a Whig organ, argued against it; by the end of the decade, both magazines were calling for Asa Whitney's "railroad to the Pacific." Nearly half the territory added to the original thirteen states was added between 1840 and 1850. Not only were Texas and California admitted as states, but with the addition of the Gadsden Purchase in 1853, both the southern and northern boundaries of the lower forty-eight states were fixed once and for all. That same year, Congress funded the four railroad surveys — and a year later the Kansas-Nebraska Act, largely driven by the railroad, aggravated the sectionalism that the Compromise of 1850 had done so little to alleviate.[12]

Of course, the lowest of land grabs is usually associated with the loftiest rhetoric, and Anders Stephanson is just one of many to observe that expansionism always appeared most "prophetic" during those moments of greatest "aggrandizement or interventionism" — "when there was a need to invest such acts with notions of essential American goodness." Ironically, O'Sullivan's earliest expression of Manifest Destiny never used those words and pointedly rejected what would later be the most binding image of Manifest Destiny — the westward course of empire. The editorial unfolded as the mystical assertion of an idea, carried in the hearts of individuals devoted to that idea. O'Sullivan argued that because "our national birth was the beginning of a new history" — a history "entirely based on the great principle of human equality" — it was therefore "destined to be *the great nation of futurity*." But as he went on to acknowledge: "American patriotism is not of soil, we are not aborigines, nor of ancestry, for we are of all nations; but it is essentially personal enfranchisement, for 'where liberty dwells,' said Franklin, the sage of the Revolution, 'there is my country.'" None of this had anything to do with "futurity" or progress as we usually think of it. It said nothing about the advancement of knowledge or better living standards, and it ignored the imperative to seize and improve land. Instead, it seemed to represent the rather vague assertion of a liberty that already existed. It was as if Americans — by which O'Sullivan meant white Anglo-Saxon Americans — carried the future with them wherever they went.[13]

Yet even as he spurned the "soil" of ancestry or empire, O'Sullivan often used spatial metaphors to make his point. As he said near the beginning of the article: "The expansive future is our arena, and for our history. We are entering on its untrodden space, with the truths of God in our minds." Several sentences later he wrote: "In its magnificent domain of space and time, the nation of many nations is destined to manifest to mankind the excellence of divine principles." Like every other aspect of society, O'Sullivan's notion of "futurity" had to exist *in* space and *as* space — and as he saw it, the "magnificent domain" of the nation would simply emerge of its own accord, peacefully, without rancor or force.

In 1845 O'Sullivan wrote another unsigned editorial for the *Democratic Review*, arguing that "it is time now for opposition to the Annexation of Texas to cease." He implored his fellow citizens to set aside their party differences and unite against Britain and Mexico, whom he accused of "hampering our power, limiting our greatness and checking the fulfillment of our manifest destiny to overspread the continent allotted by Providence for the free development of our yearly multiplying millions." Since the article was so steeped in the "unpausing struggle and excitement" of the day that O'Sullivan was willing to tolerate Texas as a slave state in order to guarantee "the freedom of our institutions," it was not until six months later, in an unsigned editorial in the *New York Morning News*, that Manifest Destiny began to symbolize the more elevated patriotism of the "great nation of futurity." Though Britain was still O'Sullivan's target, the vast territory of Oregon was now his battleground. Arguing that a boundary dispute which had festered for almost three decades needed to be settled, he declared that the United States had a right to claim "the *whole* of Oregon" instead of sharing it with Britain. In no uncertain terms he announced: "And that claim is by the right of our manifest destiny to overspread and to possess the whole of the continent which Providence has given us for the development of the great experiment of liberty and federated self-government entrusted to us. It is a right such as that of the tree to the space of air, and the earth suitable for the full expansion of its principle and destiny of growth."[14]

...

APPEARING IN THE SAME ISSUE OF THE *DEMOCRATIC REVIEW*
as O'Sullivan's article on Texas was a long and admiring article on John
Charles Frémont's *Report of the Exploring Expedition to the Rocky Mountains in the year 1842, and to Oregon and California in years 1843–4*. Of
the many elements that were to mobilize the realignment of the nation
westward, one of the earliest and most important was Frémont's expedition to the Wind River Range in Wyoming, which he carried out in
the summer and early fall of 1842. Although he barely moved west of
the Continental Divide, this was the expedition that began to codify
the Oregon Trail as an overland route to the Pacific and began to fix
the points of latitude and longitude that would eventually encompass
everything west of the Mississippi. Frémont's second expedition, lasting from May 1843 to July 1844, not only completed the Oregon Trail
survey but went on to describe a huge and meandering loop through
Oregon, California, the southern tip of Nevada, much of Utah, the
eastern half of Colorado, and the heart of Kansas. Hailed for the maps
and reports that resulted from the two expeditions, Frémont was widely
acclaimed as the nation's foremost authority on the West and soon
found himself with the nickname of "Pathfinder," taken from the title
of a James Fenimore Cooper novel. The article in the *Democratic Review*
declared his maps and reports to be "so minute and particular," so full of
"geographical, botanical, geological, and meteorological information,"
as to "enable a general to march an army, or an emigrant to move his
family to Oregon."[15]

Naturally, it was those who thought of seeing the West for themselves,
or actually moving west, who found this information most welcome.
When Francis Parkman set out in 1846 to improve his health on the
prairies and Edwin Bryant set out the same year for California, both
carried copies of Frémont's maps and reports — as did Susan Shelby
Magoffin, a teenage bride who found herself on the Santa Fe Trail for
the first time. Brigham Young was so inspired by Frémont's accounts
that in the spring of 1847 he "determined to get our wagons together,

form a grand caravan and travel through the country to the Salt Lake, 1000 miles from any civilized settlement." About the same time, the *Democratic Review* published an article entitled "California" in which it cited several passages from Captain Beechy, "of the British navy, who visited California in 1826 and '27," and several from Captain Wilkes, of the U.S. Navy, who visited California in 1841, but made no effort to quote from Frémont's report, "as it is probably in the hands of all who pursue this communication, and because it is very difficult to *select* from so large a mass of highly important and favorable testimony." By the end of the decade Frémont had become so famous as to be almost invisible as an influence. Hundreds of gold rush diaries would mimic his reports without even bothering to acknowledge them.[16]

. . .

WITHIN CONGRESS, NO ONE WAS MORE IDENTIFIED WITH the annexation of Oregon than Thomas Hart Benton — the man who had found the western side of his mind on the banks of the Mississippi, also in a dispute with Britain. Even before he was elected as one of Missouri's first senators, Benton had argued that Oregon belonged to the United States by right and by treaty, and that the forty-ninth parallel, which the British had accepted as a boundary as far as the Rockies, ought to be extended to the Pacific. In every session of Congress since 1825 he had fought for a bill that would throw the full weight of the federal government behind this claim of sovereignty. But Congress, unwilling to risk yet another war with Britain, refused to overturn the treaty of 1818, which had resulted in a joint British and American occupation of Oregon. Until Benton met Frémont in 1839, Benton's campaign seemed little more than a prolonged quarrel over map coordinates.[17]

Benton can be seen as the last great descendant of Columbus and Richard Hakluyt in American politics. He can also be seen as the self-appointed son of Jefferson. Much has been made of a meeting between the two men in 1824 — referred to by Benton's daughter, Jessie, as a "pilgrimage" to Monticello — in which the topic of local roads quickly led to a discussion of "roads for the spread of our people westward." Significantly, Jefferson presented Benton with a copy of the map Lewis and Clark had compiled during their expedition to the mouth of the Columbia River. A year later, exhorting Congress to fund a road to Santa Fe, Benton would wave this map like a flag on the Senate floor, invoking Jefferson's imagination even more than his illustrious name. Maps were not just a means or a metaphor for Benton. Like Jefferson, he regarded them as an expression of the nation's geographical predestination.[18]

In a speech delivered four years before he died, Benton reiterated a view that had guided him for four decades. Ever since the meeting with Jefferson he had envisioned not just *a* road or a series of roads but a *national* road that would hasten "the spread of our people westward." If the overland trail to Oregon and California could be seen as the first phase of that road, a transcontinental railroad would be its apotheosis. The only problem was that, as a lifelong politician, he had always envisioned this road passing through his home state of Missouri. And with Congress debating which route the transcontinental railroad ought to follow — a debate riven by rivalries between Cincinnati, Saint Louis, and Chicago as well as the usual sectional disputes — Benton again waved a map of sorts.

He began by declaring that "the line of great states which now stretch half way across our continent in the same latitudes — (Pennsylvania, Ohio, Indiana, Illinois, Missouri,) — may be matched by an equal number of states, equally great, between Missouri and California." This was little more than a rhetorical point, since the only "great state" lying between Missouri and California at the time was Texas. Stretching the point even further — by pointing to a latitude that is central to Missouri but several degrees south of Pennsylvania — he cited the survey done by Frémont in 1853–54: "He sat out, taking the winter for his time, the west for his course, a straight line his object, the mouth of the Kanzas for his point of departure, St. Louis and San Francisco the points to be connected. The parrallels of 38 and 39, covered his course." While acknowledging that, to pass through the Sierra Nevada, Frémont had to make "a slight deflection to the south, between the parallels 37 and 38," Benton clearly considered the point made: "This may be called a straight line; and so fulfills a primary condition of every kind of road, and especially of a railroad."[19]

Only someone looking at the world from a very lofty vantage point — and beholding, in Robert Smithson's words, a very "large scale system" — would make such a claim. But having settled the feasibility of five new states, bisected by a railroad following a line of latitude, Benton took yet another step backward to consider how this railroad might embody a kind of nineteenth-century version of Morton's "golden meane":

> What is the destiny of all these atlantic roads, thus pointing to the west and converging upon the central track, the whole course of which lies through the centre of our Union, and through the centre of its population, wealth and power — and one end of which points to Canton and Jeddo — the other to London and Paris; what will those lateral roads become, in addition to their original destination? They will become parts of a system, bringing our Atlantic cities nearer to the Pacific coast than they were to the Blue Ridge in the time of canals and turnpikes. And what then? The great idea of Columbus will be realized — though in a different, and a more beneficial form.

Both as a matter of form and scale, Benton's earlier campaign to annex Oregon ought to be seen in the same light. To secure the forty-ninth parallel was essentially to identify the United States as the "Zona temperata" of progress, the "golden meane" of world history. That it would be accomplished by exploring and mapping the Oregon Trail meant that Columbus's legendary Passage to India would finally have a precise latitude and longitude. If this had been nothing more than a dream before 1839, it became a reality once Benton finally met his own Columbus.

. . .

DURING FRÉMONT'S RUN FOR THE PRESIDENCY IN 1856, A story began to circulate that suggested that he and Benton had been destined to meet. It was widely known that Benton was hot-tempered and, like many southerners and westerners of the day, quick to demand "satisfaction" for real or imagined insults. Timothy Flint relates how Benton was so incensed by the son of one of Missouri's first territorial judges that, after wounding him in one duel, he decided he wasn't "satisfied" enough and later killed the man in a second encounter, eliminating "one of the most promising, and apparently the most sober and moral young men in the state." Since Greek and Roman literature was full of such vengeful bloodletting and was widely quoted in accounts of the day, it's not surprising that Benton's temper might help to create a fateful link to Frémont, as if their fortunes had been entangled from the start. There seems little question that both were staying in the same hotel in Nashville in September 1813 — Frémont as a baby, Benton carrying out his duties under Jackson. At the time, Benton and his brother Jesse were in a feud with Jackson because Jackson had served as a second to an enemy of Jesse's in a duel. When Jackson also arrived in town, a fight broke out and shots were exchanged; Jackson was carried off with his shoulder shattered by a ball from Jesse's gun; Benton fell down a flight of stairs; the fight spread to the rest of the hotel; and Frémont's parents claimed that during the melee a stray ball had passed through their room, narrowly missing the cradle Frémont was sleeping in. Whether or not the details of the story are true — and why not? — a more obvious reason the two men joined forces is that they had a like-minded understanding of the "unknowne" and a matching ambition to map it. Although Frémont would be Benton's son-in-law by the time the first expedition was funded, he was also the most qualified man in America to carry out such an expedition — and in ways even Benton wouldn't know until later.[20]

Frémont seems to have met Benton after returning from an expedition led by Joseph N. Nicollet to the Coteau des Prairies. At the time, Frémont was a protégé of the secretary of war, Joel R. Poinsett, who was also a confidant of Jackson, a Southern Unionist, and a former ambassador to Mexico. In 1835 Poinsett arranged for Frémont to help survey a railroad route from Cincinnati to Charleston, and the next year Frémont joined an army survey of the Cherokee lands in Georgia, North Carolina, and Tennessee. In 1838 Poinsett brought him to Washington DC, commissioned him a second lieutenant in the Army Corps of Topographical Engineers, and allowed him to join the Nicollet expedition in the region of what is now Minnesota and South Dakota.

In his *Memoirs* Frémont introduces Benton as "a disciple of Jefferson." He writes that, as one of the "western men" in Washington, Benton would regularly visit the rooms where Frémont and Nicollet were compiling the astronomical observations and descriptions that would allow them to map the region they'd explored. Benton expected the map to be in progress, or almost done, and was disappointed to see only a "blank projection." But after examining the raw data that were strewn about the tables, Benton and Frémont began to discuss an expedition that would move west of the Missouri to the Rocky Mountains. Frémont was quick to see the implications: "It would be travel over a part of the world which still remained the New — the opening up of unknown lands; the making unknown countries known; and the study without books — the learning at first hand from nature herself." Following one of their meetings, Frémont conveniently adopted the prophetic voice of Columbus, Hakluyt, and Morton: "The thought of penetrating into the recesses of that wilderness region filled me with enthusiasm — I saw visions." It wasn't long before Benton made it clear that the expedition was intended to be "auxiliary and in aid to the emigration to the Lower Columbia" — and by encouraging emigration and settlement, to a de facto sovereignty south of the forty-ninth parallel. Since Nicollet was gravely ill, Frémont was chosen to lead the expedition.[21]

. . .

AS IT TURNED OUT, THE EXPEDITION ITSELF WAS RELA-tively quick and straightforward. On June 10, 1842, Frémont and his party struck out from the junction of the Kansas and Missouri Rivers; moved northwest to the vicinity of Grand Island, Nebraska; followed the south fork of the Platte west to Colorado; turned north to Fort Laramie in Wyoming; headed west again to Independence Rock, South Pass, and the Wind River Range; and then more or less retraced their steps, returning to the mouth of the Kansas exactly four months later (fig. 1). This is not to say the expedition lacked vicissitudes or adventure. Over the course of those four months Frémont and his men had to deal with fast-moving prairie fires, risky river fords, treacherous buffalo hunts, pelt-

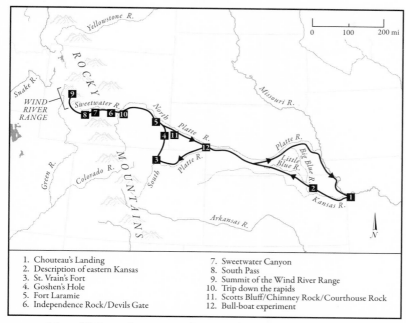

FIG. 1. Map of Frémont's 1842 expedition to the Rocky Mountains with points of interest.

1. Chouteau's Landing
2. Description of eastern Kansas
3. St. Vrain's Fort
4. Goshen's Hole
5. Fort Laramie
6. Independence Rock/Devils Gate
7. Sweetwater Canyon
8. South Pass
9. Summit of the Wind River Range
10. Trip down the rapids
11. Scotts Bluff/Chimney Rock/Courthouse Rock
12. Bull-boat experiment

ing rain, bouts of thirst, stretches of inhospitable terrain, and threatening encounters with Indians. Horses ran away, men were temporarily lost, instruments were broken or destroyed, and at one point Frémont was even threatened with a mutiny of sorts (an episode he relates by taking a page out of Caesar's *Commentaries*). But there was also an exciting climb to a summit of the Wind River Range, an equally exciting, if reckless, trip down the rapids of the upper Platte, and an opportunity to see such landmarks as Courthouse Rock, Chimney Rock, Scotts Bluff, Independence Rock, Devil's Gate, and South Pass. Moreover, the expedition often found itself stumbling across the scattered campfires and cast-off furniture of an Oregon emigrant party about three weeks ahead on the trail.

Even at the time, Frémont knew that almost none of this was actually "travel over a part of the world which still remained the New — the

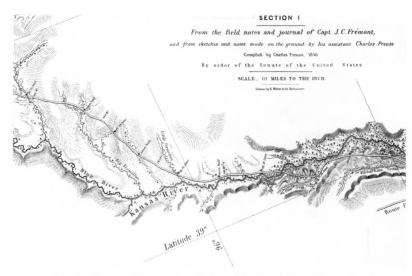

FIG. 2. Charles Preuss, *Topographical Map of the Road from Missouri to Oregon, commencing at the mouth of the Kansas in the Missouri River and ending at the mouth of the Walla-Walla in the Columbia.* Detail, section 1. Published in 1846 by order of the Senate of the United States. Image courtesy of Bob Graham.

opening up of unknown lands." Not only had these lands been the home of Indians and trappers for centuries, but they had been explored to one degree or another by several earlier expeditions, all of them lasting longer and encompassing more territory than Frémont's expedition. If nothing else, the heavy wagons carrying the emigrant party proved that a relatively familiar road to Oregon already existed. What made Frémont's brief exploration so significant, then, was the equally brief report he delivered to Congress on March 1, 1843 — a report that mainly recounted the daily events of the expedition but also included a detailed map of the route, a tabulation of the various astronomical and meteorological readings, a list of the plants collected, and, most important of all, a rationalization for Benton's agenda of annexation and expansion (fig. 2).[22]

For reasons that will become evident, this shrewd and beautiful report deserves to be seen as one of the seminal works of American expansionism. Until now, even those willing to acknowledge Frémont's practical contributions to expansionism have turned a blind eye to his more basic influence on its ideology. Understanding the nature of this influence, however, means identifying the ways in which he reduced the controversy surrounding expansionism to a matter of landscape and maps. As James Ronda has pointed out, nearly half of Jefferson's instructions to Lewis deal "with native people, either as objects of scientific study or as important peoples and tribes to be reckoned with," and the journals of the Lewis and Clark expedition are replete with a Native presence. Yet despite his own encounters with Indians, Frémont deliberately pushed them to the background — and then out of the picture altogether. Although this arc of invisibility would reach an apex as the West was widely photographed — in the words of Martha Sandweiss, "dramatic photographic vistas helped persuade countless Americans that the essence of the West was not its social communities, not the interaction between its diverse peoples, but the physical landscape itself" — its origins can be traced directly to Frémont's *Report*.[23]

The following analysis of the *Report* is divided into two parts. The first examines the way that Frémont's radical form of the picturesque helped to transform the West from a great desert into a national landscape; the second examines the way that his map of the Continental Divide, by aligning the nation's geographical predestination with the lay of the land and proving that a transcontinental railroad was both necessary and possible, helped to transform the existing space and time of western expansion. Above all, Frémont's *Report* began to create what George Kateb has called an "aesthetic craving" for expansion, implying that a nation able to encompass an entire continent would satisfy an inherent desire for beauty and order. In laying out the great swath of country "lying between the Missouri River and the Rocky Mountains, on the line of the Kansas and Great Platte rivers," the *Report* offered both an image of that orderly continental landscape and a means of achieving it. It was, in effect, a perfect semblance of Manifest Destiny for the great majority of Americans who had never actually seen the continent they were about to possess.

Sight Unseen

One

Picturesque America

The Great Desert

KNOWN AS A FIRST-RATE MATHEMATICIAN AS WELL AS A man of God, Blaise Pascal famously staked his *belief* in God on the laws of probability and once proposed a transportation system for Paris that relied on horse-drawn carriages following fixed routes and rigid schedules. As fate would have it, he was also the victim of a terrifying and improbable carriage accident. Apparently, he was driving across the Neuilly-sur-Seine bridge one day—at least a section of which had no parapet—when the two lead horses took the bit in their teeth and plummeted into the river, threatening to drag the other horses and the carriage down with them. Luckily, the traces snapped and Pascal was saved. But the episode proved so traumatic that he spent the rest of his fairly brief life believing a perilous abyss had opened up on his left side—something he tried to dispel by always placing a chair on that side, finding solace in its tangible mass and its likely location in space.[1]

Strangely enough, a somewhat similar situation existed the year Frémont set out for the Rockies, in that most Americans perceived the territory west of the Mississippi to be a kind of void or abyss to their geographic "left." In his agile, sometimes melancholy recollections of the Mississippi valley, Timothy Flint wrote that in 1818 the river "was to the great proportion of the American people," as it was to him, "a limit almost to the range of thought." As he slowly steamed down the Ohio and approached the Mississippi for the first time, he clearly felt himself to be approaching an existential boundary of some sort: "We had been looking forward to this place as the pillars of Hercules. The country on this side had still some unbroken associations with our native land. This magnificent river, almost dividing the continent, completely severed this chain." Confirming Flint's view was John Melish's *Map of the United*

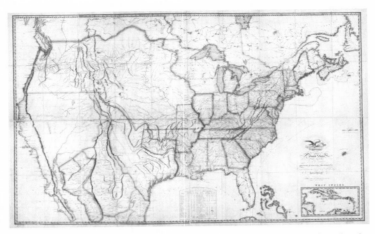

FIG. 3. John Melish, *Map of the United States*, 1816. Engraving, hand colored; 35 x 55¾ in. Map Division, New York Public Library, Astor, Lenox and Tilden Foundations, New York Public Library/Art Resource, New York.

States (1816), the first of many wall maps published in America showing the continent from coast to coast (fig. 3). East of the Mississippi there was a dense network of topography and towns, most of it accurately, if somewhat sketchily, mapped; west of the Mississippi large areas were left blank, almost nothing was named, and the entire region had, at best, a relative truth. Even calling it a relative truth might be misleading, since along with all the rivers and mountains *missing* from the map were the many imaginary features found *only* on the map.[2]

Admittedly, 1818 was also the year Britain and the United States signed a treaty drawing the forty-ninth parallel from the Great Lakes to the Rockies. Three years later Missouri joined Louisiana as the second state west of the Mississippi, and by 1826 Flint himself was forced to confess that any suggestion the "magnificent river" still represented the brink of thought "would be matter of surprise" to "the thousands of hacknied travellers on this stream." Though Flint, like most of the "hacknied travellers" he referred to at the time, never ventured more than a few miles west of the Mississippi, Josiah Gregg began his majestic *Commerce of the Prairies* (1844) by noting that the trade route from

Independence, Missouri, to Santa Fe was already deeply rutted by the time he joined his first caravan in 1831.[3]

Still, even these enterprising ventures remained isolated forays into the West and, until Frémont's first expedition, did little to alter eastern opinions of the region. In 1836 "The Report of the Senate Committee on Indian Affairs" justified its policy of "removing" Indians to territory west of the Mississippi (precisely the territory Frémont was to explore) by baldly stating: "They are on the outside of us, and in a place which will forever remain on the outside." As late as 1849 Francis Parkman could observe that setting out along the Oregon Trail was known in "the phraseology of the region" as "jumping off." And whatever Flint's familiarity with travel on the Mississippi itself, he didn't hesitate to acknowledge that "it is a common proverb of the people, that when we cross the Mississippi, 'we travel beyond the Sabbath.'"[4]

. . .

PART OF THE REASON THE MISSISSIPPI SEEMED SUCH A significant boundary to Americans was that it had long been a source of conflict between Europe and the United States. With all the hostility, diplomacy, and outright warfare over the years, a singular aspect of this conflict was that Europeans had staked a claim to the river on the basis of international law, while Americans had looked to both geography and "the Laws of Nature and of Nature's God." "From the very position of our country," Sen. James Ross had announced in 1802, "from its geographical shape, from motives of complete independence, the command of the navigation of the river ought to be in our hands."[5]

Statements of this sort would become a kind of rolling justification for possession of the entire continent—a justification that, as Albert Weinberg pointed out many years ago, increasingly relied on the idea of propinquity. A year after the Louisiana Purchase was ratified, Joseph Chandler delivered a Fourth of July oration in which he declared that Louisiana was just "the commencement of our anticipating hopes," projecting a future where "our boundaries shall be those which Nature has formed for a great, powerful, and free State." The inherent nature and flexibility of those boundaries would be revealed by a commission considering the nation's additional right to Texas a year later. Reasoning that the interior of Texas ought to be seen as an extension inward from the coastline which had been part of the Louisiana Purchase, the commission argued that "Nature seems to have destined a range of territory so described for the same society, to have connected its several parts together by the ties of a common interest, and to have detached them from others." That this reasoning often exceeded the boundaries of credulity was beside the point. Like most Europeans before them, Americans saw what they wanted to see — and "geographical shape" always conformed to the "motives of complete independence," not the other way around. In 1829, as the debate over Texas grew more antagonistic to the Mexicans, the *Nashville Republican* claimed that the Rio Grande was "designated by the hand of Heaven, as a boundary between two great nations of dissimilar pursuits" — but then defined this providential disparity by absurdly concluding: "On this side of the Rio Grande, the country is seasonable, fertile, and every way desirable to the people of the United States. On the other side the lands are unproductive, crops cannot be matured without irrigation; in short they are entirely calculated for a lazy, pastoral, mining people like the Mexicans."[6]

Regrettably, the notion of "geographical shape" could not obscure an obvious difference between latitude and longitude and the lay of the land. It was one thing for Columbus to assume that the East Indies could be reached by sailing due west from Spain and quite another to find whole continents blocking his way. The same thing was true of the colonists who expected the conditions in the Carolinas to correspond to the Mediterranean climate and soil, and no matter how confidently the Puritans claimed the territory to the north and west "by Mapp," much of what they claimed turned out to be quite different or not there at all. Although the lesson had to be learned again and again with each generation, it was evident that declaring our boundaries to "be those which Nature has formed for a great, powerful, and free State" could actually *limit* the extent of the nation as well as enlarge it. At any given point, even the abstract reach of geographical predestination had to confront the material reality of nature.

This was especially true of the period preceding Frémont's expedition to the Rocky Mountains. As Weinberg also pointed out, the history of the United States is largely the history of absolute boundaries morphing into relative boundaries. One generation's "limit almost to the range of thought" was the next generation's front yard. And yet, with all the "hacknied travellers" steaming up and down the Mississippi, not to mention all the people lobbying for the annexation of Oregon and Texas, the territory stretching from what is now Oklahoma to North Dakota remained a formidable barrier in the minds of most Americans. At least partially explored by three expeditions, the region was such a distinctly "known unknown part of America" that it had become *best* known as a vast wasteland or desert.

For a nation of farmers, this was a much greater obstacle than any apparent limit to the range of thought. The *Nashville Republican* was so quick to call the territory north of the Rio Grande "seasonable, fertile, and every way desirable" because, in Ralph Waldo Emerson's words, "the vast majority of the people of this country live by the land, and carry its quality in their manners and opinions." Half a century earlier, Hector St. John de Crèvecoeur had called the farm "the source of every good we possess," and Jefferson had taken it a step further by declaring that "those who labor in the earth are the chosen people of God." Although this rather conveniently ignored those who labored in the earth as slaves, it helps to explain why western expansion had almost always been driven by the desire for arable land. Historically, northerners had moved west in an orderly and contiguous fashion, seeking *more* land for like-minded communities, while southerners had followed a pattern of "indiscriminate locations and settlements," seeking *better* land or land they could squat. But if nearly everything west of the Mississippi was an arid and barren abyss, then there was little incentive to seek *any* land. It was precisely because Indians were assumed to be hunters and gatherers, not farmers, that the U.S. government felt justified in "removing" them to a region west of the Mississippi that was "on the outside of us, and in a place which will forever remain on the outside." Whatever the geographical predestination of the nation, the lay of the land suggested that it had reached a natural limit once it reached this region. Even those who favored the annexation of Oregon assumed the territory would be an independent republic — no longer British but separated from the United States by an area that abjured the possibility of propinquity.[7]

. . .

THE ORIGINS OF THIS PERCEIVED LIMIT CAN BE TRACED most directly to an expedition that lasted from 1806 to 1807. Led by Maj. Zebulon M. Pike, the expedition set out from the frontier town of Saint Louis, meandered through what is now Missouri, Kansas, and Colorado, and then mistakenly (or as more recent commentators have claimed, deliberately, as a form of reconnaissance) crossed into Spanish territory — at which point Pike and his party were taken into custody, questioned, treated kindly for the most part, and returned to U.S. territory. When Pike eventually wrote his report on the expedition, one of its most glaring features was a feeling of alienation and despair that seemed to grow stronger the farther west he moved.

The opening pages of the report reveal a curious and somewhat attentive eye, willing to confront the landscape on its own terms. Making his way through the broken country of eastern Kansas, for instance, Pike is moved enough to write: "We struck a beautiful hill, which bears south on the prairie; its elevation I suppose to be 100 feet. From its summit the view is sublime to the east and southeast." The next day, on a ridge dividing two rivers, he again responds with great (if essentially identical) sympathy: "The prospect from the dividing ridge to the east and southeast is sublime. The prairie rising and falling in regular swells, as far as the sight can extend, produces a very beautiful appearance." But as he moves closer and closer to the Rockies, the arid conditions seem to flatten and bleach Pike's perspective. Entries such as the one he makes on the banks of the Arkansas become more common. These banks, he remarks, "are not more than four feet in height, bordered by a few cottonwood trees;

on the north side is a low swampy prairie; on the south, a sandy, sterile desert at a small distance." Ten days later his mood is even more sere: "We observed this day a species of crystallization on the road, when the sun was high, in low places where there had been water settled; on tasting it found it to be salt; this gave some authenticity to the report of the prairie being covered for leagues." Pike does not emerge from this crystallized plain with his senses intact. The report ends with the bleakest and most sweeping assessment of all: "These vast plains of the western hemisphere may become in time as celebrated as the sandy deserts of Africa; for I saw in my route, in various places, tracts of many leagues where the wind had thrown up the sand in all the fanciful forms of the ocean's rolling wave, and on which not a speck of vegetable matter existed."[8]

This doubled image of desert and ocean could be regarded as a perfect figure of salty desolation — reminiscent of the Ancient Mariner's plaint, "Water, water, every where, / Nor any drop to drink." Indeed, it's a lot closer to the allegorical landscape of Coleridge's poem than to any prairie west of the Mississippi and is best understood as a purely geometric horizon. Whatever the specificity of certain observations in his report, Pike essentially perceived the prairie as an extremely large-scale system, with a few iconic features magnified and presumed to look about the same at every scale. Today we would see this as a form of self-similarity, a theory Benoît Mandelbrot developed in the 1970s to describe the uneven or irregular features of the world without resorting to the straight lines and smooth circles of Euclidean geometry. Mandelbrot discovered a number of natural fractals, including the shape of coastlines and the structure of plants, and perhaps the easiest way to understand self-similarity is to imagine a tree. As a geometric shape, a tree is nothing more than a series of branches. But it's a series that looks more or less the same at every point, from the newest and smallest and most delicate branches at the ends of the outermost limbs to the largest branches rising out of the main trunk of the tree. The tree grows by reproducing this shape over and over again, and thus the whole has approximately the same shape as each of its parts. Another way of putting this is that the tree is symmetrical at every scale. And this is exactly how Pike saw the prairie.

Not only does he tend to repeat himself (using more or less the same language to describe more or less the same features), but as the report gradually unfolds, it becomes clear that the sublime "swells" of eastern Kansas are just local aspects of the lengthier and more sterile "rolling waves" that define the plains and prairies as a whole. Again, Robert Smithson's terminology comes to mind: in this case, the notion of a "zero panorama," a panorama that canceled itself out by negating the distinction between near and far or large and small. This was undoubtedly a decisive and transcendent point of view. Once the horizon itself appeared uniform, forsaken, and interchangeable, Pike could treat *the entire region* between the Mississippi and the Rockies as little more than an abyss or void.[9]

Not that Americans were instantly convinced of this. Martyn Bowden has shown that atlases of the late 1700s and early 1800s typically "considered the region to be extremely fertile and productive agricultural land," primarily because Jefferson had painted such a rosy picture in the "Official Account of Louisiana." But between 1805 and 1810, as more and more information came in, the notion of the West as a great garden "gave way to one of the western interior as a fertile land interspersed with large prairies"; by 1820 or so, as data from the journals of Lewis and Clark became public, geographers such as Melish were more apt to treat the region as uncertain.[10]

This uncertainty was emphatically dispelled when an expedition led by Maj. Stephen Long up the Platte River and into Colorado confirmed Pike's point of view. Long's official report on the expedition, published in 1823, chronicled much the same landscape as Pike's, and if anything its tone was harsher and more encompassing. Describing the Platte River basin, for instance, Long writes: "The bottom lands of the river rise by an imperceptible ascent on each side, extending laterally to a distance of from two to ten miles, where they are terminated by low ranges of gravelly hills, running parallel to the general direction of the river. Beyond these the surface is an undulating plain, having an elevation of from fifty to one hundred feet, and presenting the aspect of hopeless and irreclaimable sterility." When his perspective expands to "an extent of about four hundred miles square, lying between 96 and 105 degrees of west longitude, and between 35 and 42 degrees of north latitude"—nearly all of what is now Nebraska, Kansas, and Oklahoma—he notes that the hilly country to the east "gradually subsides" to the west, "with nothing to limit the view or variegate the prospect, but here and there a hill, knob, or insulated tract of table-land." His rather numbed response is to reach for a familiar metaphor: "The monotony of a vast unbroken plain, like that in which we had now travelled nearly one hundred and fifty miles, is little less tiresome to the eye, and fatiguing to the spirit, than the dreary solitude of the ocean." Rendering this disgruntled point of view both official and beyond reproach was a map that labeled the "four hundred mile square" region a "Great Desert." This map turned out to be the most influential element of the report, reproduced and incorporated into other maps and atlases well into the 1850s.[11]

A collateral influence on eastern views of the West was James Fenimore Cooper's *The Prairie* (1827), the third, and what was intended to be the final, installment of the immensely popular Leatherstocking tales, which already included *The Pioneers* (1823) and *The Last of the Mohicans* (1826) and would later include *The Pathfinder* (1840) and *The Deerslayer* (1841). Since he was personally unfamiliar with anything west of Lake Erie, Cooper turned to Long's report as the empirical model for *The Prairie*. Like many others who had never seen the plains or prairies for themselves, Cooper found it easy to imagine the region as a great ocean desert—and it was as easterners writing for an eastern audience that both Pike and Long had so readily resorted to this metaphor. Cooper comes close to copying Long word for word at times, instinctively treating the region west of the Mississippi as a profoundly negative version of the eastern forest—an enormous and irreversible clearing, so to speak; a fallen landscape. "From the summits of the swells," he writes in the opening pages, "the eye became fatigued with the sameness and chilling dreariness" of the landscape, whose "meagre prospect ran off in long, narrow, barren perspectives, but slightly relieved by a pitiful show of coarse, though somewhat luxuriant vegetation." The cumulative effect of such imagery is a landscape that appears to be alien, degenerate, and inhospitable. Nothing in this landscape is to be appreciated for its own sake — nothing is even to be transformed — merely passed over or through.[12]

If the utter vastness of *The Prairie* harks back to the sublimity that had framed Jefferson's view from the Blue Ridge, it is more as an admonition than anything else. To be sure, the novel consistently traffics in the uniformity and magnitude that Edmund Burke had defined as essential elements of the sublime, and Burke's *Philosophical Enquiry* (1757) was so influential during this period that even Jefferson's instructions to Meriwether Lewis can be understood as a kind of sublime inventory of the facts and figures he wished to add to the knowledge of the nation. But the prairie posed a peculiar problem for the sublime. At what point did vastness and uniformity become nothing more than monotony? At what point did grandeur become "fatiguing to the spirit"? Even Americans traveling fifty miles up the Hudson had to ask themselves this question, since the "illimitable void" of the forest — as Cooper put it in *The Pathfinder* — could in certain respects be compared to the "illimitable void" of the Great Desert. Coincidentally, America's leading landscape painter, Thomas Cole, was forced to address the issue at exactly the same time Cooper was writing *The Prairie*. After delivering a painting of the Catskill Mountains to one of his most loyal patrons, he received a long and largely appreciative letter, which included the following caveat: "It is as you say a scene of wild desolation, and perhaps for that reason more monotonous in its general effect than it would otherwise have been." Cole's response was to finesse the vague reproach: "I agree with you in thinking that the general effect is rather monotonous; but the scene in Nature was so grand in its monotony as to induce me to paint it."[13]

Unfortunately, the monotony or boredom suggested by an ocean of leaves was nothing compared to the rolling waves of prairie stretching west. Whereas the "wild desolation" of the Catskills was interrupted by lightning-blasted trees, cascading waterfalls, and sun-dappled clearings, the flattened, unrelieved terrain of the prairies seemed to challenge every convention of landscape. It was, in the words of Timothy Flint, such "a new and strange world" that "there was no fixed point, no shelter for our hopes and expectations" — a sentiment echoed by Long, who also noted that "we feel the want of ascertained or fixed points of reference," and by the artist George Catlin, who went even further in his *Letters and Notes on the Manners, Customs, and Condition of North American Indians* (1841):

> For two or three of the first days, the scenery was monotonous, and became exceedingly painful from the fact, that we were (to use a phrase of the country) "out of sight of land," *i.e.* out of sight of anything rising above the horizon, which was a perfect straight line around us, like that of the blue and boundless ocean. The pedestrian over such a discouraging sea of green, without a landmark before or behind him; without a beacon to lead him on, or define his progress, feels weak and overcome when night falls; and he stretches his exhausted limbs, apparently on the same spot where he has slept the night before, with the same prospect before and behind him.

Reading these words of Catlin's, it is as if the very category of the sublime reached a limit of sorts in a landscape "without a landmark before or behind." More to the point, by saying that he is "out of sight of land," Catlin makes it evident that he is also outside the United States — signifying that the limits of the sublime actually corresponded to the limits of the nation.[14]

This would be the prevailing view of the West until well into the 1840s and early 1850s, and it contributed to what Edward Said called a "textual attitude" in which the Great Desert was repeatedly evoked in literature, journals, reports, and maps. Gregg concluded his *Commerce of the Prairies*, published a year after the *Report*, by observing: "It will now readily be inferred that the Great Prairies from Red River to the western sources of the Missouri, are . . . chiefly uninhabitable — not so much for want of wood (though the plains are altogether naked), as of soil and of water." Parkman balefully ratcheted up this rhetoric, declaring that "if a curse had been pronounced upon the land, it could not have worn an aspect of more dreary or forlorn barrenness." Meanwhile, Washington Irving had added a distinctly predatory dimension, referring to the entire territory between the Mississippi and the Rockies as a "lawless interval" filled with "new and mongrel races" and marauding bands of "savages." This may have been the most telling judgment of all, since it basically confirmed the West as an arrested state of nature. Hobbes himself, in laying out the state of nature as a condition of perpetual warfare, had cited the tribal conflicts of American Indians as his example. Irving's "interval" implied a similar congruence of space and time—an *enduring* state of nature, a *perpetual* void, a place that would *forever* remain on the outside.[15]

Yet just as the prevailing view of the West began to emerge with Pike's expedition for the army in 1806, so it began to recede with Frémont's expedition for the army in 1842. Ironically, Frémont was ordered to retrace a short stretch of Pike's route in Kansas and a more extensive stretch of Long's route in Nebraska and Colorado in an effort to locate the headwaters of several rivers they had failed to find. This time, however, the expedition was clearly intended to be a blueprint for expansion—something that many in the Oregon lobby especially were hoping to ride with all the hobbyhorsical enthusiasm of Tristram Shandy's uncle Toby. Frémont had barely returned to Washington before Thomas Hart Benton's colleague from Missouri, Sen. Lewis F. Linn, introduced yet another bill calling for a line of forts "from some point on the Missouri and Arkansas rivers into the best pass for entering the valley of the Oregon." Since Frémont had begun to survey this line during the expedition, Linn probably hoped it would lend a de facto legitimacy to his bill—and to the more general issue of western expansion. But with everyone from Pike to Irving arguing that the Great Desert was a natural barrier to expansion, Frémont had to show that it wasn't—and mainly by showing that it wasn't a desert at all. Only in this way would he be able to create a contiguity between East and West strong enough to transform the Great Desert into a relative, not an absolute, boundary.[16]

Once Frémont sat down to write the *Report*, then, he had little choice but to approach the problem aesthetically. It's true that during his second expedition he spent many hours analyzing soil samples, often noting that the land lacked water, not arability, while accumulating the kind of data that would finally refute the idea of widespread barrenness once and for all. For the *Report*, however, he clearly considered Pike and Long's *scientific evidence* far less significant than the *aesthetic* it derived from. So compelling was this aesthetic that even those who made the trip west usually saw what they expected to see, all the while assuming that the desolation in their mind's eye was just a reflection of the desolation surrounding them. The upshot was that Frémont was forced to address several related issues: (1) he had to make a "known unknown" territory known quite differently—and to an audience largely unfamiliar with the West; (2) he had to create both contrast and variety—and outright interest—where only uniformity and monotony were thought to exist; (3) he had to create a rhetorical style able to displace the impression of a Great Desert without negating the existing conventions of American landscape so completely that his style would be incomprehensible; and (4) he had to create an aesthetic continuum between East and West that would be seen as a form of propinquity. What he came up with was a fairly radical version of the picturesque.

The Hudson Valley

FRÉMONT WROTE THE *REPORT* IN THE SHADOW OF A NEW tourism industry, located east of the Alleghenies for the most part and struggling very hard to free itself from European ways of seeing. Visual habits were difficult to break, especially in the case of scenery, which had been the subject of aesthetic theory for almost two hundred years and was closely associated with "taste." American artists and writers still expected to begin or complete their training in the bastions of Old World culture, and it was not unusual to find a single studio in Rome passed from one generation to the next. Critic Henry Tuckerman lived for years in Italy before returning to America to write his *Book of the Artists*; it was in Italy that the artist Benjamin West famously compared the Apollo Belvedere to a Mohawk warrior; Washington Irving published some of his most cherished stories — including "The Legend of Sleepy Hollow" and "Rip Van Winkle" — during his long stay in England and Spain; and Cooper first published *The Prairie* in Paris, his home away from home from 1826 to 1834.

Americans who could afford it still followed some version of the Grand Tour, paying special attention to England, the Alps, and Italy. In an essay entitled "American and European Scenery Compared," included in *The Home Book of the Picturesque* (1852), Cooper wrote that "every intellectual being has a longing to see distant lands. We desire to ascertain, by actual observation, the peculiarities of nations, the differences which exist between the stranger and ourselves, and as it might be all that lies beyond our daily experience." But by the 1840s and 1850s, with a majestic and still-cryptic continent looming to the west, there was already something hollow about these words. The "distant land" of the Grand Tour had become so familiar by then that the

17

curiosity it aroused had more to do with anticipating the known than discovering the unknown. More and more Americans began to treat the layered, antiquated landscape of Europe as a decaying influence. In "Self-Reliance" Emerson wrote that "it is for want of self-culture that the superstition of Travelling, whose idols are Italy, England, Egypt, retains its fascination for all educated Americans." He went on to say that the American bound for Europe "travels away from himself, and grows old even in youth among old things"; he "carries ruins to ruins." By the time the miasmic night air of the Coliseum proved fatal to Daisy Miller, this would be a fairly common view.[17]

An American brand of tourism was an important element of the "self-culture" Emerson looked for. The itinerary Jefferson once recommended as "worth a voyage across the Atlantic to see" had expanded quite a lot in half a century. In "The Philosophy of Travel" Henry Tuckerman wrote that "Niagara, the lakes, the various magnificent mountains and lovely shores, are the shrines of our pilgrimages; and fit altars are they to kindle the worship of a free people, and inspire with elevated enthusiasm, the poets of liberty." The "magnificent mountains" he referred to — especially Mount Washington, Saddleback Mountain in Massachusetts, and Mount Holyoke — had all become notable destinations. Indeed, the crest of Mount Holyoke, with its grand prospect of an orderly valley cut by a river reversing itself, was a favorite site for short excursions and had already inspired one of America's greatest landscape paintings: Thomas Cole's *View from Mount Holyoke, Northampton, Massachusetts, after a Thunderstorm (The Oxbow)* (fig. 4). Cole, along with Irving and Cooper, was also responsible for making the Hudson Valley the most eagerly sought destination of all. As artists and writers debated the "development of nationality in American art," the diverting scenery of the Hudson Valley was often treated as emblematic of the national landscape.[18]

On the eve of the *Report*, perhaps the most representative view of American tourism was Nathaniel P. Willis's *American Scenery; or, Land, Lake, and River: Illustrations of Transatlantic Nature* (1840). The book presented itself as a "specimen" of that "class of works" in which the "enviable enjoyment" of traveling is "brought to the fire-side of the

FIG. 4. Thomas Cole, *View from Mount Holyoke, Northampton, Massachusetts, after a Thunderstorm (The Oxbow)*, 1836. Oil on canvas, 51½ x 76 in. The Metropolitan Museum of Art, New York/Art Resource, New York. Gift of Mrs. Russell Sage, 1908 (08.228). Image copyright © The Metropolitan Museum of Art/Art Resource, New York.

home-keeping and secluded as well" — or what we now call a coffee-table book. Its purpose was to allow "those whose lot in life is domestic and retired" to sit together "by the social hearth" and leisurely compare "the wild scenery of America" with the scenery of the Grand Tour to be found in other such books. Willis indicated that his aim was "to assemble as much as possible of that part of American story which history has not yet found leisure to put into form, and which romance and poetry have not yet appropriated — the legendary traditions and anecdotes, events of the trying times of the Revolution, Indian history, &c. &c."[19]

Although it might seem otherwise, Willis's emphasis on "fire-side" enjoyment was not inauthentic or trivial. Like all its later incarnations — not only *The Home Book of the Picturesque*, but also the souvenir postcard, the roadside "scenic view," and the *National Geographic* Channel — *American Scenery* was fundamentally shaped by the picturesque, an aesthetic that often made little distinction between first- and secondhand knowledge. One of its earliest proponents, the eighteenth-

FIG. 5. J. Cousen, after William H. Bartlett, *Caldwell (Lake George)*, 1840. Engraving in Nathaniel P. Willis, *American Scenery; or, Land, Lake, and River: Illustrations of Transatlantic Nature*, vol. 1, opposite p. 69. Milstein Division of United States History, Local History & Genealogy, New York Public Library, Astor, Lenox and Tilden Foundations.

century English clergyman and aesthetician William Gilpin, had generally looked to landscape painting as his model for the picturesque, and in *Observations on the River Wye* (1782) he wrote: "Of the grandeur and beauty of these scenes I can speak as an eyewitness: for though I was never on the spot, I have seen a large collection of drawings and sketches ... which were taken from them." It is easy to see why the illustrations or descriptions in picturesque guidebooks often included directions allowing the traveler to stand exactly where the artist or writer had stood, thus reproducing the expected view. Conversely, it is also why so many Americans who had seen Thomas Moran's *Grand Canyon of the Yellowstone* (1872), which juxtaposed three separate sites in a single view, felt disappointed or confused when confronted with the somewhat less orderly beauty of the park itself (see fig. 12). Naturally, Gilpin had an answer for this, too: "Exact copies can scarcely ever be entirely beautiful,

FIG. 6. H. Adlard, after William H. Bartlett, *Sing-Sing Prison, and Tappan Sea*, 1840. Engraving in Willis, *American Scenery*, vol. 2, opposite p. 47. Milstein Division of United States History, Local History & Genealogy, New York Public Library, Astor, Lenox and Tilden Foundations.

whilst he who works from imagination, culling a distance here, there a foreground, will probably make a much better landscape." A work like *American Scenery*—with its sequence of views moving from *Caldwell (Lake George)* to *Sing-Sing Prison, and Tappan Sea* to *Mount Washington, and the White Hills*—helped to make America "a better landscape" in the eyes of those who read it (figs. 5, 6). It appeased their urge to "see" these places in one way or another, and it gratified the deeper craving they had to see an American landscape both identified in the first place and treated as equal to the scenery of Europe and the Grand Tour. As its audience grew, Willis's book helped to fashion the rootless, anonymous, simultaneous community—separated from each other in space but united by the shared landscape of the book itself—that Emerson called "self-culture" and Benedict Anderson more recently called "nationalism." Susan Magoffin referred to Willis several times in her diary of the Santa Fe Trail, and always as a paragon of scenic description: "Oh, for the genius of an artist that I might pencil such scenes otherwise than in my memory, or the fancy of a Willis that I might trace with this pen a more lively and correct sketch of some of nature's grandest and most striking works."[20]

The most critical issue for a work hoping to bask in the warmth of the "social hearth" was the *kind* of scenery to be illustrated. In his preface Willis points to a landscape that is fresh, extravagant, and natural to the new republic: "Either Nature has wrought with a bolder hand in America, or the effect of long continued cultivation on scenery, as exemplified in Europe, is greater than is usually supposed. Certain it is that the rivers, the forests, the unshorn mountain-sides and unbridged chasms of that vast country, are of a character peculiar to America alone—a lavish and large-featured sublimity, (if we may so express it,) quite dissimilar to the picturesque of all other countries." In the somewhat longer introduction that follows, he writes: "It strikes the European traveler, at the first burst of the scenery of America on his eye, that the New World of Columbus is also a new world from the hand of the Creator. In comparison with the old countries of Europe, the vegetation is so wondrously lavish, the outlines and minor features struck out with so bold a freshness, and the lakes and rivers so even in their fulness and flow, yet so vast and power-ful, that he may well imagine it an Eden newly sprung from the ocean."

Essentially, Willis disrupts the language of the Grand Tour by intro-ducing what might be called a visual roughness. This is emblematic of the picturesque and, as Sidney Robinson has argued, typically "bestows on the interruption a kind of originality" that makes it look like "a new beginning." Willis's picture of "an Eden newly sprung" is just a metaphor for this "new beginning." It is a way to recalibrate the lan-guage of tourism so that America becomes ground zero. Much like Jefferson's and Filson's use of the sublime, it delineates America as a "bolder" landscape by virtue of its natural resources. However, Willis points to this "bolder" landscape not for its own sake, and certainly not as a natural paradise of some sort, but as a contrast *to* European land-scape and a contrast *within* American landscape. The very language of *American Scenery* is that of comparison and contrast, not of nostalgia for an unspoiled world. The point isn't that America has the greatest or grandest or most "wondrously lavish" scenery as such but that it has the greatest *contrast* in scenery, including the contrast between nature and artifice, resources and growth. Inevitably, it is a contrast provoked by the novelty of moving easily from one kind of landscape to another, or discovering disparate elements within the same landscape — just as a view of *The Palisades, Hudson River* gives way to *Barhydts' Lake, near Saratoga, Battle Monument, Baltimore, View from Mount Holyoke*, and *Viaduct on the Baltimore and Washington Railroad*.[21]

The picturesque is a fleeting, open-ended, inclusive, and composite aesthetic. Although it filled a theoretical gap created by Burke's rigorous separation of the beautiful from the sublime, it also destabilized, and eventually incorporated, these older and more conventional aesthetic categories. Thus the often mixed or overlapping classifications of American landscape — a landscape in which the beautiful and the sublime were still somewhat tenuous notions in any case. Willis rather vaguely refers to the "lavish and large-featured sublimity, (if we may so express it,) quite dissimilar to the picturesque of all other countries," and Catlin observes that the scenery along the Missouri could hardly be "wanting in picturesque beauty," because its flooded meadows offered "the most picturesque and beautiful shapes and colours imaginable," while its dry, eroded banks seduced the eye with "tens and hundreds of thousands of different forms and figures, of the sublime and the picturesque." In the words of Uvedale Price, a younger contemporary of Gilpin's, the pictur-esque "blended" the sublime and the beautiful but left them "perfectly distinct." Another way of putting this is that the picturesque displaced attention from individual aesthetic categories and individual elements of the landscape to the *relation between* these categories and elements. We see this quite clearly where both the beautiful and the sublime are evoked to create contrast within a landscape that is generally understood to be picturesque — as in the way Catlin opposes the "beautiful shapes and colours" of the Missouri's flooded meadows to the "different forms and figures" of its sublimely eroded banks, or the way Susan Magoffin opposes the "high mountains, thickly covered with great white rocks," to a pastoral valley marked by "its nice little cottages and court house in the center." Such double views — "marrying together grandeur and loveliness" while leaving them "perfectly distinct" — would be a common feature of American landscape. Although they could be a sign of indecision (Meriwether Lewis's excruciating attempt to describe the Great Falls of the Missouri comes to mind), they were more often the mark of novelty, ambiguity, and persistent, open-ended contrast — with Cole's *Oxbow* one of the earliest and finest examples. As Robinson also observes, the function of any element in a picturesque composition "is determined by its position in a sequence, not by its intrinsic nature," an insight that extends to both duration and scale.[22]

In many ways, *American Scenery* reflects the "large-featured" double landscape of the Hudson Valley, which, broadly speaking, began in the wilds south of Lake George (the "holy lake" of Cooper's *Mohicans*) and ended on the waterfronts of Brooklyn, Manhattan, and Staten Island. Of the 119 annotated illustrations in the book, 45 are associated with the Hudson Valley, divided fairly evenly between such views as *Black Mountain, Lake George* and scenes of the *New York Bay, from the Telegraph Station* variety. Willis located the spirit of America in a landscape "perpetually reaching forward," and the Hudson Valley was clearly reaching forward as fast and as far as any section of the country. When the Erie Canal opened in 1825, the Hudson became part of a Northeast Passage to the rich markets of the Ohio River valley and the upper Mississippi; the thick forests of the Adirondacks and the Catskills were already floating downstream to construct the closely set buildings of villages and towns; and the banks of the great river were ever more defined by the "villas" of the nouveau riche, the new marble prison near Ossining, and the fledgling academy at West Point, where all the army surveyors who followed in Frémont's footsteps would be trained. During his campaign for governor in 1838, William Henry Seward declared that, if he were elected, the Hudson River would become the nation's "true and proper seat of commerce and empire."[23]

Little wonder, then, that both Willis and the artists and writers living at the mouth of the Hudson were so quick to treat this "lavish" yet regional scenery as representative of a national landscape. If we add the illustrations of Niagara Falls and the Erie Canal to those of the Hudson Valley, more than half of *American Scenery* is devoted to the state of New York. Although there are three views of Washington DC and three of George Washington's house at Mount Vernon, nothing south of Mount Vernon is shown except Harpers Ferry and the Natural Bridge, a total of four illustrations. Nothing west of the Natural Bridge is shown at all.

. . .

SENTIMENTS AND IDEAS OFTEN SEEM MOST DEFINITIVE AT the moment they become historically obsolete, and *American Scenery* is one example. Willis was undoubtedly influenced by Irving's *Sketch Book of Geoffrey Crayon, Gent.* (1820), Timothy Dwight's *Travels in New-England and New-York* (1821–22), William Cullen Bryant's poetry, Cooper's Leatherstocking tales, Coles's landscape paintings, William Wall's *Hudson River Port Folio* (1823–24), and Basil Hall's *Forty Etchings, from Sketches Made with the Camera Lucida, in North America, in 1827 and 1828* (1829), and he was probably aware of both Coles's "Essay on American Scenery" (1836) and Emerson's *Nature* (1836). Willis's descriptions also seem to draw on the state geological surveys that were beginning to appear at the time, for example, Edward Hitchcock's *Report on the Geology, Mineralogy, Botany, and Zoology of Massachusetts* (1833) and Charles T. Jackson's *Report on the Geology of the Public Lands in the State of Maine* (1837). Thus the northeastern bias of Willis's book can be traced to an emerging consensus of what counted as "American" scenery to begin with, a growing community of artists and writers tethered to Manhattan and Boston, an expanding network of mechanized transportation that allowed them easy access to the surrounding countryside (a network largely missing in the South), and an accumulating record of scenic and scientific information focused on the Northeast.[24]

But *American Scenery* was published a year after John O'Sullivan's "Great Nation of Futurity" and a year before Catlin's *North American Indians*, and it was bracketed a little more distantly by Irving's *A Tour on the Prairies* (1835) and Frémont's *Report*. From the beginning, its influence on American culture was inversely proportional to its importance — one reason it seems so marginal or invisible today. It upheld the interests of regionalism in an era of continental expansion; it proclaimed one kind of country to be *the* country just as a much larger and more alien section of country was about to change *the* country forever. Only six years separated *American Scenery* from the western journeys of Francis Parkman, Edwin Bryant, and Susan Magoffin, but the scenery they revealed was a direct affront to Willis — Magoffin's most of all. Though she clearly looked up to Willis in her imagination, Magoffin literally lessened the landscape of *American Scenery* with each passing mile she traveled. Her frustration at not having the "genius" to record "nature's grandest and most striking works" had more to do with a meager image of landscape than a meager capacity to describe it. Inspired by the genius of the place, her journal gradually became one of the most searching and poetic accounts of the West to be written during this period. At times, her attention is so defenseless and direct that it appears to be a perfect figure of wonder.[25]

Yet even Magoffin ran a distant second to Frémont — and the *Report* was such a radical interpretation of the picturesque that it took several decades for many Americans to realize how obsolete Willis's work had become. To be sure, Frémont brings a selective and probing eye to everything he describes, and as much as anything else, the *Report* is a document of acute, firsthand observation corroborated by precise measurement. But duration and scale are also important, and Frémont instinctively turns to a kind of self-similarity to construct a prospect that extends from the mouth of the Kansas to the summit of the Wind River Range. Self-similarity does not have to imply the sameness of the Great Desert. It can also lead to systematic divergence or contrast — an endlessly oscillating interval of large and small, now and then, near and far, part and whole — which actually contributes to accuracy by multiplying contrast. Think of the description of the thawing railroad cut in *Walden* (1854), which is basically an extended study in foliate self-similarity. Likewise, the symmetries of a shifting coastline are not those of the imaginary ocean of prairie. So as Frémont slowly advances to South Pass, and then leaves it behind for the Wind River Range, both foreground and background constantly change place in the *Report*, and even the incidental detail of an abandoned beaver dam or a butterfly associated with *Asclepias tuberosa* (butterfly milkweed) finds its place in a landscape completely structured by picturesque contrast.

To depict this ephemeral, oscillating landscape, Frémont turned to a rhetoric of what might be called "topographic geology." On its face there is nothing too striking about this. After all, both topography and geology helped to define the conformities and deviations that shaped great rifts of space — and in doing so, both helped to construct an intricate, three-dimensional, essentially picturesque point of view. Moreover, as Rebecca Bedell has pointed out, geology had become almost de rigueur by this time, with artists such as Cole devoting a good deal of study to it and fashionable magazines of the day noting that geology "may be said to form a necessary part of practical and ornamental education." The *American Journal of Science* happily reported that "lectures upon geology are demanded and given in all our larger towns," while Emerson and Henry David Thoreau were just two of many contemporary writers to utilize geological metaphors. "Language is fossil poetry," Emerson says in "The Poet": "As the limestone of the continent consists of infinite masses of shells of animalcules, so language is made up of images or tropes, which now, in their secondary use, have long ceased to remind us of their poetic origin." Thoreau specifically evoked a theory known as uniformitarianism when he observed: "As in geology, so in social institutions, we may discover the causes of all past changes in the present invariable order of society."[26]

However, as Bedell also acknowledges, "Cole's finished paintings are not particularly notable for their geologic or topographic precision" — further admitting that "he often exaggerated the height and distorted the shape of the landforms in his views of American scenery." When Willis published his own version of American scenery, the view he described from Mount Holyoke took an almost gossipy approach to topographic geology: "The more extended view embraces a great variety of mountain range — Moccadhoe in the north-east, Saddle Mountain in the north-west, . . . and spurs of the Green Mountains advancing and receding in the course of the Connecticut in the north. Geologists speculate extensively on the lakes that once existed in the bosoms formed by these mountains — but we have not time to go back to the deluge."[27]

Frémont adroitly and steadfastly pushed this scenic language beyond fashion, metaphor, or gossip, more or less reducing the picturesque to the contrasts of topographic geology. Note the basic separation or opposition between geology and the picturesque that emerges in Cole's journal during a trip through the Adirondacks in 1835. "The country between Caldwell and Schroon is not very picturesque though rugged and often wild," he writes, "but its formation is very remarkable. The mountains do not run in continuous chains as is generally the case but are insolated heaps of rocks scattered confusedly about." Responding to similar or even bleaker scenery, Frémont chose to turn this point of view on its head, indicating that the "insolated heaps of rocks scattered confusedly about" were precisely what *made* the scene picturesque. Indeed, this was just the start of what would be a basic reversal in scenic language.[28]

Eastern Kansas

THE *REPORT* SEEMS TO BE THE FIRST OFFICIAL DOCUMENT of the Far West written by someone who had been trained to see that landscape beforehand and who liked what he saw. An early journal entry by the expedition's illustrator and mapmaker, Charles Preuss, includes the following comment: "Eternal prairie and grass, with occasional groups of trees. Frémont prefers this to every other landscape. To me it is as if someone would prefer a book with blank pages to a good story." Like most of those who went west, Preuss was seeing the prairies for the first time; as a German, his eye had been trained by the tilled fields, dense forests, and glaciated Alps of his native land, and apparently he thought that even sunrise and sunset lost their beauty in the "eternal" flatness of the prairie. The following comments are typical: "The same landscape. Since this morning not a tree in sight." And: "The country is getting even more monotonous." And: "Nothing new under *this* sun." But where Preuss responded to this terrain with a series of brief, dismissive gibes, focusing more commonly on badly cooked meat and missed meals, the *Report* is a cornucopia of scenic and scientific observation. Preuss's "blank page" *was* Frémont's "good story."[29]

Frémont can be included among those who sensed very early in life what deeply moved them — and his career as an explorer was in some sense lived backward, not forward, with the certainty of a geometric proof. In his *Memoirs* he recounts that he was influenced by two books. One was "a chronicle of men who had made themselves famous by brave and noble deeds, or infamous by cruel and base acts" — probably Herodotus's *Histories*, though it may have been the *Iliad* or Caesar's *Commentaries*. The other was "a work on practical astronomy, published in the Dutch," whose "language made it a closed book but for the beautifully clear maps of the stars" and the "astronomical calculations" necessary to determine latitude and longitude. Matching these interests was a love of nature so powerful that he often neglected his studies for days on end, leading to an early exit from school. Frémont referred to this period of his life as "the splendid outside days; days of unreflecting life when I lived in the glow of a passion that now I know extended its refining influence over my whole life." Thomas Hart Benton would later describe Frémont as "the young explorer who held his diploma from Nature, and not from the United States' Military Academy."[30]

Mathematics, it turned out, was a way to combine these interests. While working as a law apprentice in his early teens, Frémont was asked to survey a rice field near Charleston that had been the subject of a long-standing suit. Despite the miserable conditions he was forced to endure, the survey was so accurate that he began to attract a series of mentors. The most important were Joel R. Poinsett, who asked Frémont to help survey the Cherokee lands in Georgia and later brought him to Washington DC; Joseph N. Nicollet, who led the first two expeditions carried out by the Army Corps of Topographical Engineers; and Thomas Hart Benton, who had a hand in all the expeditions Frémont led. Apparently Frémont realized as early as the Georgia survey that his talent in mathematics could be a way back to those "splendid outside days," acknowledging that "the accident of this employment curiously began a period of years of like work for me among similar scenes." Not until he joined the Nicollet expeditions, though, would he really come into his own — eventually referring to exploration as "the true Greek joy in existence."[31]

· · ·

NICOLLET WAS A FRENCH ASTRONOMER AND CARTOGRA-pher who had sailed to the United States in 1832, eager to contribute "to the progressive increase of knowledge in the physical geography of North America." Although he was trained to calculate latitude and longitude using celestial markers and a chronometer, he was also the first to use a barometer in western exploration — an important development, since the ability to measure altitude precisely allowed him to modify the simple two-dimensional map devised by the ancient Greeks and used for centuries by European and American explorers alike. What Buckminster Fuller would later call the "informative viewability" of maps increased exponentially once the barometer came into play. Nicollet recognized that such "viewability" would be "indispensable for civil and military purposes, for physical geography, for geology, and for topography." He also described barometric data as "one of the most interesting subjects for investigation that present themselves in the vast field where pure mathematics are applied to physical phenomena."[32]

Of the various men who helped to shape his early life, Frémont undoubtedly admired Nicollet the most. If Benton and Poinsett gave him the *opportunity* to see the "unknowne," it was Nicollet who taught him *how* to see it. In a letter to Poinsett written soon after the first expedition set out in June, Frémont refers to Nicollet as "the Pilgrim of Science," and it is evident that what Nicollet taught him was a worldview as much as anything else: "Every day — almost every hour I feel myself sensibly advancing in professional knowledge & the confused ideas of Science & Philosophy wh my mind has been occupied are momently arranging themselves into order & clearness."[33]

Frémont's duties on the expedition were determined by the daily regimen of survey and measurement. "The reconnaissance of the country traversed each day," Nicollet explained, "was made by making the magnetic bearing of every point, by estimating its distance, and by making, as we went, a connected sketch or bird's eye view of the whole, and very often including distant points of importance, indicated to us by the guides, to which one of us always went to take note of." Frémont was generally given this task, which included such now-arcane procedures as "pouring out the quicksilver for the artificial horizon." Paradoxically, while the daily sketch implied a fixed vantage point — as if Frémont had simply sought the nearest hill or rise and drawn what was before him — it was actually arrived at by moving around and *constructing* a point of view. Describing the effort to survey what is now Pipestone National Monument in southwestern Minnesota, Nicollet noted: "Toward 10:00 Frémont,

Flandin and I go on horseback into the valley to study its physical and geological character. In order to grasp the relation between the valley and the surrounding prairies, we travel far and wide."[34]

Obviously the prairies were not an easy thing to survey, and in meeting this landscape on its own terms, Nicollet and Frémont showed themselves to be pilgrims of the senses as well as science. Often there were no nearby hills to ride to—or if there were, they were part of a long sequence of hills carrying to the horizon in all directions. In the opening pages of his report, Nicollet begins to describe this landscape: "There are hillocks, swells, and uplands; but they have a longitudinal and horizontal, rather than a vertical projection. In other words, it is a beautiful arrangement of upland and lowland plains, that give it an aspect *sui generis*." Although such terrain made surveying tedious as well as difficult, neither Nicollet nor Frémont tired of looking at it. Where Pike and Long saw a desert, Nicollet and Frémont saw a "vast interminable low prairie, that extends itself in front,—be it for hours, days, or weeks," a landscape where "pleasurable and exhilarating sensations are all the time felt" and "*ennui* is never experienced." They learned to judge this landscape not by some prominent feature or desired location but by the relationship of foreground to background—especially as it was revealed through time and unexpected shifts in scale. Standing on a plateau overlooking the Minnesota River, Nicollet encountered a "high, grand and beautiful prairie (1,000 to 1,100 feet)," with a view to the south that "seems limitless." He calls it a "spectacle" that is "full of grandeur because of its simplicity that contrasts agreeably with the varied and picturesque countryside the valley of the Minnesota presented to us the last 5 miles." Meanwhile, he is suddenly interrupted by a member of the party who shows him a plant "whose roots according to the Indians kill snakes when one grinds them up and rubs them on the end of a stick to present it to the animal." Not only does Nicollet unexpectedly drop his eyes to focus on the plant, but his description of how the roots are used evokes a space extremely near to hand. Abrupt transitions of this sort are typical of how he saw the prairies—and of how Frémont learned to see it, too.

Without such an awareness, the "vast interminable low prairie" simply led to even more prairie.[35]

In the section of his *Memoirs* devoted to the Nicollet expeditions, Frémont vigorously declares that "the grand simplicity of the prairie is its peculiar beauty, and its occurring events are peculiar and of their own kind. The uniformity is never sameness, and in his exhilaration the voyager feels even the occasional field of red grass waving in the breeze pleasant to the eye." While he was also instructed in the ways of the prairie by Louison Frenière, a half-breed recommended to Nicollet as a hunter and guide, it is apparent that a picturesque (or what he called a "practiced") eye was something that came easily to Frémont — as easily as surveying that difficult piece of land. Whether it was the orderly "clarity" of "Science & Philosophy," the rigors of everyday surveying, or an alertness to the "peculiar beauty" of the prairie, everything Frémont learned on the Nicollet expeditions added to a point of view that was already discriminating and precise. Once he began the *Report*, it all contributed to a compelling style.[36]

. . .

THE MOST OBVIOUS ELEMENT OF THIS STYLE IS FRÉMONT'S emphatic oscillation between scenery and science. Versed in the metrics of maps and topography, Frémont invariably wrote with a plainness — a simple emphasis on what he called "the flower and the rock" — that was common in exploration reports but unusual in scenic guides. Both then and now it could be called an aesthetic of least means. Yet he also wrote with an aesthetic ardor — an admiration for beauty, and the *experience* of beauty — that treated a flower or a rock as something more than a specimen to be pressed between the pages of a large notebook or tossed with other samples into a leather bag. Simply put, Frémont streamlined the rhetoric of tourism and occluded the rhetoric of science. And rather than preferring one to the other or reducing one to the other, he achieved this effect through sustained juxtaposition. An essential feature of Frémont's style is that scenery and science coexist as parallel and contrasting systems of description — equal and off-setting elements. Contrary to Filson in

"The Adventures of Col. Daniel Boon" or Jefferson in *Notes on the State of Virginia*, Frémont does not look for that "distant finishing" in which scenery and science converge and the eye "ultimately composes itself." Mirroring the vagaries and contradictions of the trail, the descriptions in the *Report* are relentlessly ambiguous and open-ended, and the eye is never allowed to settle or choose. On the whole, they correspond to Price's definition of the picturesque, "blending" scenery and science by leaving them "perfectly distinct."[37]

It could be said that Frémont developed such an animated, compressed, and contrasting style because his geometric imagination was so attuned to scale and duration. Maybe that is why he never limited himself, in the end, to the gap between scenery and science. Clearly, he was just as comfortable in the gap between exploration and emigration, foreground and background, past and future, motion and rest. And he always occupied an extremely unstable interval between absolute and relative space — which is to say that, even as he fixed the points of latitude and longitude that would finally reduce the West to a precise and accurate map, he chose to elaborate a landscape in which the very idea of "fixed points" was relative and transient, not absolute. The paradoxical arc of the *Report* is that its landscape had to be seen as both a point of departure and a terminus — an interval between mere country and *the* country. Almost inevitably, then, it had to unfold as a geometry of interruption and yearning.[38]

. . .

CONVINCED THAT HE SHOULD START WITH THE PHYSICAL terrain itself, Frémont chose to frame the *Report* as a narrative of verification. After specifying his orders from the Corps of Topographical Engineers and identifying the various members of the expedition, he gets things under way with the following remark: "Mr. Cyprian Chouteau, to whose kindness, during our stay at his house, we were much indebted, accompanied us several miles on our way, until we met an Indian, whom he had engaged to conduct us on the first thirty or forty miles, where he was to consign us to the ocean of prairie, which, we were told, stretched without interruption almost to the base of the Rocky mountains." A caveat of this sort — "which, we were told" — not only becomes a kind of side step or double take within the sphere of accepted knowledge, but also reveals Frémont's need to create what Steven Shapin has called an audience of "virtual witnesses" willing to accept his, and not others', view of the West.[39]

This approach might be seen as a simple appeal to firsthand knowledge. When Timothy Flint refused to review Cooper's *Prairie* for the *Western Monthly Review*, he wrote: "Of all natural scenery, one would think a prairie the most easy to imagine, without having seen it. Yet no one can present a graphic image of the distinguishing features of a prairie, until he has seen it himself." Regrettably, the most singular and persistent image of the prairie was the *result* of firsthand knowledge, appearing first in the measured language of Pike and Long and later in the more elevated rhetoric of Irving and Catlin. Faced with this situation and with a need to uphold the scientific principles of the expedition, Frémont responded with an artful strategy: he made it clear that a widely accepted fact was going to be treated as a hypothesis that needed to be *proven* by the facts. Saying no more than this, the *Report* implied that the entire nature of the prairie was now in question, not just as a double view of scenery and science but as a section of the continent, a place. It was a crucial disclaimer, a crucial shift in scale. For after exacting this interval of doubt, Frémont began to step back from the landscape of Pike and Long by moving closer to the prairie itself.[40]

The first extensive description of the prairie occurs in the entry dated Friday, June 17. The entry is one of several that actually extend over several days, and the following excerpt begins on the morning of June 19. It takes place in eastern Kansas, near the Topeka of today, as Frémont examines the left (or northern) bank of the Kansas River before heading northwest to Grand Island and the Platte (fig. 7):

> We breakfasted the next morning at half-past five, and left our encampment early. The morning was cool, the thermometer being at 45°. Quitting the river bottom, the road ran along the uplands, over a rolling country, generally in view of the Kansas, from eight to twelve

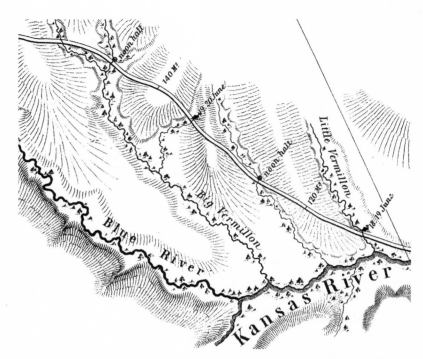

FIG. 7. Charles Preuss, *Topographical Map of the Road from Missouri to Oregon, commencing at the mouth of the Kansas in the Missouri River and ending at the mouth of the Walla-Walla in the Columbia.* Detail, section 1. Published in 1846 by order of the Senate of the United States. Image courtesy of Bob Graham.

miles distant. Many large boulders, of a very compact sandstone, of various shades of red, some of them four or five tons in weight, were scattered along the hills; and many beautiful plants in flower, among which the *amorpha canescens* was a characteristic, enlivened the green of the prairie. At the heads of the ravines I remarked, occasionally, thickets of *salix longifolia*, the most common willow of the country. We travelled nineteen miles, and pitched our tents at evening on the head-waters of a small creek, now nearly dry, but having in its bed several fine springs. The barometer indicated a considerable rise in the country — here about fourteen hundred feet above the sea — and the increased elevation appeared already to have some slight influence upon the vegetation. The night was cold, with a heavy dew; the thermometer at 10 p.m., standing at 46°, barometer 28.483. Our position was in longitude 96°14'49", and latitude 39°30'40".

The morning of the 20th was fine, with a southerly breeze, and a bright sky; and at 7 o'clock we were on the march. The country to-day was rather more broken, rising still, and covered everywhere with fragments of siliceous limestone, particularly on the summits, where they were small, and thickly strewed as pebbles on the shore of the sea. In these exposed situations grew but few plants; though, whenever the soil was good and protected from the winds, in the creek bottoms and ravines, and on the slopes, they flourished abundantly; among them, the *amorpha* still retaining its characteristic place. We crossed, at 10 a.m., the Big Vermillion, which has a rich bottom of about one mile in breadth, one-third of which is occupied by timber. Making our usual halt at noon, after a day's march of twenty-four miles, we reached the Big Blue, and encamped on the uplands of the western side, near a small creek, where was a fine large spring of very cold water. This is a clear and handsome stream, about one hundred and twenty feet wide, running, with a rapid current, through a well-timbered valley. To-day antelope were seen running over the hills, and at evening Carson brought us a fine deer. Longitude of the camp 96°32'35", latitude 39°45'08". Thermometer at sunset 75°. A pleasant southerly breeze and fine morning had given place to a gale, with indications of bad weather; when, after a march of ten miles, we halted to noon on a small creek, where the water stood in deep pools. In the bank of the creek limestone made its appearance in a stratum about one foot thick. In the afternoon, the people seemed to suffer for want of water. The road led along a high dry ridge; dark lines of timber indicated the heads of streams in the plains below; but there was no water near, and the day was very oppressive, with a hot wind, and the thermometer at 90°. Along our route the *amorpha* has been in very abundant but variable bloom — in some places, bending beneath the weight of the purple clusters; in others, without a flower. It seems to love best the sunny slopes, with a dark soil and southern exposure. Everywhere the rose is met with, and reminds us of cultivated gardens and civilization.

How different this is from the prairie that emerges in the reports of Pike and Long. How different it is from Irving's *A Tour on the Prairies*, where a similarly "toilsome march of some distance through a country cut up by ravines and brooks" suddenly reveals "one of the characteristic scenes of the Far West": "an immense extent of grassy undulating, or as it is termed, rolling country with here and there a clump of trees, dimly seen in the distance like a ship at sea." It is almost as if Frémont decides to redefine the prairie as a whole by focusing on that foreground "cut up by ravines and brooks." Easily the most unconventional aspect of his description is the way he *fractures* the landscape, deliberately matching a journey that wends its way through split and scattered terrain with a style that seems to register every sloping ridge, every pool of water, every plant in bloom, every seam of limestone, every passing shadow or breeze. All at once a static, synchronic landscape becomes diachronic and unstable. While it could be said that Frémont is just being explicit about the process that remained largely hidden as he and Nicollet moved around to construct a cartographic point of view, what emerges is a four-dimensional space—irregular, fleeting, full of contrast.[41]

Quitting the banks of a Kansas tributary to ride along the "uplands," Frémont begins to observe "a considerable rise in the country"; the next day he notes that the country is "rather more broken" and is "rising still"; and soon there seem to be ridges, ravines, and "summits" everywhere. Throughout the passage he works his way up from dry creekbed to level prairie and then down again from high ridge to river bottom, almost never keeping to a single plane, because the terrain does not allow it. On the few occasions the terrain remains flat, new obstacles and disparities force him from one side of a creek or river to the other. Gradually, he discovers that these topographic irregularities create certain environmental interruptions. After noting that the barometer indicates rising ground, Frémont announces that "the increased elevation appeared already to have some slight influence upon the vegetation." Later he writes: "In these exposed situations grew but few plants; though, whenever the soil was good and protected from the winds, in the creek bottoms and ravines, and on the slopes, they flourished abundantly." Even the *amorpha* (lead plant), so ubiquitous in the area, seemed "to love best the sunny slopes, with a dark soil and southern exposure." Contrasts of this sort structure the entire passage, with virtually every element doubled in one way or another. Upland "rolling" country gives way to even higher "broken" country; large sandstone boulders are replaced by limestone fragments; red sandstone and purple flowers "enliven" the green prairie; temperatures of 45° rise precipitously to 90°; the western bank of the Big Blue offers better ground for an encampment than the eastern bank; a "pleasant southerly breeze" becomes a "gale" and then a "hot wind"; men "suffer for want of water" on the high dry ridges, while "dark lines of timber indicate the heads of streams in the plains below"; and even as they search for water, "everywhere the rose is met with," reminding the men "of cultivated gardens and civilization."

Nowhere in all of this is there any image of the prairie as a uniform large-scale system. In fact, Frémont generally incorporates the language and imagery of sameness in a way that *adds* to the specificity of the landscape. The "rolling country" that so many people associated with water and ocean swells is mentioned only once in the *Report*, referring not to the prairie but to an area of the high plateau west of Fort Laramie, Wyoming: "The face of the country cannot with propriety be called hilly. It is a succession of long ridges, made by the numerous streams which come down from the neighboring mountain range. The ridges have an undulating surface, with some such appearance as the ocean presents in an ordinary breeze." Since Frémont invokes this image in a discussion devoted to the "nature of the road from Laramie to this point" — a discussion in which he claims that "there is no such thing as a mountain road" from the mouth of the Kansas to South Pass — he is probably trying to allay any fears that the high plateau or the Rockies will be hard to cross by associating them with the dominant image of the prairie. But the image is also quite particular — organically related to the geology and topography of that relatively circumscribed region. Adjoining regions provoke different images.

In the description of eastern Kansas, it is notable that Frémont refers to "*a* rolling country" — a temporary or local terrain — that instantly shatters into the sandstone boulders "scattered along the hills" and the limestone fragments "thickly strewed as pebbles on the shore of the sea." Not only does this image transform the prairie into something rocky and brittle rather than fluid and billowing, but it begins to look like a series of broken summits rather than an endlessly undulating plain. With his reference to the elevation of the country being "about fourteen hundred feet above the sea," Frémont goes even further, using the notion of *sea level* to turn the usual metaphor of oceanic "vastness" or being "out of sight of land" into a means of measuring the land more precisely. Although he speaks of the *amorpha* being "characteristic" and of it "still retaining its characteristic place," this, too, breaks down, as the abundance of its bloom becomes "variable," "in some places, bending beneath the weight of the purple clusters; in others, without a flower." In short, there is no attempt to define the "characteristic" nature of the landscape — except, by implication, as a terrain marked by local and contrasting features.

What's really missing in the *Report* is that horizon of sameness that so completely mesmerized everyone from Pike to Gregg. Where earlier descriptions of the prairie forced us to look up and away, insisting on a single, distant focus, Frémont's spry and discriminating eye never rests. His description reveals an extremely complex landscape, ranging back and forth in scale from limestone fragments, "small, and thickly strewed as pebbles"; to large boulders, "some of them four or five tons in weight"; to the "rich bottom" of the Big Vermillion, "about one mile in breadth"; to a "view of the Kansas, from eight to twelve miles distant." Even on the "summits" of this erratic country, he tends to look down, not away. Observing that the exposed summits seemed hospitable to "but few plants," he quickly lowers his eyes to the ravines and the creek bottoms, where, "protected from the winds," they "flourished abundantly"; reaching the Big Blue, and encamped on the uplands of its western side, he seeks yet another bottom, noting that the "clear and handsome stream" runs "through a well-timbered valley"; and riding along a "high dry ridge," his men suffering "for want of water," he again directs his gaze downward to the "dark lines of timber" indicating "the heads of streams in the plains below." It is not until the entry for July 9 (where the expedition catches its "first faint glimpse of the Rocky mountains, about sixty miles distant") and the entry for July 10 (where the sandy gravel, which gives the upper Platte the appearance of a clear "mountain stream," finally replaces the limestone and marl, which give the lower Platte its "yellow and dirty color") that Frémont really begins to draw our attention to the horizon.[42]

. . .

EVEN NOW THIS SHIFT IN EMPHASIS IS STARTLING, AND IT suggests that Frémont began to picture the West as a kind of double negative. Coincidentally or not, this was a strategy that recalled one of the earliest forms of American nationalism. Martin Brückner has shown in some detail how prior to 1750 or so the word "American" was rarely used to designate either the people or the territory of the Atlantic seaboard, except by the British, who occasionally used it to signify the lowly, backward condition of Colonial troops and society. Because the geographical space of "America" was understood to be that of a colony, the colonists themselves were essentially denied a concrete identity or location beyond "New-Englander" or "Virginian"—a clear indication that they were little more than peripheral elements of the British Empire. A typical response of the day was James Otis's *The Rights of the British Colonies Asserted and Proved* (1764), which argued that this could hardly be otherwise because the British were so ignorant of North American geography that they generally regarded the colonies "all rather as a parcel of *little insignificant conquered islands* than as a very extensive settlement on the continent." Richard Bland's *An Inquiry into the Rights of the British Colonies* (1766) stressed that by constantly referring to the colonies *as* colonies, Parliament essentially reduced them to "Non-Entities." All of this began to change, however, during the Stamp Act crisis of 1764. For one thing, the colonists turned the tables on the British by calling themselves Americans—as in Christopher Gadsden's declaration that "there ought to be no New England men; no New Yorker, known on the Continent; but all of us Americans." More radically, even though most of America remained unexplored and uncertain at the time—less a "known unknown" than "an howling wilderness" pure and simple — the colonists suddenly opted to ground their identity in the "ungrounded, ephemeral space" of the continent itself. Rather than looking to those elements of colonial society that most resembled the stable and cultivated state of British society, rather than calling themselves "Englishmen" or "His Majesty's subjects" living in the "British dominions," they suddenly chose to identify themselves with the very name, and the very territory, that had marginalized them as a political and geographical entity to begin with. Basically, the colonists decided to negate the derogatory meaning of "America" by accentuating its most elusive and negative aspects.[43]

More than half a century later, Frémont instinctively duplicated this tactic to overcome what had emerged as one of the greatest barriers to a continental nation: the Great Desert. Aware that evoking the standards of eastern or European landscape would only make it look inferior by comparison, Frémont chose to visualize the territory west of the Mississippi by accentuating its fundamental *differences* from Europe or the East. His most unique contribution to American landscape may have been to picture this territory as an object of beauty in its own right — unadulterated, unimproved, unadorned. Certainly the *Report* presented a landscape whose beauty emerged from the utility or necessary form of Nature; from the beauty of the thing itself, as Edward Weston or Wallace Stevens might have said. Almost in spite of himself, Frémont helped to canonize such geological landmarks as Courthouse Rock, Chimney Rock, Scotts Bluff, Independence Rock, and Devil's Gate. But it was mainly because he mapped their exact location and included a couple illustrations of them, not because he described them in any detail. For the most part, he sought the beauty of "perfect form" in the broken country of eastern Kansas, the "white and laminated" formations of northeastern Colorado, and the "primitive rocks" of a canyon cut by the Sweetwater River. By any contemporary standard of beauty except Whitman's or Thoreau's, possibly, these would have been regarded as marginal or nonexistent sites. Even if they were *recognized* as distinct landscapes, they would have been dismissed as incomplete, unstable, heterogeneous, random, or disorderly — the sort of sites that

Robert Smithson would later call "low profile landscapes." Such terrain was neither grand enough to evoke the sublime nor pleasing enough to evoke the beautiful, and it seemed to exclude the possibility of either historical association or future improvement.

Of course, true beauty always sets its own standard — creates its own beginning — and Frémont deliberately fashioned the *Report* to recalibrate American taste and sensibility. For an eye transported by a view of the Hudson Valley, the only thing more jarring than the actual sight of eastern Kansas would be the idea that its rising and broken terrain might merit aesthetic attention. By treating this terrain as if it were truly *worthy* of such attention while avoiding the aesthetic standards that were otherwise so important to eastern artists and writers, Frémont was able to suggest that the very elements which seemed to make the West most ugly were actually the source of its greatest beauty. In effect, he used one form of ugliness to offset another, sharing Thoreau's insight that to "double a deformity is a beauty." More sweepingly, he implied that the ugliest region of the continent might be the source of *its* most distinctive beauty, too — the region that finally rendered the American landscape distinct but equal in the eyes of Europeans and Americans alike. Thomas Cole had already suggested something of this sort in his "Essay on American Scenery." "Although the character of its scenery may differ from the old world's," he wrote, "yet inferiority must not therefore be inferred; for though American scenery is destitute of many of those circumstances that give value to the European, still it has features, and glorious ones, unknown to Europe." But much of the "Essay" is limited or compromised by Cole's devotion to the Northeast. Only glancingly does he admit that "the most distinctive, and perhaps the most impressive, characteristic of American scenery is its wildness" — and even then he emphasizes the "variety and magnificence" of the Hudson Valley skies, the diversity and decay of the eastern forest, and the marriage of "grandeur and loveliness" to be seen in the mountains of New Hampshire. Not until the West emerged as a double negative did this wildness become anything other than an exaggeration of the European landscape. And that didn't happen until Frémont wrote the *Report*.[44]

. . .

CONTEMPORARY READERS OF THE *REPORT* MADE ALMOST
no distinction between Frémont's rigorous regard for scenery and his
ardent, expressive empiricism. Certainly, they did not treat his picturesque
point of view as a separate or more "literary" element of the *Report*, and
they did not credit him with a unique style. In fact, the *Report* seemed to
lack a style of any kind, confirming it as an aesthetic of least means. An
article that appeared in the *Athenæum*, an English publication, declared,
"We have rarely met with a production so perfect in its kind as the
unpretending pamphlet containing his report." A long and approving
article in the *Democratic Review* went even further, concluding that,
"as a literary composition, it would be unjust to analyze the Report. It
is evidently the transcript of the notes made in the field; and is what
such notes would naturally be, a brief and rapid delineation of all that
was seen, and in the order in which it was seen. No attempt has been
made at fine writing."[45]

Of course, much the same thing had been said of Long's report, and
of Pike's before it, and the fact that both became so authoritative makes
it clear that empiricism did not have to be associated with the picturesque to be considered scientific. Both Pike and Long emphasized what
Geneva Gano has called a "personal and experiential involvement with
nature" — meaning that "the explorer was expected to have trained his
own eyes to recognize the 'character' of a landscape and to communicate
that character through his descriptive narrative." Yet neither sought the
characteristic features of the landscape in its contrasts, neither exhibited
anything more than a rudimentary or perfunctory awareness of scenery,
and on the few occasions they stepped back a bit to admire the landscape,
neither developed a style that consistently blended scenery and science.
Since much of what they encountered was alien to their eyes — not just
difficult to perceive as scenery but usually taken to be the actual *antithesis*
of scenery — there would be no reason for them to create such a style.[46]

Instead, they seemed to write with the desire to be a kind of camera
obscura — or as Meriwether Lewis's quixotic spelling would have it, a

"crimee obscura." Relying on much the same optics, the sixteenth-century empiricist Francis Bacon had defined the ideal observer as someone with "unimpaired senses" and a "well-purged mind." This helps to explain the mania for collecting and measuring raw data that Lewis and Clark set in motion — with the explorers themselves acting as an "unimpaired" eye for eastern and European scientists who would later tabulate and organize the data into a more truthful theory of nature. But it also implied that the explorers' "personal and experiential involvement with nature" was itself a measure of truth. If a "well-purged mind" was, as Henry Tuckerman put it, "moved within by impressions from without," those impressions were bound to be received and reflected accurately, without distortion. It is worth noting that after declaring himself "disgusted" with his "imperfect description" of the Great Falls of the Missouri — a description in which his frustrated devotion to conventional aesthetic categories compelled him to label the first fall "sublimely grand" and the second "pleasingly beautifull" — Lewis "determined to draw my pen across it and begin again, but then reflected that I could not perhaps succeed better than pening the first impressions of the mind."[47]

All of this suggests that when Frémont turned to the picturesque to express his own "impressions of the mind," it was both a break with the rhetoric of American exploration and a matter of better art, not better science. Although Frémont undoubtedly needed to prove he was a careful and reliable scientist, his greater aim was to prove that the great "ocean of prairie" was neither uniformly sterile nor utterly dreary to the eyes — and that was essentially an aesthetic enterprise. John Conron has rightly observed that the picturesque usually implies a far more animated landscape than the beautiful or the sublime, often stressing the fleeting effects of sunlight and clouds, as well as a moving point of view in which scenery is transformed "into dramatic 'incident.'" He also points out that picturesque landscapes are commonly "constructed to visualize impressions as various and changeful as the world and the consciousness they represent." Each of these elements has a place in the *Report*, as Frémont basically takes the raw data of Long's report and begins to accelerate or multiply their contrasts to create a completely different kind of geography—a geography where the beautiful and the sublime are perceived as boundaries and irregularities *within* the landscape, not as a means of reducing it to a single characteristic. Where Long finds that "the cactus ferox reigns sole monarch, and sole possessor of thousands of acres of this dreary plain," Frémont discovers that "the ground was covered in many places with an efflorescence of salt, and the plants were not numerous. In the bottoms was frequently seen *tradescantia*, and on the dry lenches were *carduus, cactus*, and *amorpha*." It is a subtle yet telling difference, with even the apparent sterility of salt morphing into the scenic "efflorescence" of *amorpha*. Evidently, Frémont felt that the way to bring the Great Desert to life was by framing his "personal and experiential involvement with nature" as an act of verification—and then elaborating verification itself as a precise yet scenic tour of "the flower and the rock." Only by presenting the Great Desert as something *worth* seeing could he incite the kind of restless interest that might provoke people to see it more *accurately*.[48]

It could be said that Frémont was the individual who led America out of the woods, creating an entirely novel landscape that Emerson, a year later, would call the "nervous, rocky West." Both Pike and Long clearly felt that the "scarcity of wood and water" was the most prominent and cheerless feature of the prairie, and a similar bias encouraged most Americans to treat the sylvan reaches of the Hudson Valley as an aesthetic ideal. Once Frémont introduced the fractured, boulder-strewn features of eastern Kansas, however, he began to redefine the American landscape as a sphere of topographic contrasts. Within the *Report* itself, flowers, and sometimes trees, would help to multiply these contrasts, but the most important element was always the ground, whether it was a sandstone boulder, a limestone fragment, the eroded face of a massive butte, or a dry ridge. The farther west he moved, the more Frémont began to reduce the *Report* to a strict examination of the ground. Along the way, he steadily transformed the arid and often desolate terrain he encountered into a new and exciting standard of scenic beauty—a distinctly "western" standard, uniquely viewed as a double negative.

That such a radical departure could be viewed as "uncolored by opinions" is a sign of how adroitly Frémont blended scenery and science in the *Report*. It helped, of course, that geology was already the science most directly indebted to the picturesque. Martin Rudwick has argued that geology actually emerged "from a synthesis of heterogeneous earlier traditions such as 'cosmogony,' mineralogy, 'géographie physique,' natural history, 'Geognosie,' and mining." It soon developed a visual language "appropriate to the subject-matter of the science," able to "complement verbal descriptions and theories by communicating observations and ideas that could not be expressed in words." Rudwick traces this visual language not to the romantic art of the era, which favored the beautiful and the sublime, but to the many military surveys and marine navigation charts that were available, to the sketches and illustrations compiled during the great voyages of discovery, and to the surveys and bird's-eye views commissioned to commemorate the great estates. Essentially, geology became a modern science by creating a "representational barrage" of maps, descriptions, stratigraphic sections, and landscapes. This made it a perfect model for the *Report*.[49]

What is most noteworthy about the *Report* is the way Frémont embraced the scenic beauty of landscape while avoiding any semblance of the "elevation" that so noticeably identified eastern artists and writers with the romantic style of scientific writing developed by Alexander von Humboldt — a list that prominently included Catlin, Irving, Emerson, and Thoreau (when he wasn't doubling a deformity) as well as Frederic Edwin Church. It was this very lack of elevation that allowed Frémont to present an aesthetic category like the double negative as if it were the record of an ideally "unimpaired" eye and a receptively blank mind, transferred whole and unaltered to the blank page. For those who believed that the mind was "moved within by impressions from without," this could only mean that the novel landscape Frémont described was actually *there*. It could not mean, as Long had said so strongly of the Great Desert, that there was *nothing* there except a weary sameness. If anything, the *Report* implied, it was the Great Desert that was not there — suggesting that in the end Frémont's act of verification, his "personal and experiential involvement with nature," was fundamentally an act of renaming.

NAMING AND RENAMING — THAT IS TO SAY, THE NOMINAL or arbitrary relationship between words and objects — is an important aspect of "Knowledge by Acquaintance and Knowledge by Description," a paper Bertrand Russell delivered in 1911. Although he would soon develop a less dualistic version of John Locke's epistemology, Russell relied on a separation of mind and matter in "Knowledge" that seems typical of nineteenth-century thought — evident, for instance, in that image of the horizon, that "meeting of the sky and the earth," that so fascinated Emerson and Thoreau as a figure of astonishment or yearning. As such, it seems quite useful in the case of the *Report*.[50]

Like many philosophical papers, "Knowledge" begins by defining its terms, arguing that "knowledge by acquaintance" is "essentially simpler than any knowledge of truths, and logically independent of knowledge of truths," while "knowledge by description" always involves "some knowledge of truths as its source and ground." Taking as his example the table he is writing on, Russell explains that "we shall say that we have *acquaintance* with anything of which we are directly aware, without the intermediary of any process of inference or any knowledge of truths. Thus in the presence of my table I am acquainted with the sense-data that make up the appearance of my table — its colour, shape, hardness, smoothness, etc." His actual "knowledge of the table as a physical object," however, is "not direct knowledge": "The table is 'the physical object which causes such-and-such sense-data.' This *describes* the table by means of the sense-data. In order to know anything at all about the table, we must know truths connecting it with things with which we have acquaintance: we must know that 'such-and-such sense-data are caused by a physical object.'" In fact, "there is no state of mind in which we are directly aware of the table; all our knowledge of the table is really knowledge of *truths*, and the actual thing which is the table is not, strictly speaking, known to us at all. We know a description and we know that there is just one object to which this description applies, though the object itself is not directly known to us." Russell goes on to explain that "common words, even proper names, are usually really descriptions. That is to say, the thought in the mind of a person using a proper name correctly can generally only be expressed explicitly if we replace the proper name by a description." The same thing is true of "all names of places," which Russell defines as "descriptions which start from some one or more particulars with which we are acquainted" and "otherwise consist wholly of concepts."

If we substitute the word "prairie" for "table," this becomes a cogent analysis of the *Report*. Frémont may have framed the *Report* as an act of verification, but it was clearly no less descriptive than any prior account of the prairie, and it brought his readers no closer than Pike or Long to any real acquaintance with the physical space defined by the word "prairie." Literally, the prairie was as absent, or unseen, as ever. What Frémont began to modify, however, was the rigid set of "sense-data" (a word Russell coined) which defined the prairie as "oceanic" and "arid." By drawing our attention to such things as the cool morning air, the uplands "rather more broken" and "rising still," the large boulders "of various shades of red," the "thickly strewed" fragments of siliceous limestone, the "variable bloom" of purple *amorpha*, and the water stand-ing "in deep pools," he significantly multiplied both the number and nature of the sense-data associated with the word "prairie." Where Pike and Long had treated "colour, shape, hardness, smoothness, etc." as a meager inventory of particulars, Frémont introduced one variable after another—a virtual explosion of visual information—which suddenly forced "the physical object which causes such-and-such sense-data" to include a much larger and more chaotic set of "particulars with which we are acquainted." The very multiplicity of these particulars implied that Frémont had developed a *mode* of description, a *style*, lucid enough for us to "know a description" of the "prairie" far more complex than anything that had appeared in Pike or Long—and to know that the singular "object to which this description applied" could only be the indirect "prairie" of the *Report*. Of course, the variety and contrast of these sense-data also implied that any descriptive style which lacked multiplicity was probably less accurate than one which accounted for it. Not only that, but the way this multiplicity gradually revealed a complex, yet coherent, landscape seemed to parallel the way the mind, "moved within by impressions from without," gradually formed itself from matter. Since the Great Desert seemed to *be* a desert because it left the mind blank—either too vast or too uniform to provoke anything other than a sensation of sameness—this may have been the most radical element of Frémont's description for those who first read his account. In any case, there is no question that the broken and blossom-strewn "prairie" which emerged in the *Report* began to replace the great "ocean of prairie" on which "not a speck of vegetable matter existed." Nor is there any question that it, and not the abyss of Pike and Long, became the "prairie" which all those who followed in Frémont's footsteps sought to verify for themselves. For just as the *Report* was not an original act of discovery but a reenactment of it through personal observation, so was every subsequent trip west both a reenactment and a verification of the *Report* itself.[51]

. . .

THERE IS, OF COURSE, NO INHERENT RELATIONSHIP BETWEEN description—even the most inventive or iconoclastic form of description—and the more formal matter of composition. When the *Democratic Review* wrote that, "as a literary composition, it would be unjust to analyze the Report" and went on to say that "it is evidently the transcript of the notes made in the field; and is what such notes would naturally be, a brief and rapid delineation of all that was seen, and in the order in which it was seen," the author seemed to be making an obvious point. On the other hand, a review of *Commerce of the Prairies* began by declaring Gregg not to be "a very practiced writer" precisely because he succumbed to a desire "to give full and just views" of everything he encountered. At one point, the reviewer became so impatient with the pace of the narrative that he literally cut it short: "We cannot follow Mr. Gregg in his journey, which those who know the usual pace of oxen will not suppose could be a very rapid one, but come with him at once to its termination in the autumn." Equally irritated by Edwin Bryant's slow and encyclopedic eye, one reviewer of his overland diary complained that it led "the weary reader on the weary traveller's track, through two hundred and forty pages of wilderness." And yet the same reviewer immediately wondered: "Why is it that Frémont's report, though a mere narrative of his progress through the wilderness, has the power to attract and interest the reader?" The answer is that Frémont always knew what to leave out and what to include, creating the *effect* of a "transcript of the notes made in the field."[52]

As much as he multiplies the sense-data of the prairie, Frémont never just accumulates information the way Long and Gregg do, and never indulges in the chaotic concatenation of events that is so characteristic of Bryant and Meriwether Lewis's longer journal entries. Sensation always implies composition in the *Report*. Frémont's very first description of the prairie begins to reveal both his topographic geology and the way in which the *Report* will be structured. What appears to be a rather random sequence of details — or a sequence of details determined more or less by the course of each day's journey — is actually a skillful and dramatic composition. With everything he includes in the description, it is obvious that Frémont chooses *not* to include a great deal more. Not only does he select details that are echoed, or exaggerated, or negated by later details, but the passage as a whole winds these contrasts tighter and tighter and then deliberately unravels the tension.[53]

Remember that the passage begins on a cool morning, in a river bottom, with plenty of water. As the party leaves the river, following the road up and over a gently rolling country, Frémont notices "many large boulders," as well as "many beautiful plants" clearly well watered. The barometer shows that there is a "considerable rise" in the country generally, with some "slight influence" on the vegetation. They camp that night on a small creek, "now nearly dry" but with "several small springs." While Frémont does not indicate the temperature at noon or sunset, he notes that at 10:00 p.m. it is almost exactly what it was when they left early in the morning. The next day the country becomes "rather more broken," with the large boulders giving way to limestone fragments that remind him of pebbles on the seashore — as if the boulders, though of different composition, had been broken down by the action of water into these smaller pieces. The sloping, ravine-cut topography is indicated by the presence or absence of plants as the party progresses from protected to exposed terrain — a steadily more extreme variation in the general "rise" of the country and evidence of a greater influence on the vegetation. The temperature at sunset is 75° — a warm day after the apparent coolness of the day before, but with plenty of water for the men to drink. On the third day the contradictions intensify. What begins as a "fine morning," with a "pleasant southerly breeze," quickly turns into a gale, "with indications of bad weather." Soon the gale itself becomes a "hot wind," bringing with it an "oppressive" atmosphere and a temperature of 90°. While the water stands "in deep pools" at noon, just several hours later the men are suffering from thirst — and this thirst is expressed by the distance between the "high dry ridge" the road follows and the timbered plains far below, accelerating the fissures within the prevailing elevation. Even the *amorpha*, while "still retaining its characteristic place," has suddenly begun to vary its bloom, sometimes ceasing to bloom at all. The aridness of that "now nearly dry" creek has overtaken both the air and the land. And yet, in the midst of this increasingly somber and shattered terrain, the rose seems to be everywhere, reminding the party of "cultivated gardens and civilization." This association instantly casts an ameliorating light over everything that has come before and adds poignancy to the observation, several sentences later, that "travelling on the fresh traces of the Oregon emigrants, relieves a little the loneliness of the road."

Contrast begets contrast in the *Report* — but of a strictly regulated order. It is not surprising that in many ways the *Report* recapitulates the history of English landscape poetry. James Turner has ably documented how contrast began as a metaphor of turmoil and wildness and then rapidly became a sign of order and balance. This is more or less what happens in the *Report*. By introducing complexity and detail into a landscape generally seen as uniform, Frémont begins to create a temporary, piecemeal *dis*order that intrinsically resists sameness and is gradually shown to be systematic at some other scale or time frame. We see this in miniature in the description of eastern Kansas, as Frémont steadily compiles an apparently quixotic or circumstantial inventory of landscape elements and then fashions them into a coherent narrative, implying a decisive shift from what Turner calls "itemization" to a "unity of structure." That the description is also a microcosm of the entire *Report* — within which it functions as a distinct and disparate section — merely confirms this sense of order.[54]

A more complex example is the apparently incongruous entry for August 6, which takes place along the Sweetwater River, in the neighborhood of South Pass, following a day of rain and cold. Quoted more or less whole, the entry reads:

> In about three miles, we reached the entrance of a *kanyon*, where the Sweet Water issues upon the more open valley we had passed over. Immediately at the entrance, and superimposed directly upon the granite, are strata of compact, calcareous sandstone and chert, alternating with fine white and reddish white, and fine gray and red sandstones. These strata dip to the eastward at an angle of about 18°, and form the western limit of the sand and limestone formations on the line of our route. Here we entered among the primitive rocks. The usual road passes to the right of this place; but we wound, or rather scrambled, our way up the narrow valley for several hours. Wildness and disorder were the character of the scenery. The river had been swollen by the late rains, and came rushing through with an impetuous current, three or four feet deep, and generally twenty yards broad. The valley was sometimes the breadth of the stream, and sometimes opened into little green meadows, sixty yards wide, with open groves of aspen. The stream was bordered throughout with aspen, beech, and willow; and tall pines grew on the sides and summits of the crags. On both sides, the granite rocks rose precipitously to the height of three hundred and five hundred feet, terminating in jagged and broken pointed peaks; and fragments of fallen rock lay piled up at the foot of the precipices. Gneiss, mica slate, and a white granite, were among the varieties I noticed. Here were many old traces of beaver on the stream; remnants of dams, near which were

lying trees, which they had cut down, one and two feet in diameter. The hills entirely shut up the river at the end of about five miles, and we turned up a ravine that led to a high prairie, which seemed to be the general level of the country. Hence, to the summit of the ridge, there is a regular and very gradual rise. Blocks of granite were piled up at the heads of the ravines, and small bare knolls of mica slate and milky quartz protruded at frequent intervals on the prairie, which was whitened in occasional spots with small salt lakes, where the water had evaporated, and left the bed covered with a shining incrustation of salt. The evening was very cold, a northwest wind driving a fine rain in our faces; and at nightfall we descended to a little stream, on which we encamped, about two miles from the Sweet Water. Here had recently been a very large camp of Snake and Crow Indians; and some large poles lying about afforded the means of pitching a tent, and making other places of shelter. Our fires to-night were made principally of the dry branches of the artemesia, which covered the slopes. It burns quickly, with a clear oily flame, and makes a hot fire. The hills here are composed of hard, compact mica slate, with veins of quartz.

We might see this region as a more extreme or "primitive" version of the rising yet broken country of eastern Kansas, with many of the same kinds of contrast. After moving from an "open valley" to where "the hills entirely shut up the river," the party turns into a ravine that leads to "a high prairie" and "hence, to the summit of the ridge," which seems to represent a "regular and very gradual rise." "Wildness and disorder" are all around. The "fine white and reddish white" sandstones are darkened by the wetness of a "fine rain," and crude "blocks of granite" lie in piles "at the foot of the precipices." Even in the midst of wetness and "rich, soft grass," the prairie is "whitened in occasional spots with small lakes, where the water had evaporated, and left the bed covered with a shining incrustation of salt." A new element is the "many old traces of beaver on the stream," with the felled trees lying near the remnants of their dams morphing into the "large poles" left lying about a recently deserted "camp of Snake and Crow Indians," appropriated by Frémont for his own camp. As in the earlier description, the region emerges as a diverse and completely three-dimensional landscape.

Whatever its resemblance to eastern Kansas, however, it is the juxtaposition of this terrain to South Pass that matters most. On the whole, the distance between Devil's Gate and South Pass is covered quickly and cursorily in the *Report* — except for the August 6 entry, which seems to be a kind of small-scale diversion. Only as Frémont begins to characterize the pass itself does it become clear why he might have suddenly focused on a rugged canyon rather than the "usual road" that passed to the right of it. South Pass forms an unusual section of the Continental Divide. It is so nondescript, and the ascent to it so gradual, that "with all the intimate knowledge possessed by [Kit] Carson, who had made this country his home for seventeen years, we were obliged to watch very closely to find the place at which we had reached the culminating point." After noting that it is even difficult to "fix positively the breadth of this pass," Frémont goes on to declare: "It will be seen that it in no manner resembles the places to which the term is commonly applied — nothing of the gorge-like character and winding ascents of the Allegheny passes in America; nothing of the Great St. Bernard and Simplon passes in Europe." Eventually, he compares the "elevation we surmounted immediately at the Pass" to the "ascent of the Capitol hill from the avenue, at Washington" — and then extends this relatively short incline to include the whole region. "Approaching it from the mouth of the Sweet Water, a sandy plain, one hundred and twenty miles long, conducts, by a gradual and regular ascent, to the summit, about seven thousand miles above the sea; and the traveller, without being reminded of any change by toilsome ascents, suddenly finds himself on the waters which flow to the Pacific ocean."

As an instance of sudden and deliberate contrast, it is hard to imagine a better way of showing what South Pass *isn't* than by highlighting a "gorge-like" canyon that more truly resembles the "Allegheny passes in America" and the "Great St. Bernard and Simplon passes in Europe." If nothing else, this juxtaposition helps to reveal exactly what South Pass *is*, namely, the kind of "culminating point" that makes it a perfect spot for heavy, overburdened wagons to cross the Continental Divide. Of course, it is typical of Frémont's geometrical imagination to turn the "regular and very gradual rise" of a ridge overlooking the canyon into a "sandy plain, one hundred and twenty miles long" — as if the lay of the land, rising like "the Capitol hill from the avenue," naturally draws the nation west. But even something as incidental as the felled trees becomes an aspect of this providential incline, signifying that the legendary fur trade (the trade so coveted by the British that they refused to relinquish the Oregon Territory) is about to be overtaken by the tents and "other places of shelter" associated with a wave of emigrants. An obvious inference is that the Continental Divide ought to be seen as an historical divide and that the road to the future is about to run through South Pass.

Not that Frémont is content to leave it at this. In the opening paragraph of the *Report* he flatly states that his orders are "to explore and report upon the country between the frontiers of Missouri and the South Pass in the Rocky mountains" — indicating, more or less, that the pass will be his final destination and the climax of the narrative. Yet even before he reaches the pass, he begins dropping hints that he is looking past it. When he breaks a thermometer at Fort Laramie, he marks the "misfortune" by noting that he has promised himself "some interesting experiments in the mountains." When he breaks a barometer a few days later, he says for the first time that he has brought it along "principally for mountain service." By the time he rids himself of the party's wagons, burying them in a cache to be retrieved later, all pretense is gone — he is leading a mountain expedition. This means that whatever Frémont says or implies about South Pass, it cannot be seen as the pinnacle of the *Report*. In some sense it must fall short — must look as level narratively as it does literally — in order to draw the expedition on. And this is exactly what the trip through the canyon achieves. With its "wild and disorderly" terrain and its juxtaposition to the pass, it creates an expectation of roughness that can only be satisfied by moving beyond a smooth and almost indiscernible "culminating point." Indeed, such a long and arrested incline suggests that roughness even needs to be exaggerated, encouraging us to feel that only a large-scale diversion to the Wind River Range will dispel the anticipation provoked by the small-scale diversion to the canyon.

So it is that South Pass itself turns out to be the real diversion. Having been the destination or background of the expedition since the first day, the pass now appears to be little more than a foreground to the Wind River Range—the prairie to its summit. As Smithson might have put it, it is here that the long and linear arc of the Oregon Trail becomes the labyrinth of the high mountain range. No wonder Frémont has less to say about the gentle yet momentous pass than the sheer, inconsequential canyon. As usual, it is largely through the length and direction of his gaze that he reveals the subjectivity of his composition.

. . .

WALTER BENJAMIN ONCE OBSERVED THAT "HISTORY DECAYS into images, not into stories." The aphorism appears in a paragraph about historical materialism, but its impetus appears to be an insight about photography. Benjamin, a philosopher as well as a critic, was among the first to recognize that photography would create a boundless universe of images in which a single instant of history could symbolize an entire era—a condition even truer today than seventy or eighty years ago, as we all wander around with iconic images in our heads, ignorant or forgetful of anything but the simplest context. While it is not an obvious point of reference, it helps to keep this distinction in mind when thinking of the *Report*. For Frémont constantly and insistently substituted images for stories; that is to say, topographic geology alone became the story he chose to tell.[55]

A curious aspect of the expedition is that Frémont actually brought a daguerreotype camera along, evidently hoping to photograph the high plains and the Rockies for the first time. Since the camera is never mentioned in the *Report*, we only know this because a stray voucher is part of the public record and because Preuss added it to the many other things he mocks in his journal: "Yesterday afternoon and this morning Frémont set up his daguerreotype to photograph the rocks; he spoiled

FIG. 8. Charles Preuss, *Chimney Rock*. Engraving in John C. Frémont, *Report on an Exploration of the Country Lying between the Missouri River and the Rocky Mountains, on the Line of the Kansas and Great Platte Rivers*. Printed by order of the United States Senate, 1843. Image courtesy of Bob Graham.

five plates that way. Not a thing was to be seen on them." Comparing Preuss's journal to the *Report*, it appears Frémont tried to photograph Devil's Gate, South Pass, and a view of the Wind River Range, only to give up after botching every exposure. That he waited until the high plains to make his first plate suggests that photography — or what Smithson called the "Cartesian eye" of the camera — was supposed to verify the rawest form of topographic geology. Frémont may have chosen to photograph South Pass to corroborate its ascending flatness, but the other sites had no intrinsic interest, except as "wild and disorderly" scenery. Discovering this suppressed element makes it even clearer that he set out to construct a landscape without any of the historical associations that supposedly made European landscape so superior to the United States. Of the six etchings that eventually appeared in the *Report* — none of them showing anything east of Scotts Bluff and Chimney Rock — five were strictly geological landscapes (figs. 8, 9). The only exception was a view of Fort Laramie, which helped to illustrate the military aims of the expedition. Image and text were of a piece in the *Report* — pictures, not stories.[56]

FIG. 9. Charles Preuss, *Devil's Gate*. Engraving in Frémont, *Report on an Exploration*. Printed by order of the United States Senate, 1843. Image courtesy of Bob Graham.

By contrast, a book like Willis's was conceived as a series of illustrated texts, with the texts themselves devoted to "that part of the American story history has not yet found leisure to put into form, and which romance and poetry have not yet appropriated — the legendary traditions and anecdotes, events of the trying times of the Revolution, Indian history, &c. &c." When Willis described the view from Mount Holyoke, for example, less than half the text was devoted to the view itself; most of it was a chronicle of the crucial land transactions and the history of Indian warfare in the region. While he may have argued that the contrasts of American scenery made it equal or superior to Europe in certain respects and that Americans generally looked to the future, not the past, in their landscape, Willis shared an almost universal yearning to associate the new landscape with an ancient and authentic history — a "legendary tradition." For a nation so insecure about its place in the world, images were not informative or eloquent enough to stand alone. Willis explicitly referred to the texts as "the intellectual portion" of the book and the etchings as "the embellishments."[57]

It has often been pointed out that by situating the Leatherstocking tales among the Catskills, the Adirondacks, and the shores of the Great Lakes, Cooper, too, began to create a landscape rife with history. His literary model was Sir Walter Scott, whose Waverly novels offered a romantic version of English and Scottish history and were extremely popular on both sides of the Atlantic. Looking for a Native version of Scott's legendary heroes, Cooper turned to an emblematic figure of the Enlightenment—the noble savage. Here he found a precedent in Irving's *Sketch Book of Geoffrey Crayon, Gent.*, which had appeared three or four years before *The Pioneers*. In addition to "The Legend of Sleepy Hollow" and "Rip Van Winkle" (indigenous versions of German folk tales), the *Sketch Book* included two essays—"Traits of Indian Character" and "Philip of Pokanoket: An Indian Memoir"—each of which identified the American landscape with Indian legends and traditions. What is most notable about the essays is the note of nostalgia they strike. While admiring the Indians' "loftiness of spirit" and admitting that "the rights of the savage have seldom been properly appreciated or respected by the white man," Irving nevertheless concludes: "They will vanish like a vapor from the face of the earth; their very history will be lost in forgetfulness; and 'the places that now know them will know them no more for ever.' Or if, perchance, some dubious memorial of them should survive the lapse of time, it may be in the romantic dreams of the poet, to people in imagination his glades and groves, like the fauns and satyrs and sylvan deities of antiquity." Obviously, this is a history both granted and revoked at the same moment; a history that metaphorically links the landscape of America with antiquity, or even the state of nature, while exterminating the agents of that history. The fantasies of an *Ivanhoe*-like chivalry that suffuse both the Leatherstocking tales and Irving's western narratives merely extend this vision of an obsolete people to the entire continent, constructing a past that has no future. Thus Cooper's now famous title: *The Last of the Mohicans*.[58]

What was true of Irving and Cooper, and even more bookishly of Willis, was also true of Catlin and Thoreau. Catlin presented *North American Indians* as an extended description of "the character and condition of those tribes living entirely in a state of nature." Like many others, he viewed the Mandans as the "remains" of the mythical "*Welsh colony*—the followers of Madoc"—who had set sail for the New World in 1170 only to become lost to history. He also claimed that certain customs and "the character of their heads" were evidence that many Indian tribes had mixed with descendants of the "lost tribes of Israel." At the same time, he documented a number of Indian creation myths which, if they evoked the Noachian deluge, also challenged it and linked America to an alternative cosmos. The Mandan image of earth being carried on the shell of a tortoise—part of a larger story in which the shell was pierced by a tribe of white people, now dead, who unleashed a flood that drowned all but one man—seems to have struck Thoreau, in particular, since he refers to it more than once. More significantly, Thoreau came to see Indian languages as a link to some ancient alignment of word and object. Two of the essays included in *The Maine Woods* (1864), "Chesuncook" and "The Allegash and East Branch," haphazardly pursue the idea that Indian nomenclature somehow represented the language of nature itself. At one point Thoreau happily notes that even when the guide Joe Polis spoke English, he "generally added the syllable *um* to his words," translating the sonorants of civilization into a "wild and refreshing sound, like that of the wind among the pines, or the booming of the surf on the shore." As an absent or suppressed figure of European colonization, the Indian appears over and over again in *Walden*, *Cape Cod* (1865), and *A Week on the Concord and Merrimack Rivers* (1849)—and Thoreau's dying words were said to have been "moose" and "Indian."[59]

What's so conspicuous about the *Report* is how implacably Frémont resists this effort to make the western landscape credible by investing it with a history that reaches back to the "sylvan deities of antiquity," the state of nature, or an American version of Genesis. Written for Congress and the army but with a popular audience in mind, the *Report* presents a landscape that is almost entirely free of the refined associations expected of scenic guides such as Willis's as well as the more savage associations expected of western narratives such as Irving's and Catlin's. However much this served the interests of settlers over the years, reinforcing the idea that the West was simply an empty space waiting to be filled, it was a very original and iconoclastic decision at the time. The Great Desert was such an overwhelming image of desolation and emptiness that it seemed to demand some sort of human presence. A powerful metaphor of the abyss cried out for an offsetting metaphor of agency and desire. Frémont would furnish this metaphor by identifying the continent with the nation — but only after identifying the continent itself as a purely physical landscape.[60]

This is not to say that reading history into the landscape would have been all that straightforward for Frémont in any case. After all, it is hard to wax nostalgic about the vanishing Indian if you're proposing a line of forts to lessen their existing threat to emigrants; it is just as imprudent to extol Spanish contributions to the West if a war with Mexico is imminent. Frémont is clearly more comfortable with the less impending history of French occupation, introducing each and every one of his men, most of them of French heritage; evoking the songs of Canadian voyageurs as he shoots the rapids of the upper Platte; and briefly describing a fur trader named Chabonard whose camp is on an island nicknamed Saint Helena. He is also untroubled by the fabled past of fur trading, if only because he can equate it with the abandoned beaver dam along the Sweetwater. But what little history he does include almost always exists *in* the landscape, not *as* landscape — one reason the many prairie fires he describes emerge as more of an atmospheric effect than a long-standing form of Indian land use. Even when he expresses satisfaction that "the name of 'Long's peak'" has "been adopted and become familiar in the country" and briefly accounts for several other "American" names, he still restricts his emphasis to the terrain itself. A telling comparison can be made between Irving's description of Scotts Bluff and Frémont's of Goshen's Hole. Irving devotes two sentences to what the bluff looks like and two paragraphs to the "melancholy circumstance" of how it came to be named for a man who died nearby, whereas Frémont ignores the biblical reference altogether and spends almost half a page explaining why the terrain "might very naturally be called a hole in the hills."[61]

This comparison also reveals how adamantly Frémont resists the temptation to read some "fancied resemblance" into the landscape by associating it with picturesque castles and ruins. Echoing Catlin's account of a Missouri riverbank as an "ancient and boundless city in ruins," Irving's account of Scotts Bluff reads as follows: "On the 21st, they encamped amidst high and beetling cliffs of indurated clay and sandstone, bearing the semblance of towers, castles, churches, and fortified cities. At a distance, it was scarcely possible to persuade oneself that the works of art were not mingled with these fantastic freaks of nature." Though Frémont appears to adopt this imagery when he describes Goshen's Hole, it is the first and only time he does so, and it has little to do with picturesque ruins. To begin with, he takes great pains to delineate the lay of the land not only as it appears before him but at a much larger scale: "Looking back upon the spot, at a distance of a few miles to the northward, the hills appear to shut in the prairie, through which runs the creek, with a semi-circular sweep, which might very naturally be called a hole in the hills. The geological composition of the ridge is the same which constitutes the rock of the Court-house and Chimney, on the North fork, which appeared to me a continuation of this ridge. The winds and rains work this formation into a variety of singular forms." Only on the heels of these relatively precise observations does Frémont suggest that the overall effect of the formation is that of "a massive fortified place" — and even here almost all of his metaphors evoke "an old fortified town" rather than an architectural fantasy. The rock of the region "much resembles masonry at a little distance," he writes; a nearby hill terminates "on either extremity in enormous bastions"; and sometimes the terrain looks like "a solitary house, with many chambers," the sort of "natural defenses" that create a refuge "perfectly secure from any attack of prowling savages." The single-mindedness of this metaphor, and Frémont's sudden use of it, is explained a paragraph or two later when he sees Fort Laramie for the first time. For the fort — "a quadrangular structure, built of clay," its "lofty walls, whitewashed and picketed, with large bastions at the angles" to protect the "apartments" that open into a central yard — is pictured in exactly the same terms.

Just like his description of the canyon before South Pass, then, Frémont indulges in a lengthy and apparently gratuitous episode to create a contrast or correspondence with something that comes immediately after. In this case, the image of "a massive fortified place" helps to advance his agenda of a future line of forts figured by the "singular forms" of the terrain—hardly an image of picturesque ruins. Indeed, the glaring incongruity of this extended metaphor makes it clear just how much an emphasis on topographic geology freed Frémont from a conventional view of landscape. The so-called classical landscape—that bedrock of literary and artistic allusion—is *literally* reduced to bedrock in the pages of the *Report*; and what was latent or partial in earlier surveys and scenic accounts of the West suddenly becomes the "hard bottom and rocks in place" of Thoreau's famous point d'appui—the "place where you might found a wall or a state." The Great Desert, it turns out, is simply a diluvial, downstream version of the Rockies.[62]

That such a radical aesthetic resulted in one of the most influential government reports ever written still seems a bit improbable. However, it can probably be attributed to three factors. For one thing, the landscape that emerged in the *Report* was generally confirmed by those moving west along the overland route—a process of acceptance that accelerated as the "textual attitude" of emigrants and travelers was increasingly shaped by the rhetoric of topographic geology. For another, geology itself began to provide a history that sidestepped the need to take Indians or the "sylvan deities of antiquity" into account—an important consideration, since it essentially emptied the West of any Native presence. Most important of all, Frémont used the elements of topographic geology to create a landscape that derived from the West's primitive and contrasting beauty—not the agrarian ideal that had made it seem so ugly and forbidding by comparison. No longer did the Great Desert have to seem fertile to seem worthy of attention. As soon as it *became* worthy of attention, in fact, it ceased to be the Great Desert.[63]

Courthouse Rock

ONE OF THE MANY THOUSANDS WHO FOLLOWED FRÉMONT
west was the editor and journalist Edwin Bryant. His diary of that
experience, published in 1848 as *What I Saw in California*, was a fairly
typical account of the overland trail in the decade or so after Frémont
first mapped and described it. Next to the *Report*, this was the account
most read by those about to go west or on their way west, especially
during the gold rush, when it was often reprinted under the title *Rocky
Mountain Adventures*. Like a majority of those who made the grueling
overland journey, Bryant felt that the "pleasures" of the trip "derived
almost exclusively from the sublime and singular novelties presented to
the vision." Yet he often analyzed how difficult it was to see these novelties through existing landscape conventions, recapitulating the dilemma
that Frémont had both raised and resolved to some extent in the *Report*.
What makes *What I Saw* so typical is that it is both a firsthand response
to the western landscape and a record of how that landscape gradually
came to resemble Frémont's topographic geology.[64]

Bryant was raised in the Northeast and had lived no farther west than
Kentucky before he set out for California. Coincidentally, he was the
cousin of William Cullen Bryant, whose long reverie of a poem, "The
Prairies" (1832)—with its imagery of "unshorn fields," "airy undulations,"
and "encircling vastness"—had helped to create the prevailing view of the
prairie in the first place. Although Bryant had obviously read the *Report*
very carefully and carried it with him as he traveled, the knowledge it
represented was no less secondhand at this point than his cousin's poem.
It is hardly surprising, then, that as the prairie finally opens out before
him, it provokes the following outburst of wonder and bewilderment:

I had never before beheld extensive scenery of this kind. The many descriptions of the prairies of the west had forestalled in some measure the first impressions produced by the magnificent landscape that lay spread out before me as far as the eye could reach, bounded alone by the blue wall of the sky. No description, however, which I have read of these scenes, or which can be written, can convey more than a faint impression to the imagination of their effects upon the eye.

It is an experience that will be repeated over and over again among those moving west — the sudden confusion that arises as an eye "forestalled" by expectation and convention is abruptly overwhelmed by the thing itself. The obvious conclusion is that expectations shaped by eastern hills and forests could not encompass such an open and treeless terrain. But even if Bryant expected the prairie to look the way it looked in Frémont's description of eastern Kansas and not the way it looked in his cousin's poem, it is apparent that he has to *learn* to see it that way by acquainting himself with the prairie's "extensive scenery" firsthand. Since he is not composing backward, the way Frémont was, it is not unreasonable for him to conclude at this point that "no description" will be adequate to the "magnificent landscape" that "lay spread out before" him. What follows, however, is a gradual accommodation to that landscape, as Bryant slowly sheds a secondhand aesthetic ignorant of the West and begins to develop a firsthand aesthetic that more or less confirms the *Report* — if only negatively or out of frustration at times.[65]

It is evident from the opening pages of *What I Saw* just how far Bryant needs to travel to see what he is looking at. His early descriptions of the prairie are nothing more than poetic conceits masquerading as firsthand observation. For the most part, he simply treats it as a grander or more sublime version of the eastern landscape. Confronted with his first view of the prairie, he exclaims, "I had never before beheld extensive scenery of this kind"; in the aftermath of his first storm on the prairie, he declares, "I had never previously witnessed any meteoric displays comparable with it." Over the next several weeks he sees "the most perfect and brilliant rainbow I ever beheld"; a stretch of country that "presents greater pastoral charms than I have witnessed in the oldest and most densely populated districts of the United States"; a repeat of "the most brilliant rainbow I ever beheld"; a second storm, which again provokes him to write that "a more sublime and meteoric display, I never witnessed or could conceive"; and a second stretch of country which appeared to be "the most desirable, in an agricultural point of view, of any which I have ever seen." Even as he begins to see the landscape differently and in greater detail, Bryant tends to fall back on this echolalic exaggeration when he doesn't know what else to say — proving, once again, that Lewis's faltering yet ecstatic description of the Great Falls was no fluke.[66]

Obviously, the sublime was still the rhetoric of speechlessness it had been for many others in the West. In Bryant's case, this futility reaches a kind of crescendo in the area of western Utah now known as the Great Salt Lake Desert. Within the space of a dozen pages he claims that "neither prose or poetry, nor the pencil of the artist, can adequately portray" the beauty of the desert; that the terrain is "a mixture of brown and hoary barrenness, aridity, and desolation, of which no adequate conception can be conveyed by language"; and that "no words can describe the awfulness and grandeur of this sublime desolation." This is just a more extreme version of what drives him to exaggeration in the narrative's early pages. Unsure of how to evaluate or compose the desert in his own mind, Bryant finds it even harder to describe it for those who have never seen such a landscape. Both here and throughout *What I Saw* the sublime represents a significant gulf between word and object — a gulf that arises when the usual images and associations fall profoundly short of the landscape itself. (Describing exactly the same "thirsty, sweltering, longing, hateful" area in *Roughing It*, Twain finds himself "glad, for the first time," that he has brought along his thick unabridged dictionary, because "we never could have found language to tell how glad we were" to reach the other side "in any sort of dictionary but an unabridged one with pictures in it.") Even if we take into account that Bryant is usually writing as an advocate of the trail, exaggeration in general is a sign of this linguistic gulf. Whenever he finds himself bewildered by the landscape, he just substitutes enthusiasm for description and calls it the grandest or most desolate he's ever seen. In the end, it's nothing more than the Great Desert acclaimed for its barrenness instead of condemned for it. The abyss is still an abyss—unseen and unsaid. As Emerson famously wrote, "The ruin or the blank that we see when we look at nature, is in our own eye. The axis of vision is not coincident with the axis of things." This is not the double negative of the *Report*.[67]

Yet gradually, in fits and starts, Bryant's axis of vision begins to revolve, aligning itself not only with the axes of latitude and longitude Frémont had surveyed, but also with the contours and morphology of the terrain he had described. Very early in the narrative, Bryant is apt to see things in the most general and uniform terms: "It is impossible for me to convey to the reader the impressions made upon my mind of these measureless undulating plains, with their ground of the freshest verdure, and their garniture of flame-like flowers, decorating every slope and hill-top." But just a few pages later—in a description of the party's train of wagons "strung out two or three miles in length"—he offers his first compelling glimpse of the prairie: "The views of this long procession, occasionally sinking into the depressions of the prairie, and then rising therefrom and winding along the curves of the ridges to avoid the wet and soft ground, were highly picturesque." There is an inchoate awareness of boundaries in this description and an openness to the picturesque instead of the sublime. Like Frémont before him, Bryant is beginning to see the landscape by focusing on its breaks and transitions—with ground "garnished" to the horizon giving way to "wet and soft ground" separated by high dry ridges. Still, this is hardly an emphatic difference, and it emerges as a single lowly rise in a landscape still leveled by exaggeration. It is not until three weeks later, in the area of eastern Kansas where Frémont first described the prairie, that everything Bryant has learned finally takes hold:

> Our march, as usual, has been over the high table-land of the prairie, occasionally dotted with one or more small trees, indicating the localities of springs or pools of stagnant water. The undulations and ravines have been less frequent, the surface of the country presenting

before us an expansive inclined plane, which we have been climbing the entire day. We crossed several affluents of the Blue, with sandy and gravelly beds; the waters having ceased to flow, stand in pools of considerable depth. The soil as we advance is becoming sandy and less fertile, and the grass and other vegetation is much shorter and thinner. Vegetation appears to be very backward, many of the trees being bare of foliage; and the flowers which one hundred and fifty miles back were dropping their blossoms, are here budding and bursting into bloom.

Compared to his earlier descriptions, both the amount of detail Bryant includes and the way in which he frames it are remarkable. For the first time, duration and scale really interrupt the "measureless undulating plains" of his imagination. All at once we see a landscape that is not all sameness and surface. It's true this landscape is never as rough or irregular as Frémont's and nowhere near as three-dimensional, but it is elaborated through a similar set of edges and inclines. Among other things, it includes the same contrasts between high tablelands and ravines, the same "increased elevation," the same disparity in vegetation; it even includes a similar acceleration in contrast as the passage develops and ends with the same mitigating bloom of flowers. What makes it especially important, however — and especially indebted to Frémont — is that it finally ruptures the silence of the sublime. Once again, the picturesque represents a new beginning.[68]

As it happens, this is also the moment Bryant's interest in geology and mineralogy begins to surface. The surest sign of this hard knowledge is that his eye becomes more exacting and alert and his voice becomes even more like Frémont's. Of the Platte he writes: "The breadth of the river bottom on the southern side, is from two and a half to four miles. The bluffs, as we advanced up the stream, become more elevated and broken. Sometimes they present a sloping, grassy surface, blending gently with the level plain; — at others, they assume the form of perpendicular, or overhanging precipices, with a face of bare and barren sand, so compact as to appear like solidified rock." Four days farther to the west he writes, as Frémont had written: "As we advance up the Platte, the soil becomes less fertile. The vegetation is thin and short. The river to-day has generally been eight or ten miles from us on our right. Ledges of calcareous rock frequently display themselves in the bluffs." And in an area of the Black Hills west of Fort Laramie he describes a scene that recalls Frémont's view from the summit of the Wind River Range: "We encamped, this afternoon, in a small, oval-shaped valley, through which flows a rivulet of pure, limpid water. The valley is surrounded on all sides by high, mountainous elevations, several of which are composed of granite-rock, upheaved by the subterranean convulsions of nature; others are composed of red sandstone and red clay. A volcanic debris is thickly scattered in places." Since Bryant's interest in geology was undoubtedly influenced by the *Report*, and he is clearly going over the same ground as the *Report*, it's perfectly understandable that much of *What I Saw* reads as unacknowledged imitation of Frémont's topographic geology, often simulating or duplicating descriptions in the *Report*, even where Bryant views them from a slightly different vantage point or displaces them to a different location altogether. Less apparent, perhaps, is that imitation was basically a form of liberation in this instance. The more Bryant sounded like Frémont, the more he sounded like a better version of himself — still fraught and overexcited, certainly, but able to actually picture the landscape instead of burying it in metaphor and exaggeration. We might say that the descriptions he was reading secondhand in the *Report* allowed him to translate the sense-data he was seeing for himself into a style that expressed his own impressions — impressions that revealed a keen eye and a humid imagination but that otherwise left him stunned or speechless, paralyzed by the unbridgeable gap between word and object.[69]

To see the West at all, then, Bryant had to learn to see it as a double negative. Only by opening his eyes to the most singular, disorderly, unstable, marginal, and alien features of the West was he able to regard it as anything more than an exaggerated or contrary version of the East; only by reducing his view to the horizon of topographic geology was he able to open his eyes to begin with; and only by mastering the least aesthetic of means was he able to depict the natural beauty of a landscape that seemed to lack a beauty of any sort.

. . .

UNFORTUNATELY, BRYANT EXHIBITED A NEW KIND OF speechlessness in his effort to depict Courthouse Rock, Chimney Rock, and Scotts Bluff—features that had already emerged as geographic landmarks and that he clearly wished to enshrine as national landmarks. Frémont had purposely set this process in motion when he compared the rising elevation of South Pass to "the ascent of the Capitol hill from the avenue, at Washington," and he would make an even bigger issue of Independence Rock, which he eventually describes twice, coming and going. Those who came after Frémont merely elevated other prominent features of the trail to the same status. Stephen Fender has argued that this was especially true of those traveling west during the gold rush because they viewed themselves as part of a national phenomenon. But if Bryant, Francis Parkman, Horace Greeley, and Mark Twain are any indication, almost everyone who took to the overland trails seemed to be, in the words of Brigitte Bailey, "visualizing and gazing on behalf of the nation." This was the nature of travel writing during this period, whether in the form of published essays, private journals, or letters back home. On the other hand, almost no one seemed sure of *how* to describe these new landmarks. It was as if the ambition to verify them as national monuments came into conflict with the need to portray them as natural terrain.[70]

All of this is evident in *What I Saw*, beginning with Courthouse Rock as it rises to meet Bryant on the horizon. Estimating that he is still twenty-five or thirty miles away, Bryant writes that he "saw an elevated rock, presenting an imposing and symmetrical architectural shape. At this distance its appearance was not unlike that of the capitol at Washington; representing, with great distinctiveness of outline, a main building, and wings surmounted by domes." In an effort to examine the bluff "more closely than could be done by an observation from the trail," he and a companion mount their horses and ride in the direction of the rock—only to get caught in quicksand. With their way delayed, and worried that they will not be able to overtake their party by nightfall, they eventually stop several miles short of their destination. Thus Bryant's final word on the subject: "The rock appeared, from the nearest point where we saw it, to be from 300 to 500 feet in height, and about a mile in circumference. Its walls so nearly resemble masonry, and its shape an architectural design, that if seen in an inhabited country, it would be supposed some collossal edifice, deserted and partially in ruins."[71]

Superimposing the Capitol, the edifice of federal law, on a bluff already identified with a courthouse began to confirm the West as a naturally patriotic landscape. As the first of several features indicating that the prairie was finally giving way to the high plains and the Continental Divide, Courthouse Rock was especially meaningful to emigrants moving along the trail—exceeded only by South Pass and Independence Rock as a symbol of progress and national purpose. William Wadsworth noted in *The National Wagon Road Guide* (1858) that "it has doubtless derived its name from the peculiarity of its form as a national object, its colossal size, and remarkable isolation." Just as they would with Independence Rock—also lying isolated and mysterious in otherwise level terrain—people felt an irresistible impulse to climb Courthouse Rock and an even greater urge to leave their names and the year of their passage.[72]

But Bryant's description of the sentinel-like bluff is noticeably distant and abstract. For some reason he abandons the grainy, three-dimensional style he has been developing since eastern Kansas—a style structured by the breaks and continuities in the landscape, with few elevated associations or ornate literary flourishes—and resurrects the rhetoric of romantic travel. In this case, his mimicking of Frémont merely proves how little he has learned. Although he appropriates Frémont's illustrious image of the Capitol and evokes the stratum of marly masonry that Frémont extends from Goshen's Hole to "the rock of the Court-house and Chimney," the effect is nothing like the *Report*. The *Report* is very careful to present South Pass and Goshen's Hole as real places, describing them in great detail as specific sites within a surrounding terrain. But the quicksand that mires Bryant and his companion insures that Courthouse Rock remains little more than an architectural profile, its "great distinctiveness of outline" rendering the "collossal" natural land-mark strictly two-dimensional and emblematic. Indeed, the singularity of its profile is so simplified by Bryant that he never bothers to mention the adjoining fragment of bluff now known as Jail Rock.

Nor does any of this stop once Chimney Rock rises on the horizon. If anything, the closer Bryant draws to Chimney Rock, the more he seems to distance himself from the *Report*. Frémont had consciously used the example of Chimney Rock to criticize those who saw or named the landscape "according to some fancied resemblance": "It looks at the distance of about thirty miles, like what it is called — the long chimney of a steam-factory establishment, or a shot-tower in Baltimore." Other than noting that it "consists of marl and earth limestone" and that "the weather is rapidly diminishing its height, which is now not more than two hundred feet above the water," Frémont was content to leave it at that, convinced that Preuss's illustration would "render any description unnecessary" (see fig. 8). *What I Saw* turns this approach on its head, as a sloppy version of the *Report*'s statistics and mineralogy (in which the rock appears to be "several hundred feet" high and "composed of soft rock") almost instantly morphs into a tale of "fancied resemblance." For after gazing at the "singularly picturesque and interesting" scenery on either side of Chimney Rock (scenery that, in Preuss's illustration, seems to be pushing Chimney Rock itself out of the picture), Bryant is suddenly seized by a paroxysm of literary tourism: "There are four high elevations of architectural configuration, one of which would represent a distant view of the ruins of the Athenian Acropolis; another the crum-bling remains of an Egyptian temple; a third, a Mexican pyramid; the fourth, the mausoleum of one of the Titans." He goes on to refer to the bluff in the near background as "ranges of castles and palaces" and those in the distance as "pyramids, spires, and domes." And he concludes on a supremely sublime note: "The illusion is so perfect that no effort of the imagination is required to suppose ourselves encamped in the vicinity of the ruins of some vast city erected by a race of giants, contemporaries of the Megatherii and the Ichthyosaurii."[73]

It is hard to ignore the suspicion that Bryant reacts in this way not because he lacks a language for the scenery, per se, but because he lacks a language for its *greatness*. It says a lot about Bryant's evolving eye that, in the middle of the Utah desert, and always on the edge of speechlessness, he actually writes some of the most precise descriptions to be found in *What I Saw*. In fact, when he reaches western Nevada, a landscape nearly as alien as western Utah, his analysis of some "remarkable boiling springs" — though it recalls several descriptions in Frémont's second report and ends in a Blakean image of "infernal steam-power" — is probably his most sure-footed and compelling description of all. Still, there is no hint of greatness in any of these desert views, no attempt to present them as anything larger or other than physical space. So when Bryant tries to elevate the West, tries to make us see it as a patriotic or national landscape, he seems to lose his bearings. If he knows that topographic geology helps him to apprehend a landscape he might otherwise think of as wasted, or dreary, or downright hostile to the senses, he is not alert enough to see that it might also be a rhetoric of grandeur.[74]

Like so many others desperate to see metaphorical greatness where material greatness seemed to be lacking or hard to describe, Bryant turns to the ruins of the Grand Tour. Already these ancient ruins were a model for many American institutions — exhibiting, in the words of Benedict Anderson, "that image of antiquity so central to the subjective idea of the nation." Jefferson had specified as early as 1786 that Virginia's new capitol ought to emulate something "already devised, and approved by the general suffrage of the world," namely, "the Maison quarrée, erected in the time of the Caesars"; later, when asked his advice about the Capitol in Washington DC, he indicated that he would "prefer the adoption of some one of the models of antiquity, which have had the approbation of thousands of years." For at least the next century and a half, statehouses and courthouses all over the country would duplicate the columns, entablatures, porticos, and rotundas of classical Greek and Roman architecture. That there was always a slightly absurd side to this reflex is shown by Henry Adams's sardonic view of the nation's capital seventy years into its history: "As in 1800 and 1850, so in 1860, the same rude colony was camped in the same forest, with the same unfinished Greek temples for workrooms, and sloughs for roads." But looking to validate what was often called the great "experiment" of liberty — Lincoln would famously refer to the "*proposition* that all men are created equal" and characterize the Civil War as "*testing* whether that nation, or any nation so conceived and so dedicated, can long endure" — Americans commonly chose to build their civil edifices in the proven image of Athenian democracy and Roman republicanism.[75]

This obsession with ruins would be a significant influence on those taking the overland trails. As surveyors, and emigrants, and eventually tourists equated their own trajectory with that of John O'Sullivan's "great nation of futurity," they sought a rhetoric of grandeur that would include, if not exactly describe, the western landscape. The "fancied resemblance" of so many early descriptions is a sign that, for most people, the West had to be appropriated as an object of the imagination before it could be seen as a material object. "We cannot see anything," Thoreau once observed, "until we are possessed with the idea of it, take it into our heads, — and then we can hardly see anything else." For easterners writing with an eastern audience in mind, the path of least resistance was simply to borrow the rhetoric of nationalism that already existed.[76]

. . .

HISTORY SHOWS THAT BRYANT'S IRRESOLUTE EFFORT TO describe Chimney Rock would be typical of those traveling west in the 1840s and 1850s. Ironically, a stammering, sublime form of speechlessness would be most characteristic of those who wished to glorify the West — a situation that gave Twain's wry reference to his unabridged dictionary a good deal of bite. It gradually became apparent, however, that Frémont's *Report* offered a rhetoric of grandeur which avoided this magnified silence by proposing a more singular and organic image of the nation. Clearly, the natural history that had so profoundly shaped the nationalism of everything from Jefferson's *Notes* to Willis's *American*

Scenery was very appealing in the form of topographic geology — and topographic geology itself became a splendid model for a nation seeking to identify its destiny and progress with the continent. In effect, it was propinquity writ large.

If there was something in particular that really raised the profile of topographic geology in American culture and advanced it as a rhetoric of nationalism, it was the western surveys. To be sure, topographic geology was of little interest to Zebulon Pike (who seemed most concerned that Indians respect the American flag) and of only secondary interest to Stephen Long (who clearly regarded vegetation as the most important measure of things). But as we've seen from the Nicollet and Frémont expeditions, and as William H. Goetzmann has shown more generally, it dominated almost every survey of the West from the late 1830s through the 1870s — with Congress explicitly authorizing surveys after 1867 to make it their principal objective. On a less utilitarian level, topographic geology also became a kind of horizon of knowledge during this period. One of the century's most radical theories — evolution by means of natural selection — was both inspired by the geological theory of uniformitarianism and confirmed by a growing fossil record that helped to confirm uniformitarianism as well. Western surveys had a lot to do with this, since much of the evidence for steady, global change was in the form of fossils discovered in the prairies and high plains. Frémont's contribution to this record was modest, but in the next several decades data began accumulating from a variety of sources.[77]

The early surveys of Ferdinand V. Hayden were both typical and significant. During the 1850s, Hayden made several trips to the Dakotas and Montana, gathering data for what would become the standard stratigraphic model for the West — a profile of geological layers ranging from the earliest era of earth history to the present. This model was especially important to John S. Newberry, who had helped to train Hayden. During an expedition to explore the Colorado River basin in 1857, Newberry became the first geologist to see the sheer vertical walls of the Grand Canyon. Examining the exposed layers of granite, shale, limestone, and sandstone, Newberry quickly recognized that he was looking at a unique cross section of the earth's crust—and that by looking deeper into the canyon, he was looking deeper into time. It's not surprising that the accumulating evidence of the West added weight to the notion of what is now called "deep time," first proposed by the uniformitarian geologist James Hutton and epitomized by his observation that "we find no vestige of a beginning, no prospect of an end."[78]

The grandeur of deep time turned out to be extremely important to American landscape. With evidence pouring in from the surveys of the 1840s and 1850s, America looked older every day—and on a magnificent scale. Goetzmann points out that by 1860 the various core samples used to construct stratigraphic columns were numerous enough to trace "whole formations" from "the Dakota Badlands to the Llano Estacado of Texas"—a far more extensive and precise version of Frémont's attempt to link Goshen's Hole and the bluffs of Courthouse and Chimney Rocks. That so much of this evidence seemed peculiar to the West added still another dimension to its claim on the imagination. Soon Americans were so possessed by the grandeur of the West that they could hardly see anything else. The upshot was that the natural history of the United States became a legitimate substitute for the human history of Europe and the Mediterranean.[79]

Yellowstone

IT MAY BE HARD TO PINPOINT WHEN DESCRIPTIONS OF
the West generally divested themselves of Old World references in favor
of the strictly figurative elements that Anne Farrar Hyde has referred
to as "geology, color, shape, and size." But it seems accurate to say that
this process began as early as Frémont's *Report* and accelerated fairly
rapidly with the reports of Capt. Howard Stansbury's expedition to
the Great Salt Lake, Lt. James Simpson's expedition to the lands of
New Mexico, the great railroad surveys of the mid-1850s, Lt. Joseph
C. Ives's expedition to the Colorado River, Clarence King's Fortieth
Parallel Survey, Hayden's survey of the Yellowstone region, Lt. George
Wheeler's surveys west of the hundredth meridian, and John Wesley
Powell's surveys of the Colorado Plateau. At the same time, Karl Bod-
mer's paintings of formations along the upper Missouri, Alfred Jacob
Miller's paintings of the prairies and the high plains, Catlin's paintings
of formations along the lower Missouri, and Preuss's illustrations for
Frémont were just the first of thousands of images to appear in official
government reports, travel guides, promotional tracts, daily newspapers,
monthly journals, and East Coast galleries. The photographic record of
Timothy O'Sullivan, William H. Jackson, and Andrew J. Russell was
particularly stunning (fig. 10). Still, it wasn't long before works such as
Frederic Edwin Church's paintings of the Andes and Albert Bierstadt's
of the Rockies and Sierra Nevada — each executed on a scale evoking
the great history paintings of Europe — made it clear that topographic
geology was also a suitable subject for the most ambitious and exalted
landscape paintings (fig. 11). All of this culminated in a system of federal
parks that would soon join the republican grid and the transcontinental
railroad as among the earliest manifestations of a full-blown national

FIG. 10. Timothy O'Sullivan, *Green River near Flaming Gorge, Wyoming*, 1872. Albumen print, 8 x 10⅝ in. Library of Congress, Prints and Photographs Division, Washington DC.

landscape. Even the first of these — Yellowstone — was viewed through a lens of pronounced geological contrast that holds true to this day.[80]

. . .

IT IS WELL-KNOWN BY NOW THAT THE CAMPAIGN TO MAKE Yellowstone a national park was largely orchestrated by the Northern Pacific Railroad. Hoping that the so-called general traveling public would follow its tracks to the wonders of Montana, the Northern Pacific (1) hired Nathaniel P. Langford, who had visited the region in 1870, to deliver a series of public lectures in Philadelphia, New York, and Washington DC; (2) arranged for several articles written by Langford and illustrated by Thomas Moran to appear in *Scribner's Monthly*; (3) helped to pay for Hayden's expedition to the Yellowstone region in 1871; (4) made sure the expedition included William H. Jackson as well as Moran; and

FIG. 11. Albert Bierstadt, *Merced River, Yosemite Valley*, 1866. Oil on canvas, 36 x 50 in. The Metropolitan Museum of Art, New York/Art Resource, New York. Gift of the sons of William Paton, 1909 (09.214.1). Image copyright © The Metropolitan Museum of Art/Art Resource, New York.

(5) convinced Hayden to insert a recommendation in his official report to Congress that Yellowstone be set aside as a national park. The publicity juggernaut set in motion by the railroad easily overcame what turned out to be weak and unorganized opposition.[81]

After clarifying that the Yellowstone region was "unadapted to agriculture, mining or manufacturing purposes" — an opinion expressed by the *Virginia City Daily Territorial Enterprise* but taken from Langford and repeated many times during congressional debates — the effort to reserve it as a national park focused almost exclusively on the condensed topographical contrasts that were so characteristic of the region. Hayden was still assembling the men and equipment for his own expedition when Rep. William D. Kelley of Pennsylvania, relying on the report of the 1870 expedition, delivered an address in which he hailed "the characteristics of a hitherto unexplored section of Montana, the wonders of which not only exceed those of Niagara and the geysers of California, but rival in magnitude and extraordinary combination those of the Yo

FIG. 12. Thomas Moran, *The Grand Canyon of the Yellowstone*, 1872. Oil on canvas, 84 x 144 in. Smithsonian American Art Museum, Washington DC/Art Resource, New York. Lent by the Department of the Interior Museum.

Semite, the cañons of Colorado and the geysers of Iceland." When the Senate passed its version of the Yellowstone bill in January 1872, the *Helena Daily Herald* exclaimed: "If it contains the proportions set forth in Clagett's bill, it will embrace about 2,500 square miles, and include the great canyon, the Falls and Lake of the Yellowstone, with a score of other magnificent lakes, the great geyser basin of the Madison, and thousands of mineral and boiling springs. Should the whole surface of the earth be gleaned, another spot of equal dimensions could not be found that contains on such a magnificent scale one-half the attractions here grouped together." When the bill passed both houses of Congress a month later, the *New York Times* observed: "Perhaps, no scenery in the world surpasses for sublimity that of the Yellowstone Valley; and certainly no region anywhere is so rich, in the same space, in wonderful natural curiosities." Meanwhile, Moran was putting the finishing touches on his magnificent paean to the new park — *The Grand Canyon of the Yellowstone* (fig. 12).[82]

. . .

ALTHOUGH *THE GRAND CANYON OF THE YELLOWSTONE WAS* completed several months after the park bill was signed into law, the monumental, eight-by-twelve-foot painting quickly became the most visible symbol of the new park and a national icon in its own right: exhibited in New York in May 1872 and bought by Congress a month later. After touring a number of eastern cities, it was placed in the Senate lobby — the first "pure landscape" to be part of the Capitol collection and an obvious companion piece to Emanuel Leutze's *Westward the Course of Empire Takes Its Way*, which already decorated the stairway of the Capitol and was often cited as the visual embodiment of Manifest Destiny (see fig. 24). Viewing the Grand Canyon, either in the Senate lobby or in reproduction, would be among the most compelling reasons Americans of that time chose to see Yellowstone for themselves.[83]

As we might expect, Moran's first images of Yellowstone were created sight unseen. When Langford submitted the manuscript for the two-part essay that would appear in *Scribner's Monthly* as "The Wonders of the Yellowstone," the magazine asked Moran to illustrate it, even though he'd never been west of Lake Superior. Working from Langford's text as well as from the sketches and descriptions that had inspired Congressman Kelley to single out Yellowstone's "extraordinary combination" of canyons and geysers, Moran essentially repeated the secondhand process that had led to Cooper's *Prairie*. As Scott Herring has sardonically observed, Moran ignorantly turned a couple of acclamatory narratives into a series of picturesque and sublime fantasies. His attempt to depict the Devil's Slide in Montana, for instance — which Langford had described as having walls that "were as even as if they had been worked by line and plumb," walls that "might readily be mistaken for works of art as of nature" — resulted in a feature that looked "like a foot-bridge in a formal garden," but on the scale of the Great Wall of China (fig. 13). Another etching, entitled *Great Cañon of the Yellowstone*, was equally fanciful, with a view from a rocky riverbed (in real life, deep underwater) that made it look like a forbidding fissure rather than a majestic canyon.[84]

THE DEVIL'S SLIDE, MONTANA.

eyond them, and two of the company to ep guard until one o'clock ; then to be ieved by two others, who were to watch daylight. This divided the labor among en, who were to serve as picket-men each week.

ese precautionary measures being fully rstood, we left Boteler's, plunging at into the vast unknown which lay before Following the slight Indian trail, we eled near the bank of the river, amid the lest imaginable scenery of river, rock, and untain. The foot-hills were covered with dure, which an autumnal sun had sprinkled h maroon-colored tints, very delicate and autiful. The path was narrow, rocky, and neven, frequently leading over high hills, in ent and descent more or less abrupt and lifficult. The increasing altitude of the route vas more perceptible than any over which

we had ever traveled, and the river, whenever visible, was a perfect mountain torrent.

While descending a hill into one of the broad openings of the valley, our attention was suddenly arrested by half a dozen or more mounted Indians, who were riding down the foot-hills on the opposite side of the river. Two of our company, who had lingered behind, came up with the information that they had seen several more making observations from behind a small butte, from which they fled in great haste on being discovered. They soon rode down on the plateau to a point where their horses were hobbled, and for a long time watched our party as it continued its course of travel up the river. Our camp was guarded that night with more than ordinary vigilance. A hard rain-storm, which set in early in the afternoon and continued

FIG. 13. Thomas Moran, *The Devil's Slide, Montana*, 1871. Print with text, *Century Illustrated Monthly Magazine*, May 1871. General Research Division, New York Public Library, Astor, Lenox and Tilden Foundations.

Still, Moran's imagination was so stimulated by the drawings and descriptions he had worked from that when he heard about Hayden's expedition to Yellowstone he went to *Scribner's Monthly* with a proposal to exchange sketches and eyewitness reports for the money he would need to join the expedition. Inexplicably, his longtime employer turned him down. Almost immediately, however, the president of the Northern Pacific agreed to the proposal and arranged for a letter to be written to Hayden, suggesting that Moran, an artist "of rare genius," would be a "desirable," and free, addition to the expedition. Moran eventually spent forty days in the wilderness, both afoot and on horseback, exploring a region roughly the size of Connecticut. He slept "out in the open air" for the first time in his life, discovered that the altitude and rough life left him feeling easily "used up" the first few days, and witnessed an accident, typical of western expeditions, in which a horse stumbled and nearly killed its rider. All the same, there was never any doubt that the region lived up to his longing for exotic scenery.[85]

Throughout the trip, Moran spent many hours with Hayden, learning how to see and depict this strange terrain correctly. He also worked closely with Jackson, the two of them drawing and photographing together as they began to select the vantage points that would eventually reduce the majestic and contrasting terrain to the series of iconic features that now mark the standard tour of the park. It wasn't long before Moran came to see the canyon formed by the Yellowstone River as emblematic of the entire area. At the head of the canyon was a magnificent waterfall (now known as the Lower Falls), and not only were its craggy rhyolite walls grand in themselves, but their mottled, heat-induced coloring was the reason the region had been named Yellowstone in the first place. Moran spent more than three days scouting and sketching the site, his longest stay in any one spot. While he was still there, he began using Jackson's photographs as a visual aid — partly in the way earlier artists had used the camera obscura to frame and reduce scenes to two dimensions, partly in the way artists of his own day cut and pasted features to make composite views. By the time he returned to New York, he had arrived at what he believed to be the perfect picture: a spectacular vista of the jutting, encrusted rocks and the mist-shrouded falls, seen from a point slightly below the canyon rim but still high enough to glimpse the distant plumes of steam rising from the geysers to the west. Of course, anyone who has been to the site knows that the painting does not present a realistic vista — not even when the site is viewed from what is now called Artist's Point, where there is a reproduction of the painting available for comparison. Essentially, *The Grand Canyon of the Yellowstone* is a composite of realistic elements that have been pasted together to create an imaginary or ideal — or what we now call a "virtual" — view. As Henry Tuckerman once said of Frederic Church's work, Moran "advanced from the faithful rendition of details to a comprehensive realism in general effect."[86]

Moran may well have had this laudatory appraisal — written by one of the period's leading art critics about one of its leading artists — somewhere in the back of his mind as he began to compose the *Grand Canyon*. Certainly his explanation of the enormous painting, appearing in a survey of American artists published a decade later, shows exactly the same regard for geological realism transformed into pictorial idealism; and it follows a paragraph in which he singles out Church as "a man of refinement":

> Topography in art is valueless. The motive or incentive of my *Grand Canyon of the Yellowstone* was the gorgeous display of color that impressed itself upon me. Probably no scenery in the world presents such a combination. The forms are extremely wonderful and pictorial, and, while I desired to tell truly of Nature, I did not wish to realize the scene literally but to preserve and convey its true impression. Every form introduced into the picture is within view from a given point, but the relations of the separate parts to one another are not always preserved. For instance, the precipitous rocks on the right were really at my back when I stood at that point, yet in their present position they are strictly true to pictorial Nature; and so correct is the whole representation that every member of the expedition with which I was connected declared that he knew the exact spot which had been reproduced. . . . The rocks in the foreground are so carefully drawn that a geologist could determine their precise nature. . . . I elaborated them out of pure love for rocks.

Both this explanation and the painting itself make it clear why the *Grand Canyon* so quickly became a national icon. Though Moran proclaims "topography in art" to be "valueless," what he means by this is a narrow realism that violates "pictorial Nature." Plainly, the painting's nearest antecedent was the work of Bierstadt, Church, and Cole — and its more distant model was the juxtaposed, contrasting landscape of Frémont's *Report*. The *Grand Canyon* simply conveyed a more immediate and arresting grandeur, emerging as the apotheosis of a topographic geology that had begun in the broken reaches of eastern Kansas and then gradually migrated west as a rhetoric of nationalism. To put it a little simply, perhaps: if the American imagination had been associated with the forest for two and a half centuries — a cultural arc that takes us from John Smith's *Generall Historie of Virginia* (1624) to Cooper's Leatherstocking tales — now it was the reign of rocks that prevailed. Rocks created a propinquity between East and West that had not been possible when trees were the aesthetic standard for landscape.[87]

Strictly as a matter of art, the *Grand Canyon* also emerged as a national icon because it added a western dimension to some of the elements of the Hudson River school most indebted to European painting — notably, the solitary tree or stand of trees that, like a side-screen on a stage, framed nearly every scene, and the glorious morning or evening sky that took up half of each picture and gave it such a resplendent light. Both these elements were associated with the seventeenth-century French artist Claude Lorrain, and simulating Claude was often a way for American artists to cast their own landscape in the reflected glow of European landscape while also pointing to its native contrasts — especially the contrast between past and future that seemed so prevalent in scenes of sunrise and sunset. As John Brett, a nineteenth-century English artist, coolly observed: "Sentiment in landscape is chiefly dependent on meteorology."[88]

Moran obviously pays homage to these conventions, but he is able to incorporate and subvert them at the same time. For one thing, the towering yet trimly shaped conifer to the left probably came from a tree he sketched at the Borghese Villa in Rome, not from anything he saw in the northern Rockies. Since he had noted very early in the diary he kept of the expedition that "pine & fir" appeared "to be the only trees that grow upon the Mountains in the west," he may have wanted to add a little variety to the existing species in the area. A more plausible explanation is that he wished to exaggerate the comparison between European and American landscape, utilizing an element of the classical Italian countryside to frame a starkly western scene. Whether he transplanted this noble tree or concocted it out of thin air, its thick, sturdy trunk and immense height dwarfed anything in Europe or the Northeast and completely altered both the carefully calibrated scale and the finely balanced contrast of the Hudson River school. Implicitly, it proclaimed the "nervous, rocky West" to be both grander and of greater contrast than anything east of the Mississippi, and thus far more emblematic of a national landscape.[89]

Augmenting this iconoclasm was the way Moran shifted from meteorology to geology. Remarkably, there is almost no sky in *Grand Canyon*, and what little remains is so compressed by the rim of the canyon that it cedes most of its gilded luminescence to the rhyolite walls below. Suddenly, it is not the encircling arch of heaven but the subterranean sphere of rocks that colors the entire landscape. Nor is this the only reversal, since Moran also suppresses the surrounding vegetation in favor of rocks — most notably, in the ecru area that stretches from the head of the falls to the distant geyser basin, which is really twelve or thirteen miles of dense forest. Both the amount of space they occupy and the size of the painting itself signify that Moran expects these precipitous and elaborate rock formations to bear the emotional weight of the picture. In fact, since the picture is plainly a more glaring assault on the *regionalism* of the Hudson River school than on its *style*, he probably chose the stunning site precisely because its ochre walls could be seen as equivalent to the providential light that had so often graced the sky in American painting. Jackson, whose black-and-white photographs of the region are just as spectacular in their way, later told an interviewer that the painting had become a national icon largely because of its "wonderful coloring."[90]

Sometimes it is hard to see past this "wonderful coloring." Rarely has the ineffable been so earthbound. But Moran's greater purpose was a "comprehensive realism" that would idealize the entire region. Again and again he stressed that "probably no scenery in the world" presented "such a combination" of color and form, suggesting that only the juxtaposition of different, even incompatible, points of view would allow him "to preserve and convey its true impression" within the space of a single painting. Certainly this is what we confront in the finished work: a view that cannot be seen *except* as a painting. While there are many signs of this, perhaps the most subtle is the way he lowers both the rim of the canyon and the height of the intervening plateau to create a nonexistent view of the geyser basin. Admittedly, the basin is just a few wispy plumes of steam, more than matched by the chilly veil of mist rising from the falls. But added to the hoary encrusted rocks of the plateau and the aureate volcanic walls of the canyon, the geysers are a reminder that everything in sight has resulted from the long-term effects of heat and cooling, creating the impression that even the most incongruous elements of the scene are part of a single large-scale system. Of course, it is hardly coincidental that this large-scale system is basically a collage of the topographic features that had received the most attention as Congress debated the bill to make the region a park. For his first great success, at least, Moran's "comprehensive realism" was little more than an aesthetic confirmation of Congress's legislative agenda — one of several reasons the painting was purchased so quickly for the Senate lobby.[91]

Inspired by the beauty and success of his Yellowstone trip, Moran soon headed even farther west, joining John Wesley Powell's survey of southern Utah and northern Arizona before returning to New Jersey with sketches and studies for what was clearly intended to be a companion piece to the *Grand Canyon* — a work he called *The Chasm of the Colorado* (fig. 14). The new work was exactly the same size as the *Grand Canyon*, had almost the same title, and was acquired just as quickly by Congress. With this purchase, Congress not only embraced the last remaining area of the Great Desert but set in motion a trajectory of consolidation that would soon add many other areas of the West to the national park system. Less than five years after Yellowstone and the

FIG. 14. Thomas Moran, *The Chasm of the Colorado*, 1873–74. Oil on canvas, 84 x 144¾ in. Smithsonian American Art Museum, Washington DC/Art Resource, New York. Lent by the Department of the Interior, Office of the Secretary.

canyons of the Colorado Plateau were first revealed to a disbelieving public, and less than fifteen years after Yosemite and the giant sequoias were first photographed, Americans had clearly come to believe that even the most distant, alien, or primitive regions of the continent were an essential part of their national landscape. As the *New York Herald* put it, just after the bill making Yellowstone a national park was signed into law:

> Why should we go to Switzerland to see mountains, or to Iceland for geysers? Thirty years ago the attraction of America to the foreign mind was Niagara Falls. Now we have attractions which diminish Niagara into an ordinary exhibition. The Yo Semite, which the nation has made a park, the Rocky mountains and their singular parks, the canyons of the Colorado, the Dalles of the Columbia, the giant trees, the lake country of Minnesota, the country of the Yellowstone, with their beauty, their splendor, their extraordinary and sometimes terrible manifestations of nature, form a series of attractions possessed by no other nation in the world.[92]

All the Different Parts of Our Country

THAT "THIRTY YEARS AGO" THE *NEW YORK HERALD* REFERRED to was the very moment Frémont set out for South Pass and the Wind River Range, compiling the descriptions, maps, and data that began to turn the double negative of the West into the positive we think of it as today. Advancing in a relatively straight, if serendipitous, line, the *Report* helped to transform both the rhetoric of American scenery and the direction of its gaze. Later, on his second expedition, Frémont added the Great Salt Lake, The Dalles of the Columbia, the Sierra Nevada, Lake Tahoe, and the San Joaquin valley to the inventory of national scenery, and on his third expedition he named the Golden Gate. Soon these and other landmarks were heralded not just as "worth a voyage across the Atlantic to see" but as "a series of attractions possessed by no other nation in the world." Adjusting its sense of scale, as well as its sense of place, to include a landscape that had often been overlooked or reviled, the nation gradually set its sights on the entire continent. In the words of Timothy Flint, the landscape of the East and the landscape of the West were finally "brought into *juxtaposition*."[93]

Just how much this shift in textual attitudes can be attributed to Frémont's unusual version of the picturesque should now be apparent. The *Report* was *so* unusual that it bestowed "a kind of originality" on the American landscape — and even where this "new beginning" was only partially understood, it still helped to create a continental landscape shaped by its topographic contrasts. A continental landscape implied that individual landmarks or regions were less important than the way they related to each other; it exaggerated the self-similarity that Frémont had first exposed among the boulders and shards of eastern Kansas; and as a "series of attractions" that stretched from East to West, it enhanced the novelty and variety of American scenery while further separating it from European scenery. It was just a matter of time before Americans concluded that the nation needed to embrace these multiplied contrasts to see itself whole.

If only because the comparison to *American Scenery* is so obvious and unavoidable, perhaps the clearest sign of this metamorphosis is a publication entitled *Picturesque America: or, The Land We Live In*, issued semimonthly from 1872 to 1874, then collected as a two-volume set edited by the ubiquitous octogenarian William Cullen Bryant. Like Willis's *American Scenery*, Bryant's *Picturesque America* included a series of disconnected "subjects" or views, with no intrinsic relation to each other except as contrasting national scenery. Also like *American Scenery*, its format was that of the illustrated essay, though cheaper engraving techniques allowed for multiple illustrations, while Willis had been limited to one for each essay. The single greatest difference was the geographical reach of *Picturesque America*, which now extended from coast to coast. Volume 1 began on the coast of Maine and ended on the coast of California, making its continental approach both figurative and literal. True, this perspective was still hedged a bit, since only fifteen of the sixty-five "subjects" can really be considered west of the Alleghenies—and of those, only eight were west of the Mississippi. But the two-volume set included essays titled "The Great National Park" and "The Yosemite Falls" as well as three essays illustrated by Moran: "The Cañons of the Colorado," "The Rocky Mountains," and "The Plains and the Sierras" (where etchings of the Devil's Slide and Devil's Gate in Utah show how far the rhetoric of topographic geology had advanced since Preuss's etchings for the *Report* and Moran's for *Scribner's Monthly*) (figs. 15, 16). It also included thirteen essays on scenery south of the Mason-Dixon Line, indicative of the effort after the Civil War to unite the country by latitude as well as longitude. And in keeping with an aesthetic that constantly redeployed the boundary between nature and art, there were many urban views not just of Boston, New York, Philadelphia, and Washington D C but of Saint Augustine, New Orleans, Buffalo, Cleveland, Detroit, Charleston, Saint Louis, Cincinnati, Milwaukee, and Chicago.[94]

184 *PICTURESQUE AMERICA.*

Whoever follows the nomenclature of Weber Cañon would be led to think the enemy of mankind held there at least undisputed sway. All the great glories of the view are marked as his. The Devil's Gate—a black, ragged opening in one part of the great gorge, through which the foaming waters of the river rush white and noisy—is one, but it is well named. A very spirit of darkness seems to brood over the place. On each side, the broken cliffs lie in shadow; the thundering water roars below; there is no verdure but a blasted tree here and there; great bowlders lie in the bed of the stream and along the shore. In the distance, seen through the gap, there are black hills and mountain-summits overlooking them. And there is a cool wind here, that is like a breeze blown across the Styx, and that is never still, even in the hottest summer day.

Devil's Slide, Weber Cañon.

It is worth the while to think, in this wonderful valley, of the engineering skill that was needed to carry the iron road through its depths. All through the cañon are evidences of the difficulties of the task. Here a truss-bridge and web-like trestle-work carry the rails from one point of the rocky wall to another beyond the stream; here, for a great space, the road-bed is cut from the very sides of the great cliffs, where the gorge narrows and leaves no room for more than sand and river. And, as if to mock at it all, Nature has tried her hand, too, at construction, with a success at once weird, sublime, and grotesque. On the left hand of the route,

FIG. 15. Thomas Moran, *Devil's Slide, Weber Cañon*, 1874. Print with text in William Cullen Bryant, ed., *Picturesque America*, ca. 1872–74, vol. 2, p. 184. Milstein Division of United States History, Local History & Genealogy, New York Public Library, Astor, Lenox and Tilden Foundations.

DEVIL'S GATE, WEBER CAÑON.

FIG. 16. Thomas Moran, *Devil's Gate, Weber Cañon*, 1874. Print with text in Bryant, *Picturesque America*, vol. 2, p. 183. Milstein Division of United States History, Local History & Genealogy, New York Public Library, Astor, Lenox and Tilden Foundations.

In a preface that often echoed Willis's in *American Scenery*, Bryant declares that "it is the design of the publication entitled 'PICTUR-ESQUE AMERICA' to present full descriptions and elaborate pictorial delineations of the scenery characteristic of all the different parts of our country." As with Yellowstone, it is the great contrast in American scenery that makes it so distinct and grand: "On the two great oceans which border our league of States, and in the vast space between them, we find a variety of scenery which no single country can boast of." Evoking the usual comparisons to Europe, Bryant writes that "a rapid journey by railway over the plains" soon "brings the tourist into a region of the Rocky Mountains rivalling Switzerland in its scenery of rock piled on rock." But he quickly notes that "Switzerland has no such groves on its mountain-sides, nor has even Libanus [the Lebanon Mountains], with its ancient cedars, as those which raise the astonishment of the visitor to that Western region." Right after this, to exaggerate both the contrast within American scenery and its divergence from European scenery, Bryant observes: "Another feature of that region is so remarkable as to have enriched our language with a new word; and *cañon*, as the Spanish write it, or *canyon*, as it is often spelled by our people, signifies one of those chasms between perpendicular walls or rock — chasms of fearful depth and of length like that of a river, reporting of some mighty convulsion of Nature in ages that have left no record save in these displacements of the crust of our globe." Then, in a sign of just how far the desert has risen in the public's estimation and imagination, even an emblematic easterner like Bryant feels the need to declare: "Nor should we overlook in this enumeration the scenery of the desert, as it is seen in all its dreariness, not without offering subjects for the pencil, in those tracts of our Western possessions where rains never fall nor springs gush to moisten the soil." Of course, Bryant is now speaking of the *real* deserts of Utah, Nevada, and Arizona, not the Great Desert of old. Twain had already made this point in *Roughing It*, referring to a stretch of Nevada that includes Carson Sink as "the Great American Desert — forty memorable miles of bottomless sand."[95]

All in all, it could be said that Frémont's picturesque panorama of nearly fifteen hundred miles and Bryant's of more than three thousand miles were just expanded versions of Willis's equally elided view up the Hudson Valley. But since the variety and contrasts of these scenic landscapes emerged from a kind of slurred or blended propinquity, that very expansion helped to create a perception that the nation had no limits short of the "vast space" between the "two great oceans which border our league of States." No longer did declaring that "our boundaries shall be those which Nature has formed" imply a restriction of any sort. No longer did the Great Desert imply "a limit almost to the range of thought" or "a place which will forever remain on the outside." Confirming the decision to set aside Yellowstone Park, *Picturesque America* proved that arability was not the only measure of a shapely, contiguous nation. Such a nation could also be considered beautiful and whole when the land that was most suitable "to agriculture, mining or manufacturing purposes" was juxtaposed with the land that was least suitable — which is undoubtedly what Bryant meant by "all the different parts of our country." If any further proof was needed, just two decades later — or exactly fifty years after the *Report* was published — Katharine Lee Bates would climb to the summit of Pike's Peak in Colorado, cast her eyes eastward to the still droughty fields of Kansas and Nebraska and westward to the sheer gray peaks of the Rockies, and begin to compose "America the Beautiful" — showing once and for all that the territory Pike himself had first stigmatized as a great sandy desert was now considered splendid enough to symbolize the nation. As a matter of scenery, anyway, latitude and longitude were now perfectly aligned with the lay of the land.

. . .

UNFORTUNATELY, NONE OF THIS COULD BE TAKEN FOR granted at the time Frémont wrote the *Report*. That was the nature of his originality — even he could not be sure that his effort to identify the abstract space of geographical expansion with the "country lying between the Missouri River and the Rocky Mountains, and on the line of the Kansas and Great Platte rivers" would be accepted by a population that had been virtual witnesses to the Great Desert for two generations. Knowing that the region *beyond* the Great Desert included South Pass and the Wind River Range only added to his uncertainty. These topographic features were already known to be part of a continental divide, and the divide itself had long looked like an even greater barrier to expansion than the Great Desert — a barrier where the conflict between geographical predestination and the boundaries "fixed by the hand of nature" seemed almost insurmountable. Certainly it appeared to be a worrisome obstacle to those who wished to annex Oregon, since emigrants had to cross the divide to reach the remote territory. How were "the ties of a common interest" that supposedly linked the interior of Texas to the rest of the nation supposed to incorporate something as imposing as the Continental Divide?

It is here that Frémont's decision to push past the gentle incline of South Pass to a summit of the Wind River Range is shown to be such a stroke of genius. Frémont repeatedly, and bombastically, refers to the wild and precipitous summit as "the loftiest peak of the Rocky mountains," and his account of climbing it might lead us to see the episode as little more than a romantic interlude in which the explorer himself emerges as a kind of scientific hero. Yet it is also the rhetorical peak of the *Report* — the point at which Frémont finally begins to associate the geographical predestination of the nation with the space between the "two great oceans which border our league of States." Having exceeded the Great Desert as a barrier to western expansion, Frémont uses his trip to South Pass and the summit to suggest that the Continental Divide would also unite, not obstruct, a continental nation. Within months, this inspiring picture would significantly shape Asa Whitney's project for a railroad to the Pacific and begin to transform American views of progress and expansion.

Two

Westward the Course of Empire

The Mouth of the Oregon

ONE OF THOREAU'S MOST LUMINOUS AND ENDURING WORKS is an essay entitled "Walking." Delivered as a lecture in 1851 and then amended off and on until his death in 1862, the essay rather jauntily describes how he sets out each day for "a Nature such as the old prophets and poets, Menu, Moses, Homer, Chaucer, walked in," evoking an allusive sense of adventure that falters only when he finds that he has "walked a mile into the woods bodily, without getting there in spirit." In a text as peculiar and meandering as the course of his rambles, Thoreau suddenly asks himself: "What is it that makes it so hard sometimes to determine *whither* we will walk?" Attempting to answer the question, he claims that there is "a subtle magnetism in Nature, which, if we unconsciously yield to it, will direct us right." For Thoreau himself, yielding to this magnetism means that he always heads in the same direction on his walks: "between west and south-southwest." He describes this process — in which his "needle" is sometimes "slow to settle" — as if he were setting out on a pilgrimage or an eccentric "sort of crusade": "I turn round and round irresolute sometimes for a quarter of an hour, until I decide, for the thousandth time, that I will walk into the southwest or west. Eastward I go only by force; but westward I go free." Almost immediately, he locates this essentially philosophical geography in the real world: "I must walk toward Oregon, and not toward Europe. And that way the nation is moving, and I may say that mankind progress from east to west."[1]

Naturally, the first reference to Oregon in American literature gets it wrong. It appears in William Cullen Bryant's "Thanatopsis" (1817): "Take the wings / Of morning, pierce the Barcan wilderness, / Or lose thyself in the continuous woods / Where rolls the Oregon" — a river, in other words, and a misnamed one at that, since it was really the Columbia he was speaking of. Bryant probably based his information on explorer Jonathan Carver's *Travels Through the Interior Parts of North-America* (1778), where it is identified, sight unseen, as "one of the four most capital rivers on the Continent of North America" (the so-called river of the West) and said to "traverse upwards of two thousand miles." The poem was written nearly a decade after Lewis and Clark had journeyed down the Columbia, but information about the area was still sketchy, and works like Carver's would influence public opinion well into the 1840s. For his part, Jefferson had sent the two explorers in that direction because by 1803 trade with China had become America's most lucrative foreign market, and he expected them to verify and map the long-sought Northwest Passage that would complete a river route across the continent. A limited amount of evidence, and a preference for proportion, led Jefferson to believe that the geography of the continent was symmetrical, with a single chain of mountains in the West equal in height and direction to the Alleghenies in the East. The same wishful thinking led him to believe in a short passage through those mountains equivalent to the road to "Frederic town" he had described from the summit of the Blue Ridge Mountains. An English explorer, Robert Rogers, had actually reported in 1772 that a single portage of "about twenty miles" separated the Missouri and the mythical Oregon—exactly the same distance that separated Jefferson from "Frederic town." Unfortunately, just as Columbus discovered the Atlantic to be much wider than his maps showed, so did Lewis and Clark find the Rockies not just wider than Rogers's account but higher. It turned out that Rogers's short and simple portage was actually a journey of 340 miles over very rough ground.[2]

Almost from the beginning, the idea of "Oregon" was aligned with nationhood. For the most part, the nation moved west in search of land—the course of history epitomized by Jefferson's belief that people began to feel uneasy when the local population exceeded more than ten per square mile and Daniel Boone's famous statement on leaving Kentucky that he needed "more elbow-room." But with the return of the Lewis and Clark expedition in 1806 and the founding of Astoria in 1811, Oregon entered the national consciousness as both a gateway to the markets of the Pacific Rim and a territorial dispute with Britain. Of the two great struggles over annexation in the 1840s — Oregon and Texas — Oregon clearly came closer to the abstract principles of John O'Sullivan's "great nation of futurity." Many southern Democrats hoped that Texas would be divided into five new states, preserving a balance in Congress that safeguarded the "peculiar institution" of slavery; many northern Democrats went along with this because they hoped that free blacks would migrate west rather than north, leaving white workers with less competition for jobs; meanwhile, both northern and southern Whigs feared that adding Texas would encourage the nation to expand ever farther south and west, provoking a war with Mexico and creating an indefinite sphere of slavery. Neither party or section seemed to see Oregon in this way — at least partly, of course, because it would open or streamline markets for every section of the country, but also because it looked as if protracted emigration to the territory would eventually result in a peaceful settlement with Britain, and the territory itself seemed too distant at the time to threaten the balance of Congress. Accelerating emigration to Oregon would be one of Frémont's principal goals in the *Report*. And this goal helped to shape its most thrilling and symbolic episode: the trip to "the loftiest peak of the Rocky mountains."[3]

. . .

IN 1825 THOMAS HART BENTON DELIVERED A SPEECH ON the Senate floor that comes as close as any single event to being the origin of the *Report*. Although he had often written and spoken on the subject of Oregon before, this was Benton's most synoptic statement to date and the start of a campaign to sway his Senate colleagues that would last nearly two decades. Like many others who would argue for the annexation of Oregon over the years, he spent much of his time defending American claims to the territory. But after emphasizing that these claims could only be enforced through occupation, he devoted the final paragraphs of his speech to two important questions: "What are to be the advantages of this occupation?" and "What the effect upon this Union?"[4]

Benton begins by saying that the occupation of Oregon would secure the fur trade of the Rocky Mountains "for a century to come" — a justification that will actually be obsolete by the time of Frémont's expedition, as indicated by the abandoned beaver dam he describes in the canyon near South Pass. Almost instantly, however, economics gives way to national security, with Benton suggesting that a military presence was needed to prevent British and Russian fur traders from provoking local Indians against American interests in the West. He refers to the Indians as "among the best horsemen in the world" and insists they are ready to issue "in clouds from the gorges of the Rocky Mountains," eager to sweep "with the besom of desolation" all the way to the Missouri and Mississippi. Looking even farther west, Benton argues that occupation would also provide "a naval station on the coast of the Pacific" powerful enough to control the entire Columbia basin and able to offer the kind of security that was missing when Astoria had to be sold to the British in 1813. He then returns to economics, claiming that occupation would establish the "communication between the valley of the Mississippi and the Pacific ocean" that had been "the object of Mr. Jefferson in sending out Lewis and Clark." And finally, in yet another shift of direction, he points to what he calls "the greatest of all advantages to be derived" from occupation: the out-and-out "exclusion of foreign Powers." Obviously, the country he most hopes to exclude is Britain, which he accuses of "inconsistency" for "following the 49th parallel to the summit of the Rocky Mountains, and refusing to follow it any further."

Unfortunately, Benton's entire argument roused the specter of Charles de Secondat, baron de Montesquieu, the eighteenth-century political theorist who had concluded that "it is in the nature of a republic to have only a small territory." Both *Considerations on the Causes of the Greatness of the Romans and Their Decline* (1734) and *The Spirit of the Laws* (1748) pursued this line of reasoning — especially the *Laws*, where Montesquieu most forcefully equated the limits of a republic with natural as well as moral boundaries. Comparing Asia and Europe, for example, he noted that Asia "has broader plains; it is cut into larger parts by seas; and, as it is more to the south, its streams dry up more easily, its mountains are less covered with snow, and its smaller rivers form slighter barriers." Such a geography led him to conclude that, because it was easily overrun, Asia would always be ruled by large empires and "always be despotic." In Europe, on the other hand, where the natural divisions of high mountains, hard-to-ford rivers, and numerous local seas led to "many medium-sized states," a "government of laws" would not be "incompatible with the maintenance of the state." Focusing on the issue of appropriate size, Montesquieu argued that a large republic would generally favor "large fortunes, and consequently little moderation in spirits," resulting in the kind of man who looked for greatness "only on the ruins of his homeland." But a republic that remained small would generally mean that the public good, lying "nearer to each citizen," would be "better felt, better known," while at the same time, *abuses* against the public good would be "less extensive" and "less protected" by bad laws. Rome became his most instructive example of a good republic gone bad: "It is a matter of common observation that good laws, which have made a small republic grow large, become a burden to it when it is enlarged." While "Rome was made for expansion" in Montesquieu's view, "it lost its liberty because it completed the work it wrought too soon."[5]

Many Americans were receptive to this social geography because it corroborated the idea of "compact settlement," which had shaped the early townships of New England and was the model for the national grid, which was steadily moving west. In 1677, in the wake of King Philip's War, the General Court of Connecticut had declared that the "woefull experience in the late warr" showed that "living in a single and scattering way, remoate from townships and neighborhood," led to a weakened community and to "heathenish ignorance and barbarisme." Two years later the clergyman Increase Mather drafted a report of the Boston synod that harshly declared, "There hath been in many professors an insatiable desire after Land, and worldly Accomodations," so much so "as to forsake Churches and Ordinances, and to live like the Heathen, only that they might have Elbow-room enough in the world." But as Perry Miller, Sacvan Bercovitch, and various others have pointed out, even the fanaticism of compact settlement carried with it a moral imperative to civilize the New World — the oft-invoked "errand into the wilderness" that, along with the "insatiable desire after Land," pushed the Puritans farther and farther west and was inherent in the republican virtue associated with the national grid.[6]

Jefferson grappled with the issue of density and dispersal for forty years. He began as a fairly doctrinaire disciple of Montesquieu, but to justify the Louisiana Purchase, if nothing else, his views steadily evolved over the years. In a letter written to John C. Breckinridge just after the purchase, Jefferson suggested that the new territory might develop in two stages: (1) "The best use we can make of the country for some time, will be to give establishments in it to the Indians on the East side of the Missipi, in exchange for their present country, and open land offices in the last, & thus make this acquisition the means of filling up the Eastern side, instead of drawing off it's population"; (2) "when we shall be full on this side, we may lay off a range of States on the Western bank from the head to the mouth, & so, range after range, advancing compactly as we multiply." Though this indicated he was already beginning to modify Montesquieu to incorporate the "range of States on the Western bank," Jefferson had not yet renounced the theoretical need for limits. In the same letter he suggested that "future inhabitants" of the "Missipi States" might "see their happiness" in Union but might also "see their interest in separation" into smaller republics. A few years later, however, he was willing to disavow Montesquieu in theory as well as practice — in part by refining his view of a republic. Writing to John Taylor in 1816, he defined a "pure republic" as "a government by its citizens in mass, acting directly and personally, according to rules established by the majority." Such a government "is evidently restrained to very narrow limits of space and population," and Jefferson doubts "if it would be practicable beyond the extent of a New England township." What *would* be "practicable on a large scale of country or population" is a republic "where the powers of the government, being divided, should be exercised each by representatives." A month before he had written much the same thing to a different correspondent, expressing his belief that "a government by representation is capable of extension over a greater surface of country than one of any other form." And in 1817, in a letter to the French diplomat whose queries had inspired him to write the *Notes on the State of Virginia* more than three decades earlier, he would wax even more magnanimous: "I have much confidence that we shall proceed successfully for ages to come, and that, contrary to the principle of Montesquieu, it will be seen that the larger the extent of country, the more firm its republican structure, if founded, not on conquest, but in principles of compact and equality."[7]

Though Benton was the ideological heir of Jefferson, fears of dispersal pressured the debate about Oregon from the beginning. Long's *Account of an Expedition from Pittsburgh to the Rocky Mountains* had appeared just two years before Benton's speech and had made it clear that the territory "lying between 96 and 105 degrees of west longitude, and between 35 and 42 degrees of north latitude" was so dry and "destitute of woodland" as to be "uninhabitable by a people depending upon agriculture for their subsistence." Since the "republican structure" Jefferson had in mind was inherently agricultural — embodied in the "range after range" of the national grid — Long's report suggested that there might be a practical limit to the "greater surface" of the nation after all. The report specifically addressed this issue in its final volume, noting that, "viewed as a frontier," the region might "prove of infinite importance to the United States, inasmuch as it is calculated to serve as a barrier to prevent too great an extension of our population westward, and secure us against the machinations or incursions of an enemy that might otherwise be disposed to annoy us in that part of our frontier."[8]

Knowing that many of his colleagues shared this view and needing to answer the question he himself had posed about the effect of occupation "upon the Union," Benton included a short passage near the end of the speech that is clearly a tactical ploy — utilizing the *idea* of limits to enclose and expand the nation at the same time:

This republic should have limits. The present occasion does not require me to say where these limits should be found on the north and south; but they are fixed by the hand of nature. . . . Westward, we can speak without reserve, and the ridge of the Rocky Mountains may be named, without offense, as presenting a convenient, natural, and everlasting boundary. Along the back of this ridge the western limit of this republic should be drawn, and the statue of the fabled god Terminus should be raised upon its highest peak, never to be thrown down. In planting the seed of a new Power on the coast of the Pacific ocean, it should be well understood that, when strong enough to take care of itself, the new Government should separate from the mother empire, as the child separates from the parent at the age of manhood.

Not since Jefferson's purchase of the Louisiana Territory were such contrary ideas so brazenly juxtaposed. First, Benton recognizes Long's "barrier to prevent too great an extension of our population westward," then he nullifies it by proposing a temporary extension. Rather deftly, in fact, he redefines a spatial issue as a matter of time — aware long before Robert Moses would make it a principle of city planning that "once you sink that first stake, they'll never make you pull it up." Essentially, he proposes an absolute boundary only to make it relative.[9]

But history was against Benton in 1825. With the War of 1812 resulting in an uneasy standoff with Britain, most of his colleagues preferred the status quo to a more aggressive approach. It would be another seventeen years before Frémont's expedition to South Pass set out — and during that interval of time, no Oregon bill of any kind was approved by Congress. Even as the expedition got under way, the Tyler administration was negotiating the Webster-Ashburton Treaty with Britain, reaffirming the joint occupation of Oregon Territory. The treaty was signed the day Frémont reached the foothills of the Wind River Range.

Even so, Benton's concluding words in 1825 anticipated many of the issues that would define western expansion for the next forty years. Significantly, it was a period in which elbow room became one of the most important measures of progress. Thus Benton, after claiming that the "infant Power" on the Pacific would protect the interests of the "mother empire," looked to the occupation of Oregon as the logical advancement of nationhood: "Gentlemen may think that this is looking rather deep into the chapter of futurity; but the contrary is the fact. The view I take is both near and clear. Within a century from this day, a population greater than that of the present United States will exist on the west side of the Rocky Mountains." He confidently contends that such a "calculation is reducible to mathematical precision. We double our numbers once in twenty-five years, and must continue to do so until the action of the prolific principle in man shall be checked by the same cause which checks it in every race of animals—the stint of food." Since anyone in attendance would have known that Benton was referring to Robert Malthus's famous "principle of population," this was bound to seem more sinister than reassuring. Malthus had argued that any unchecked population added to its numbers geometrically, while its food supply never grew more than arithmetically. It was a "calculation" that led him to predict—contrary to, say, Turgot, Adam Smith, and Condorcet, who had argued that free trade was the "only possible preventative against scarcity"—that every nation in the world would eventually face a chronic shortage of food. What Benton had in mind, however, was yet another version of American exceptionalism. If, earlier, he had used time to redefine space, now he used space to redefine time. For after invoking a rigorous principle of degeneration, he quickly showed how to delay its inexorable chronology: "This cannot happen with us until every acre of our generous soil shall be put in requisition; until the product of more than a thousand millions of acres shall be insufficient to fill the mouths which feed upon them." The obvious conclusion was that America would falter as a nation unless it actually "requisitioned" every acre of its "generous soil," beginning, paradoxically, with Oregon, the soil farthest from its existing frontier.[10]

Westward the Course of Empire

THE TRAJECTORY OF BENTON'S SPEECH MAKES IT CLEAR
that space and time could not be separated in the debate over Oregon — just as they could not be separated during the disagreements that
arose after King Philip's War and the Revolutionary War. Americans
always understood expansion to be a figure of history and progress as
much as settlement, and during the protracted debate over Oregon,
each side operated with a different view of time as well as space. More
accurately, perhaps, each side viewed the relationship *between* space
and time differently.[11]

Progress was generally a negative force in Montesquieu. Because he
associated any form of government — whether a monarchy, a republic,
or what he called "despotism" — with distinct institutions and locales,
he was far more interested in typology than history. One commentator
has astutely called this typology a "logical grammar" in which each form
of government was defined "as a kind of geometrical figure composed
of 'necessary relations.'" On the whole, Montesquieu looked to design,
not development, to explain the different forms of government. And
since the ideal republic was shaped by an ideal locality — situated on a
large scale within the "Zona temperata" so important to Benton and
Thomas Morton and on a smaller scale within the natural boundaries
formed by mountains, valleys, or seas — he inevitably treated progress
as the intemperate violation of space. If a republic began to exceed its
natural limits, moving forward in space could only mean moving backward in time; the farther it exceeded these limits, the sooner it would
degenerate into lawlessness, corruption, and loss of public virtue; taken
to an extreme, it could mean a return to the ignorance and barbarism
that had long been associated with the state of nature.[12]

FIG. 17. Thomas Cole, *The Course of Empire: Arcadian State*, 1836. Oil on canvas, 39¼ x 63¼ in. Collection of the New-York Historical Society. Accession #1858.2.

Toward the end of the eighteenth century, economists such as Smith and Malthus would take a more linear view of history while still viewing degeneration as a variable. Smith's *Wealth of Nations* (1776) assumed that every civilization passed through four distinct and hierarchical stages, of which the "lowest and rudest state" was hunting and fishing, the second was pasturage, the third was agriculture, and the final stage was commerce, where a steadily advancing division of labor resulted in a large-scale system of manufacturing and trade as well as an ever-expanding sphere of luxury or "opulence." But as Emma Rothschild has aptly remarked, the fundamental objective of Smith's "new science" of political economy was to depict the "irregular order" of a system marked by "profound insecurity." Lord Kames, a Scottish contemporary of Smith's, wrote that "great opulence opens a wide door to indolence, sensuality, corruption, prostitution, perdition"—a point of view that is evident in one of Thomas Cole's most celebrated works, *The Course of Empire* (1836) (figs. 17, 18, 19). Smith himself feared that factory work would be so debilitating that a "man whose whole life is spent in performing a few simple operations, of which the effects too are, perhaps, always

FIG. 18. Thomas Cole, *The Course of Empire: Consummation*, 1836. Oil on canvas, 51¼ x 76 in. Collection of the New-York Historical Society. Accession #1858.3.

FIG. 19. Thomas Cole, *The Course of Empire: Desolation*, 1836. Oil on canvas, 39¼ x 63¼ in. Collection of the New-York Historical Society. Accession #1858.5.

the same, or very nearly the same," would have "no occasion to exert his understanding, or to exercise his invention." We find a similar sentiment in *Walden* when Thoreau worries that "men have become the tools of their tools."[13]

Robert Malthus's far bleaker "principle" of fertility—what Benton called the "prolific principle in man"—suggested that degeneration was not just a threat to progress but its inevitable result. Drew McCoy has pointed out that most eighteenth-century thinkers believed the basic impetus for progress was population growth, "which promoted a search first for supplementary sources of food and eventually for additional sources of employment that could support increased numbers of people." Malthus simply argued that these "supplementary sources of food" would ultimately fall short of a population that was doubling every twenty-five years, provoking a permanent state of poverty within society. Aware that Malthus had taken his rate of population growth from Benjamin Franklin's "Observations Concerning the Increase of Mankind," Americans seemed to find this conclusion especially ominous.[14]

During the revolutionary period, when it was clear that conditions in England were already forcing people out of agriculture and into a far more miserable and insecure life of manufacturing, Franklin and Jefferson and many other colonists began to see everything west of the Alleghenies as a kind of safety valve that might delay or even suspend the course of history. Montesquieu had taught them that "the founders of the ancient republics had made an equal partition of the lands. This alone produced a powerful people, that is, a well-regulated society." He had also taught them that "it is not sufficient in a good democracy for the portions of land to be equal; they must be small, as among the Romans." Since Americans were anxious about civil union and haunted by the poverty and dependence that seemed to accompany wage labor, many began to feel that an equal division of the land would not only help to bring forth a new nation but perpetually suspend its current stage of development. Of course, this would only be possible if there was enough land to keep dividing—and thus the importance of that austere grid of townships and sections that began in the Ohio River valley around 1785 and then worked its way west, year by year, decade by decade, until it reached the Pacific Ocean. The grid was basically an attempt to overcome history by design — as close as anything in the nation's history to a static, geometric model of agrarian republicanism. Certainly Jefferson assumed that the slowly migrating grid would make sure the grim horizon of opulence and poverty continued to recede before the eternal present of a happy husbandry. Utilizing the purity of space to retard the corruptibility of time, the republic would be reborn each time the grid advanced — and like the self-similarity of the grid itself, agrarian virtue would hold true from the forty-acre farm to the nation as a whole.[15]

. . .

THE GREAT IRONY OF THIS EFFORT TO DELAY OR CIRCUM-vent progress was that it actually accelerated the nation's commitment to a linear and eschatological view of history. For more than a century there had been two separate versions of this eschatology, one religious, the other secular, although they often overlapped. In the Puritan version, which lasted well into the 1840s and 1850s, America was a sort of end that represented the beginning of the end. Convinced that their errand into the wilderness had taken them to the last remaining quadrant of earth, the Puritans firmly believed they had fulfilled the promise of Psalms 2:8 — "Ask of me, and I shall give thee the heathen for thy inheritance, and the uttermost parts of the earth for thy possession" — while also believing that these "uttermost parts" embodied the glory of the latter days prophesied in Isaiah, Jeremiah, and Revelation. John Mellen, in *A Sermon Delivered before the Governor* of Massachusetts in 1797, was plainly speaking for many others when he declared that "if we maintain our rate of western expansion," we will achieve that "which the scripture prophecies represent as constituting the glory of the latter days." Although the nation was barely west of the Alleghenies at this point, Mellen's declaration implied that reaching the western edge of the continent had to be seen as the end of these days, the end of progress, the end of history — the moment when "the mountain of the LORD's house shall be established in the top of the mountains, and shall be exalted above the hills; and all nations shall flow unto it" (Isaiah 2:2).[16]

Both a resplendent sky and the golden glow of Greek mythology seemed to light the secular version of this tradition, which was best articulated by George Berkeley, a bishop as well as a philosopher and mathematician. Berkeley's image of progress appeared in a poem entitled "On the Prospect of Planting Arts and Learning in America" (1726), and like its more biblical counterpart, it identified the ultimate progress of arts and learning with the western edge of the continent and the beauty of the closing day. Reviving the medieval doctrine of *translatio studii*, in which culture rose to new heights as it advanced from east to west, the poem closed with the following words:

> There shall be seeing another golden Age,
>   The rise of Empire and of Arts,
> The Good and Great inspiring epic Rage,
>   The wisest Heads and noblest Hearts.
>
> Not such as *Europe* breeds in her decay;
>   Such as she bred when fresh and young,
> When heav'nly Flame did animate her Clay,
>   By future Poets shall be sung.
>
> Westward the Course of Empire takes its Way;
>   The four first Acts already past,
> A fifth shall close the Drama with the Day;
>   Time's noblest Offspring is the last.

It wasn't long before the westward course of empire became one of the most resonant images in American history. We see its lengthening shadow in Hector St. John de Crèvecoeur's *Letters from an American Farmer* (1784), where he writes: "Americans are the western pilgrims, who are carrying along with them that great mass of arts, sciences, vigour, and industry which began long since in the east; they will finish the great circle." We see it again in the final words of *The Pioneers*, where Cooper says of Leatherstocking that "he had gone far towards the setting sun — the foremost in that band of pioneers who are opening up the way for the march of the nation across the continent." It is also the figure Thoreau had in mind when he wrote: "I must walk toward Oregon, and not toward Europe. And that way the nation is moving, and I may say that mankind progress from east to west." Eventually, it would inspire the mural that still adorns the U.S. Capitol, Leutze's *Westward the Course of Empire Takes Its Way*.[17]

What the Puritan and secular images of progress had in common was a horizon of perfectibility that ended at its highest stage. Both the errand into the wilderness and the westward course of empire explicitly associated the "finish'd bliss" of expansion with the end of history itself. There was, however, another view of progress in which expansion could be projected as a horizon of indeterminate, not absolute, perfectibility — and that was the marquis de Condorcet's *Sketch for a Historical Picture of the Progress of the Human Mind* (1795). Like Pascal, Condorcet's understanding of probability fundamentally shaped his view of progress and civilization; like Pascal and Smith, his views were often elaborated within the sphere of moral philosophy. Only in the final months of his life, while evading arrest by the Jacobins of the French Revolution, did Condorcet turn to history itself to frame the role of progress in human affairs. Finished just before he was captured and found dead in his cell (making it one of the most heartbreaking and imaginative leaps of faith ever recorded), the *Sketch* was the first systematic challenge to the repetitive, decline-and-fall scenario of Montesquieu, C. F. Volney, and Edward Gibbon — a challenge that looked to the history of empiricism, not the history of empires, for its model. Such a model assumed that even as empires rose and fell, truth and knowledge as a whole advanced and would keep on advancing indefinitely. Not surprisingly, it was Condorcet's *Sketch*, together with William Godwin's *Enquiry Concerning Political Justice and Its Influences on General Virtue and Happiness* (1793), that provoked Malthus to formulate the grimly contrary, dystopian future in which "selfishness would be triumphant," the "subjects of contention would be perpetual," and "not a single intellect would be left free to expatiate in the field of thought."[18]

It could be said that this last point — the status of intellectual freedom — was the most important to Condorcet, who along with Montesquieu and Smith and many other thinkers of the era owed much of his epistemology to John Locke's *Essay Concerning Human Understanding* (1690). One of the most radical aspects of Locke's epistemology was its nominalism. As a theory of language, it suggested that while words "stand for ideas," and "all our notions and knowledge" depended on "common sensible ideas" that were later "transferred to more abstruse significations," language (and therefore knowledge) itself was a relatively arbitrary sphere in which "the names that stand for things" were always "made by men" and mediated by history. Derived from this was a sociology of knowledge in which the nature of our ideas and conduct was largely determined by such social factors as upbringing and education — or what Locke himself called the "law of opinion or reputation." Perhaps the most important consequence of this sociology was its emphasis on education, for it implied that such things as anarchy, vice, and poverty were less a matter of malevolence or greed than of error arising from ignorance and superstition.[19]

To counteract the "poison of enthusiasm and superstition" that left so many people in society "mutilated and deformed," Smith had declared science to be the "great antidote" — and Condorcet, as Rothschild points out, argued that "even the constitution of one's own country" should be taught "as a matter of information, or as if one" were "speaking about a fact." Actually, facts would structure the *Wealth of Nations* far more than the *Sketch*, which was written as an outline for a much longer and more detailed work. But both Smith and Condorcet looked to the give-and-take of scientific discourse, along with the gradual accumulation of scientific knowledge, as the model for a free and virtuous society. It was "this new step in philosophy," Condorcet wrote, "that has for ever imposed a barrier between mankind and the errors of its infancy, a barrier that should save it from relapsing into its former errors under the influence of new prejudices." As a result of this barrier, "a new doctrine" had arisen that would "deal the final blow to the already tottering structure of prejudice — the doctrine of the indefinite perfectibility of the human race."[20]

Condorcet makes it clear from the opening pages of the *Sketch* that the doctrine of "indefinite perfectibility" will be his guiding principle. Outlining the goals of the *Sketch*, he resolutely declares: "Its result will be to show by appeal to reason and fact that nature has set no term to the perfection of human faculties; that the perfectibility of man is truly indefinite; and that the progress of this perfectibility, from now onwards independent of any power that might wish to halt it, has no other limit than the duration of the globe upon which nature has cast us." Though Rothschild is right to say that this outline is basically "an evaluation of probabilities," its trajectory is unmistakable. Among other things, Condorcet imagines the "abolition of inequality between nations" and the "progress of equality within each nation"; an end to "our murderous contempt for men of another colour or creed"; an acceleration of those "sciences whose progress depends on repeated observations over a large area"; an early version of social security keyed to the statistics of life expectancy; equal access to education (for women as well as men); and the advantages of a universal language. He even assumes (in the paragraphs that left Malthus so skeptical) that the progress of science and technology would permanently postpone the moment when "the amount of ground" might prove inadequate to "each successive generation." Thus Condorcet more or less ends the *Sketch* with the following question: "Do not all these observations which I propose to develop further in my book, show that the moral goodness of man, the necessary consequence of his constitution, is capable of indefinite perfection like all his other faculties, and that nature has linked together in an unbreakable chain truth, happiness and virtue?"[21]

We know now that a rationalism of this sort could just as easily result in a "war to end all wars" and the absurd self-incrimination portrayed in Arthur Koestler's *Darkness at Noon*, suggesting, in Rothschild's words, that Condorcet was "a visionary of the enlightenment and also of the counter-enlightenment." At the time, however, this point of view seemed both exact and liberating, especially to someone like Jefferson, who sometimes associated the frontier of the new nation with the frontier of knowledge and history and always found comfort in reducing the errors and lacunae of understanding by adding to his collection of weather data, population statistics, plant and animal species, and so on. Writing to William Green Munford in 1799, Jefferson announced that he was "among those who think well of the human character": "I consider man as formed for society, and endowed by nature with those dispositions which fit him for society. I believe also, with Condorcet, . . . that his mind is perfectible to a degree of which we cannot as yet form any conception." Typically, Jefferson resorted to an inventory, a "survey of what is already known," to illustrate both the adequacy of the human mind and how much it had yet to achieve, concluding that "as long as we may think as we will, & speak as we think, the condition of man will proceed in improvement." Such optimism was consistent with his belief that America represented at least a temporary exception to Malthus's iron law of population: "Here the immense extent of uncultivated and fertile lands enables every one who will labor to marry young, and to raise a family of any size. Our food, then, may increase geometrically with our laborers, and our births, however multiplied, become effective."[22]

Even so, Jefferson's horizon of perfectibility was severely compromised. Ultimately, it was the availability of space, not the advancement of knowledge or technology, that defined his and many other Americans' view of progress in the early days of the republic. If the limits of the human mind seemed as indefinite as the future, the future itself still stopped on the shores of the Pacific. It was there that "the immense extent of uncultivated and fertile lands" finally ran afoul of the multiplying generations to come, jump-starting Malthus's state of sustained degeneration. Benton tried to postpone this contraction by calculating that "it will require more people than a century can produce" before "the product of more than a thousand millions of acres shall be insufficient to fill the mouths which feed upon them." But this "mathematical precision" just affirmed the closed space of progress.[23]

. . .

PROGRESS WAS SUCH A COMPELLING AND CONTENTIOUS issue in the decades bracketing Frémont's expedition to the Wind River Range that Major L. Wilson has approached the entire period as a relentless struggle among contending views of space and time. His brief yet original essay, "The Concept of Time and the Political Dialogue in the United States, 1828–48," makes it clear that the fear of density and degeneration that had encouraged Benton to invoke the name of Malthus was still opposed by a fear of expansion that had also forced him to raise a statue of the "fabled god Terminus" on the "everlasting boundary" of the Rocky Mountains. Framing progress as an issue of freedom, Wilson argues that "it mattered greatly whether one brought to the task of building society a view of freedom as something complete at the beginning or end of the process." In the first case, "freedom might lead to unfreedom" as society "thickened" and developed over time; in the second, a more perfect freedom would arise only "as richer social conditions were created." Although the essay adds to the historiography of Manifest Destiny as a party and sectional dispute limited to the 1840s and early 1850s, it also suggests a way past this approach.[24]

In Wilson's view, Whigs of the day, especially New England Whigs, overwhelmingly favored the second option, envisioning a relatively limited republic that had to consolidate or delay itself in space in order to advance itself in time. For them, the nation was not "a political arrangement" for some existing form of free society but a way of accelerating the "positive means" by which such a society might emerge. Worried about too little development rather than too much, they found the so-called American System of internal improvements a particularly fine blueprint for "qualitative change through time rather than quantitative growth across space." We see this very clearly, for instance, in the philosophy of Henry Adams, who wrote that "to the New England mind, roads, schools, clothes, and a clean face were connected as part of the law of order or divine systems. Bad roads meant bad morals." In keeping with this "law of order or divine systems," Whigs almost invariably viewed the western frontier as a looming menace to perfectibility. Not only was it a sphere of lawlessness and chaos, but its alluring emptiness threatened to drain the labor force and loosen the social ties that made their compact and happy realm possible, actually reversing the course of history. Thus Daniel Webster's stubborn opposition to the annexation of Texas: "There must be some limit to the extent of our territory, if we would make our institutions permanent."[25]

Another way of putting this is that Whigs located the horizon of Condorcet's indefinite perfectibility within the fixed boundaries of Montesquieu's republic, essentially transforming a space Jefferson had hoped would limit or arrest progress into a space where progress was both a means and an end. For Democrats, on the other hand, the frontier to the west was both a constant source of hope and renewal and the sine qua non of nationhood — a policy which implied that the only way to enlarge the nation's freedom was by utilizing both the availability and the purity of space to retard the corruptibility of time. Summoning Isaiah Berlin's notion of "positive" and "negative" freedom, Wilson argues that Jackson viewed western expansion as a policy of planned decentralization, leading to a nation of relatively unlimited space ruled by relatively limited government. He traces this policy to Jefferson's well-known belief that each generation should be free of the debts and obligations of the generation before. Derived from Condorcet's views of contracts, the belief actually led Jefferson at one point to propose that the nation renew its laws and institutions every nineteen years. A more practical solution was to make land available to each succeeding generation, especially since there was a good deal of latitude in how territories seeking statehood had to model their own constitutions on that of the United States. When Jackson appealed to Congress to reduce the price of public lands, he made it clear that "the speedy settlement of these lands, constitutes the true interest of the Republic." Although the Homestead Act, which granted free land to any adult willing to build on it and farm it for five years, would not become law until 1862, Jackson was the most forceful president since Jefferson to govern as if the nation's virtue and happiness were guaranteed by its western frontier.[26]

These basic disagreements about space and time would persist through much of the 1840s, evident in the pages of quasi party organs such as the *Democratic Review* and the *American [Whig] Review* and often compressed to a simple dispute between "new territory" and "no territory." In 1846 an editorial in the *Democratic Review* stated outright that "the task of the American people for the present century, is clearly to take and occupy the northern continent of America"; the editorial went on to accuse the Whigs of having "sought to *prevent* the occupation of territory" by confining "the swelling population in a limited territory" and casting "without the pale of the Union him whose exigencies or enterprise carried him beyond an imaginary line as a boundary." A year later, in the middle of the Mexican War, an editorial in the *American Review* blamed the armed conflict on the Democrats, called it a "spectacle of backsliding and crime," countered with a skeptical "we are not sure that even South America is to escape," and ended with a quote from Webster in which he declared that "we want no accession of territory; we want no accession of new States. The country is already large enough."[27]

Only toward the end of the decade, as *both* the *Democratic Review* and the *American Review* began to endorse a railroad to the Pacific, would the debate over progress and the westward course of empire really change. Among other things, it was then that Frémont's view from the "loftiest peak of the Rocky mountains" began to take hold as an image of a nation whose progress transformed every absolute boundary into a relative one. *So* relative was this boundary, in fact, that it actually blurred the boundary between the two parties until the Kansas-Nebraska Act reignited the sectional conflicts that would quickly fracture each of them. As Nathaniel Hawthorne (whose stories were regularly published in the *Democratic Review*) declared in 1853, "The two great parties of the nation appear — at least to an observer somewhat removed from both — to have nearly merged into one another; for they preserve the attitude of political antagonism rather through the effect of their old organizations, than because any great and radical principles are at present in dispute between them."[28]

The Loftiest Peak of the Rocky Mountains

THE SUMMIT OF THE WIND RIVER RANGE WAS PROBABLY Frémont's destination from the moment he was chosen to lead the expedition. He was the only one to see it this way, however. Benton plainly had South Pass in mind, hoping for an accurate survey of the quickest and easiest wagon route to Oregon; Sen. Lewis F. Linn, Benton's colleague from Missouri, had been agitating for several years for a survey of military posts to protect the Oregon emigrants; and Col. John J. Abert, chief of the Corps of Topographical Engineers, seemed to envision a hydrological expedition, initially instructing Frémont to "make a Survey of the Platte or Nebraska river, up to the head of the Sweetwater." Each of these notions fell short of the view that eventually appeared in the *Report*.[29]

In his autobiography, published more than a decade after the events, Benton claimed that the expedition was "upon its outside view the conception of the government, but in fact conceived without its knowledge, and executed upon solicited orders, of which the design was unknown." Evoking Jefferson's stealth and duplicity in making the Louisiana Purchase, Benton essentially argued that he and the rest of the Oregon lobby had been able to secretly plan and conduct an official army expedition, indirectly committing the Tyler administration to a policy of annexation and emigration it openly opposed. Not only was the expedition supposedly funded by a special appropriation of $30,000, added to the army's budget for the year, but when Abert gave Frémont the order "to go to the frontier beyond the Mississippi" (Benton was never very clear when it came to western geography), Frémont had "carried it back, and got it altered, and the Rocky Mountains inserted as an object of his exploration, and the South Pass in those mountains named as a particular point to be examined, and its position fixed by him."[30]

Plots of this sort always seem more plausible if they also seem justified and successful. Since the Tyler administration was so hostile to Oregon emigrants, and the popularity of the *Report* made that antagonism irrelevant, it is easy to see why Benton's story held up for so long — reprised by Frémont, Allan Nevins, and many others. The truth, on the other hand, seems to be that the expedition was largely shaped by the existing budget and agenda of the Corps of Topographical Engineers. As Vernon Volpe has discovered fairly recently, "Frémont's 1842 expedition was part of an ongoing plan for extensive scientific explorations of the Rocky Mountain regions," and it was "approved and the funds authorized according to the usual unremarkable bureaucratic procedures." Volpe's most telling point is that Joel R. Poinsett (Martin Van Buren's secretary of war at the time) had gone before Congress in 1839 and again in 1840, urging an ambitious program of exploration that would extend "our researches over the Rocky Mountains to the shores of the Pacific Ocean." "It is believed," Poinsett said in 1839, "that these explorations, cautiously and slowly conducted, will prove much more useful in their results, both as regards the geography and natural history of that portion of our country, than the great expeditions which have preceded them." So when Senator Linn also went before Congress in 1840, asking the army to survey a line of military posts, Poinsett and Abert agreed that such a line "would be productive of the most beneficial effects upon the commerce of the whole region" but saw it mainly as an excuse to increase the budget of the corps and extend its surveys "to the passes of the Rocky Mountains." Even a diversion Frémont made to St. Vrain's Fort in western Colorado — a diversion that admittedly went beyond his official instructions and clearly represented a de facto approval of Linn's proposal — was well within the scope of the corps's planning "So. west of the Missouri."[31]

What wasn't within the scope of either Benton's or Abert's blueprint for the expedition was Frémont's trip to the summit of the Wind River Range. Despite the coyness he shows in the *Report* — waiting until he nears South Pass to reveal that he has brought the barometers along "principally for mountain service" — Frémont must have had the summit in mind from the start. Aside from outfitting the expedition with the most accurate barometers, chronometers, and thermometers he could buy, he was so eager to reach the summit and so concerned about the time available to reach it that he ignored the survey of the Kansas River called for in his instructions and actually neglected to fix the exact location of South Pass until he came down from the mountain. As it turned out, this decision was extremely farsighted — probably more farsighted than even he understood at first, and certainly more farsighted than Benton's obsession with South Pass and Abert's more general interest in rivers.

The grounds for this decision are not hard to figure. Again, Jefferson's description of the Blue Ridge was probably a distant influence, since in addition to calling the Alleghenies "the spine of the country between the Atlantic on one side, and the Missisipi and St. Laurence on the other," Jefferson had also written that "the mountains of the Blue ridge, and of these the Peaks of Otter, are thought to be of a greater height, measured from their base, than any others in our country [meaning Virginia], and perhaps in North America." Both the Lewis and Clark expedition and the Long expedition had proven this supposition to be wrong, so the more immediate impetus seems to have been Washington Irving's *Adventures of Captain Bonneville* (1837). Aware that many now believed the Wind River Range to be the highest point in North America (yet another misconception dating back to Robert Rogers and Jonathan Carver, who had referred to the region as a single "height of land"), Irving devoted an entire chapter of *Bonneville* to the ascent of a summit near the southern edge of the range. At the end of the chapter, acknowledging that the captain had lacked the instruments to measure its height, he called on others to rectify this situation — and included his personal view that the highest peak was actually farther north: the one measured by "Mr. Thompson, surveyor to the Northwest Company; who, by the joint means of the barometer and trigonometric measurement, ascertained it to be twenty-five thousand feet above the level of the sea."[32]

On its face, it is hard to think of a more direct source than this for the comment Frémont made just after discovering his last barometer was broken: "A great part of the interest of the journey for me was in the exploration of these mountains, of which so much had been said that was doubtful and contradictory." But if confirmation is needed, we also have Preuss's word for it: "The last barometer, with which we wanted to measure the mountains tomorrow, was broken when we unpacked it. Fortunately, it could be repaired. Otherwise we would not have climbed the mountains."[33]

. . .

SUMMITS OCCUPY A PECULIAR PLACE IN THE AMERICAN imagination because they are literally a way to put things in perspective. When Boone worked his way up to that "eminence" in Kentucky, it was mainly to separate himself from the surrounding forest and see what lay ahead; for all the pleasure he found in it, the beauty that struck his eye was serendipitous. The same thing is true of Jefferson's trip to the Blue Ridge, which begins and ends, after all, as a large-scale view of mountain ranges and a verification of American maps. Howard Mumford Jones has compared this view to the view of Fort William Henry in *The Last of the Mohicans*, and the comparison is apt: as Leatherstocking overlooks the fort from a nearby mountain, he sees the tents and batteries emerging in the uncertain light as "a scene which lay like a map" beneath his feet. In fact, summits are a recurring figure in the Leatherstocking tales. *The Pioneers*, the first of the series, opens with a bird's-eye view of Templeton, and two of the most resonant episodes in the novel are Judge Temple's view of the future from the top of "Mount Vision" and Leatherstocking's view of "all creation" from a rocky ledge in the Catskills. Since summits were sought from the first landfalls in America, they always seemed to represent the origin or final proof of knowledge.[34]

A natural preference for higher ground made the metaphorical associations of summits that much stronger. In his *Memoirs*, Frémont observed that whenever "the eye ranges over a broad expanse of country," the effect of this space "reacts on the mind, which unconsciously expands to larger limits and freer range of thought." Wachusett was a mere "nineteen hundred feet above the village of Princeton," yet when Thoreau and his companion reached its summit they felt as if they had "travelled into distant regions, to Arabia Petrea, or the farthest east" and were now "privy to the plan of the universe." Loftier mountains did not necessarily inspire loftier rhetoric, but they seemed to give freer rein to the patriotic imagination of Americans. In "Scenery and Mind," an essay included in *Home Book of the Picturesque*, the Reverend Elias L. Magoon wrote that "the lofty genius of Alexander" — "nourished by the majestic presence of mount Olympus" — was just one of many instances in which "grand natural scenery" proved to be "the nursery of patriotism the most firm and eloquence the most thrilling." Arguing, as Montesquieu had earlier, that "the physical aspect and moral traits of nations are in great measure influenced by their local position," Magoon adopted an essentially topographic point of view to prove that "liberty has ever preferred to dwell in high places": "The transition from the monotonous plains of Lombard to the bold precipices of Switzerland is, in outward nature, exactly like that, in inward character, from the crouching and squalid appearance of the brutalized peasant, to the independent air and indomitable energy of the free-born and intelligent mountaineer."[35]

Americans were especially obsessed with the providential metaphor of Mount Pisgah, taken from Deuteronomy 34: "And Moses went up from the plains of Moab unto the mountain of Nebo, to the top of Pisgah, that is over against Jericho. And the LORD showed him all the land" — the promised land of Israel — which Moses himself was never to set foot in. Nothing is more emblematic of American culture than this vista of what the clergyman John Cotton in 1630 had called "Gods promise to his plantations." Lamenting the "hideous and desolate wilderness" that seemed to press in on every side of Plymouth Colony, William Bradford wrote of his fellow Pilgrims: "Neither could they, as it were, go up to the top of Pisgah to view from this wilderness a more goodly country to feed their hopes; for which way soever they turned their eyes (save upward to the heavens) they could have little solace or content." The promise of "a more goodly country" can be discerned in the "small catch of smooth blue horizon" that Jefferson spied from the top of the Blue Ridge as well as "the beautiful level of Kentucke" that abruptly unfolded before Boone. The Reverend Magoon explicitly linked the metaphor to the westward course of empire when he observed that "the advancement made during the past sixty years abundantly indicates that the grand goal which Berkeley descried from afar, by a Pisgah-view on the border of the land he himself was not permitted to penetrate, will yet be triumphantly attained."[36]

Frémont also understood the advantages of "a Pisgah-view," and it was on the summit of the Wind River Range that he hoped to construct an image of "a more goodly country" that would be unified by the topographic geology of the continent—a promised land in the sense of "*all* the land" (later echoed in Bryant's "all the different parts of the country"). As usual, the surest way to do this was by focusing on the physical features of the summit and letting the "facts" speak for themselves. Above all, Frémont needed to compose his description of the summit as if its optimistic or providential image of nationhood followed strictly from the lay of the land. Whereas Long's bleak assessment of the Great Desert had suggested an objective "barrier" to expansion, Frémont's more meticulous and informed view of the Wind River Range would be the means to ascend and surpass that barrier.

Of course, focusing on the facts was also a way to discredit Irving. A singular aspect of the *Report* is that Frémont devotes the first three-quarters or so to challenging the accounts of Pike and Long and then shifts his attention to Irving's western narratives once he reaches the summit. Almost all of the summit description can be read as a rejoinder to Irving's immensely popular and influential books. Not only were they considered up-to-date and accurate, but as Stephanie LeMenager has rightly pointed out, they reaffirmed the idea that everything west of the Mississippi was a "virtually landless space" unsuited to expansion. *A Tour on the Prairies* may have stopped short of the Rockies, substantiating nothing more odious than the Great Desert, but both *Astoria* and *Bonneville* pictured the region beyond the Great Desert as such "an irreclaimable wilderness" that it seemed to be an enduring obstacle as well. This was an alarming problem for Frémont—and his response was to create a work that implicitly debunked the accuracy of the three earlier narratives.[37]

. . .

FRÉMONT DOES NOT EVEN SEE THE FOOTHILLS OF THE WIND River Range until fifty pages into the *Report*, and his hike to the "loftiest peak" of the range — over ridges and through valleys that turn out to be dead ends or just the first of many — occupies another ten pages of delays. But the summit view itself emerges abruptly and tumultuously and is fairly short:

> Putting hands and feet in the crevices between the blocks, I succeeded in getting over it, and, when I reached the top, found my companions in a small valley below. Descending to them, we continued climbing, and in a short time reached the crest. I sprang upon the summit, and another step would have precipitated me into an immense snow-field five hundred feet below. To the edge of this field was a sheer icy precipice; and then, with a gradual fall, the field sloped off for about a mile, until it struck the foot of another lower ridge. I stood on a narrow crest, about three feet in width, with an inclination of about 20° N. 51° E. As soon as I had gratified the first feelings of curiosity I descended, and each man ascended in his turn; for I would only allow one at a time to mount the unstable precarious slab, which it seemed a breath would hurl into the abyss below. We mounted the barometer in the snow of the summit, and, fixing a ramrod in a crevice, unfurled the national flag to wave in the breeze where never flag waved before. During our morning's ascent, we had met no sign of animal life, except the small sparrow-like bird already mentioned. A stillness the most profound and a terrible solitude forced themselves constantly on the mind as the great features of the place. Here, on the summit, where the stillness was absolute, unbroken by any sound, and the solitude complete, we thought ourselves beyond the region of animated life; but while we were sitting on the rock, a solitary bee (*bromus, the humble bee*) came winging his flight from the eastern valley, and lit on the knee of one of the men.

> It was a strange place, the icy rock and the highest peak of the Rocky mountains, for a lover of warm sunshine and flowers; and we

pleased ourselves with the idea that he was the first of his species to cross the mountain barrier — a solitary pioneer to foretell the advance of civilization. I believe that a moment's thought would have made us let him continue his way unharmed; but we carried out the law of this country, where all animated nature seems at war; and, seizing him immediately, put him in at least a fit place — in the leaves of a large book, among the flowers we had collected on our way. The barometer stood at 18.293, the attached thermometer at 44°; giving for the elevation of this summit 13,570 feet above the gulf of Mexico, which may be called the highest flight of the bee. It is certainly the highest known flight of that insect. From the description given by Mackenzie of the mountains where he crossed them, with that of a French officer still farther to the north, and Colonel Long's measurements to the south, joined to the opinion of the oldest traders of the country, it is presumed that this is the highest peak of the Rocky mountains. The day was sunny and bright, but a slight shining mist hung over the lower plains, which interfered with our view of the surrounding country. On one side we overlooked innumerable lakes and streams, the spring of the Colorado of the gulf of California; and on the other was the Wind river valley, where were the heads of the Yellowstone branch of the Missouri; far to the north, we just could discover the snowy heads of the *Trois Tetons*, where were the sources of the Missouri and Columbia rivers; and at the southern extremity of the ridge, the peaks were plainly visible, among which were some of the springs of the Nebraska or Platte river. Around us, the whole scene had one main striking feature, which was that of terrible convulsion. Parallel to its length, the ridge was split into chasms and fissures; between which rose the thin lofty walls, terminated with slender minarets and columns, which is correctly represented in the view from the camp on Island lake. According to the barometer, the little crest of the wall on which we stood was three thousand five hundred and seventy feet above that place, and two thousand seven hundred and eighty above the little lakes at the bottom, immediately at our feet. Our camp at the Two Hills (an astronomical station) bore south 3° east, which, with a bearing afterward obtained from a fixed position, enabled us to locate the peak. The bearing of the *Trois Tetons* was north 50° west, and the direction of the central ridge of the Wind river mountains south 39° east. The summit rock was gneiss, succeeded by sienitic gneiss. Sienite and feldspar succeeded in our descent to the snow line, where we found a feldspathic granite. I had remarked that the noise produced by the explosion of our pistols had the usual degree of loudness, but was not in the least prolonged, expiring almost instantaneously. Having now made what observations our means afforded, we proceeded to descend. We had accomplished an object of laudable ambition, and beyond the strict order of our instructions. We had climbed the loftiest peak of the Rocky mountains, and looked down upon the snow a thousand feet below, and, standing where never human foot had stood before, felt the exultation of first explorers.

This is easily the most portentous and complex passage in the *Report*: overtly statistical and impressionistic, yet shaped from first to last by a careful juxtaposition of the seen and the unseen. On the one hand, it features a precise tabulation of the barometric and astronomical readings that enable Frémont to fix the elevation and location of the peak—pretty accurately, as it turns out, although there is still some question whether he climbed the peak that now bears his name. These measurements weave their way through the entire description, adding a glorious exactitude to everything they touch. Frémont has already cited a desire to fix some astronomical positions as the reason for diverting to St. Vrain's Fort, so to justify a venture that violated "the strict order" of his instructions even more blatantly, the scientific findings on the summit have to seem that much more remarkable and precise. This is undoubtedly why he refers to the "highest" or "loftiest" peak of the Rockies three times and why he feels such "exultation" at "standing where never human foot had stood before." On the other hand, it is Frémont's impulsive leap to the "unstable precarious slab" that really sets the tone of the passage—as a matter of curiosity and as an instance of "laudable ambition" in the midst of "a terrible solitude." What's more, the "terrible convulsion" at Frémont's feet morphs extremely quickly into the invisible horizon of the whole continent — a far grander version of the transition from foreground to background than Jefferson describes in the *Notes*. Thus facts assume the density of feelings and symbols at virtually every turn in the passage, the result of a deftly composed episode that relies on four simple yet emblematic elements: the barometric reading, the national flag, *bromus* the humble bee, and the topographic geology of the site.[38]

{ THE BAROMETRIC READING }

IN THE PAGES LEADING UP TO THE SUMMIT DESCRIPTION Frémont had begun to refine his claim that the barometer was "principally for mountain service" by identifying it as "the only means of giving" the peaks that rise before him "authentically to science." Even his description of the ingenious repair Preuss referred to, though a relatively crude replacement of a broken cistern, was couched in the language of accuracy and precision: "Among the powder-horns in the camp I found one which was very transparent, so that its contents could be almost as plainly seen as through glass. This I boiled and stretched on a piece of wood to the requisite diameter and scraped it very thin, in order to increase to the utmost its transparency. I then secured it firmly in its place on the instrument, with strong glue made from a buffalo, and filled it with mercury, properly heated." As soon as Frémont reaches the summit, however, he turns the barometer into an oddly paradoxical form of objectivity. All at once a figure of mechanism and statistical certainty becomes a way to verify the priority of the naked eye and his own authority as an eyewitness.

Frémont's greatest obstacle in writing the *Report* was not the Great Desert or the Rocky Mountains — it was his own credibility. Not only was he less experienced than either Pike or Long (who had each surveyed a great deal more territory over a longer period of time than he had), but the act of verification that had set his own report in motion explicitly contradicted their accounts. Since any challenge to the prevailing view of the West had to come from a more credible account of the terrain in question, Frémont could not just be another eyewitness—he had to be an *expert* witness. That is why the trip to the summit is so important. Whatever the truth of his precise and picturesque descriptions to this point, they could not be counted on as a source of credibility. If anything, the intrinsic nature of these descriptions—radical enough to find interest and beauty in the very features of the West that had long been considered irredeemably ugly and dispiriting—made it more likely they would be mistrusted. Nor were his accounts of bad weather, river fords, prairie fires, buffalo hunts, and Indian war parties any help, since these read as pro forma nods to the sort of hardships and adventures expected of anyone traveling west at the time. Thus it is not until he reaches the summit—an episode he has been leading up to for many pages—that Frémont truly emerges as an expert witness. Certainly, that is where his accurate measurement of "the loftiest peak of the Rocky mountains" most clearly certifies him as the most credible and reliable witness to date. Even more than being the first to set foot on the convulsive crest, he is the first to give it grandly, definitively, and "authentically" to science. Such authenticity seems so intrepid and undeniable that it transcends his lack of experience and suggests that *everything else* in the *Report* is both credible and valid.

. . .

THE PRECEDENT FOR THIS CREDIBILITY CAN BE TRACED to the works of Francis Bacon, who viewed the mind as a kind of primitive or naive mirror, reflecting "the genuine light of nature." As this metaphor suggests, Bacon was deeply influenced by the mechanics of seeing. Advances in precision-ground lenses were already creating a revolution in telescopes, microscopes, and spectacles, and he was quick to recognize how radically these instruments would extend and correct the sphere of human vision. Aside from arguing that science ought to rely on firsthand observation and detailed experimentation, he was among the very earliest to propose an essentially cybernetic view of knowledge (of which Lewis's wish to see like a "crimee obscura" can be seen as one example). To refute those who believed the senses were not a source of truth — and specifically those who believed "the knowledge of man extended only to appearances" — Bacon argued: "Here was their chief error: they charged the deceit upon their senses; which in my judgment, notwithstanding all their vacillations, are very sufficient to certify and report truth, though not always immediately, yet by comparison, by help of instrument." One of the most vigorous proponents of this view was Thoreau, who near the end of *A Week on the Concord and Merrimack Rivers* exclaimed: "What wonderful discoveries have been, and may still be, made, with a plumb-line, a level, a surveyor's compass, a thermometer, or a barometer! Where there is an observatory and a telescope, we expect that any eyes will see new worlds at once."[39]

Although Bacon's emphasis on eyewitness testimony clearly influenced Locke's *Essay*, and thus Smith's and Condorcet's view of error and social progress, Thoreau's reference to "new worlds" suggests that it was also an important element of the nation's identity. Partly because its natural resources needed to be assessed and partly because it was such a vast and exotic source of pure knowledge, firsthand accounts of the New World had been extremely valuable all along. Obviously the earliest accounts were from Europeans who had sailed across the Atlantic and then returned to their native countries with various specimens and descriptions of their experience. But as more and more settlements took hold in the New World, Europeans increasingly looked to a network of colonial correspondents for the observations and specimens that would allow them to discover what Bacon had called the "true axioms" of nature. There was even reason to believe that the colonists' exposure to a rawer setting might leave their senses less "impaired" than Europeans'. In theory, anyway, this seemed to foreshadow an independence of sorts — where the colonies would still be peripheral to the political centers of Europe for a while but fundamental to the advancement of knowledge and civilization. It was Berkeley, after all, one of the great philosophers of empiricism, who had argued that world history would culminate on the western shores of the New World.

According to Susan Scott Parrish, this trajectory of independence began to accelerate once wonder gave way to curiosity. Throughout the sixteenth and seventeenth centuries, the New World was often associated with a supernatural abundance and a bewildering population of hybrid species, including the opossum, the first marsupial to be seen by Europeans, which was described by the captain of the *Pinta* as a "monstrous beaste with a snowte lyke a foxe, a tayle lyke a marmasette, eares lyke a batte, handes lyke a man, and feete lyke an ape, bearing her whelpes aboute with her in an outwarde bellye much lyke unto a greate bagge or purse." The European response to such prodigies, portents, divine providences, or monsters, as they were called, was largely a matter of awe and amazement. Toward the end of the seventeenth century, however, natural history began "systemizing the abiding and rational text of creation" through "the clarifying tools of dissection, numeracy, mechanical analysis, and universal nomenclature," and by the middle of the eighteenth century wonder had completely given way to curiosity. As Parrish notes, curiosity "was a uniquely capacious term, explaining not just a disposition toward inquiry but the subsequent acts of close and careful investigation." In effect, it meant that "men became or remained curious" as long as they "witnessed curiosities" and possessed "the capacity to describe them." Since Europeans were so curious about America that "they made themselves in practice open to any testifier or collector who could satisfy that curiosity," it was now apparent that the mere "act of close and careful investigation" gave colonial eyewitnesses an authority they had never had before. Simply put, empiricism "*gave* authority where political empire took it away."[40]

By the time Jefferson began to compile a garden book devoted to nearly six decades of plantations at Monticello, a farm book divided into such topics as tobacco and slaves, and a notebook recording thousands of meteorological readings, it was clear that Americans had happily embraced empiricism as a confirmation of their singularity and independence, pointedly deriving their independence from "the Laws of Nature, and of Nature's God." It is hardly coincidental that Jefferson's *Notes on the State of Virginia* was largely an examination of American nature. Nor is it coincidental that Jefferson's celebrated instructions to Lewis and Clark were fundamentally an order to observe, record, collect, and measure everything they came into contact with — accompanied by an order to avoid dangerous situations as much as possible, since "in the loss of yourselves, we should lose also the information you will have acquired."[41]

Yet both the meticulous, patriotic *Notes* and the extraordinary expedition it inspired were clearly conceived as a more exacting and informed response to earlier eyewitness accounts of America — and it is this, more than anything else, that makes them so emblematic. Comparisons of this sort were especially true of later expeditions to the West, where the curiosity that had supplanted wonder was itself supplanted by credibility. No longer was the simple "act of close and careful investigation" a warranty of authority. Once the garden of the late 1700s had morphed into the desert of the 1820s and 1830s — and then morphed again into the more ambiguous accounts of Catlin, Flint, and Gregg — the very idea of what counted as "the West" was largely a matter of who you chose to believe. To the millions of Americans who had never seen the West for themselves, the issue of credibility was especially fraught.

. . .

ONLY THE HUMORLESS OR NAIVE WILL BEGRUDGE THE FACT that Frémont's own credibility turned out to be a kind of scientific sleight of hand. The *Report* makes it clear that Frémont actually figured out the summit he ought to climb by examining the profile of the Wind River Range and then heading for the peak that "exhibited more snow to the eye than any of the neighboring summits" — what he calls the "main peak" or "Snow peak." Though snow is never a precise or accurate measure of elevation (especially in the Wind River Range, where there are more than forty peaks over thirteen thousand feet), this is never mentioned; nor does Frémont mention that many of the peaks in the Wind River Range were actually invisible to him when he made his choice, or that almost any peak can look higher or lower if approached from a different direction. Even worse is that his corroborating evidence seems equally vague and visual: "From the descriptions given by Mackenzie of the mountains where he crossed them, with that of a French officer still farther to the north, and Colonel Long's measurements to the south, joined to the opinion of the oldest traders of the country, it is presumed that this is the highest peak of the Rocky mountains." It becomes apparent, then, that Frémont's claim of having reached and recorded "the loftiest peak of the Rocky mountains" derives solely from the authority of his naked eye. And yet, in the passage itself, all that matters is the abstract and objective *barometric reading*, which proves decisive.

Frémont has foreshadowed the definitive nature of this reading by mourning the loss of every barometer or thermometer as a loss of certain knowledge. Just before he repairs the shattered cistern, for instance, he writes of how grief-stricken the men are that it broke: "The height of these mountains, considered by the hunters and traders the highest in the whole range, had been a theme of constant discussion among them; and all had looked forward with pleasure to the moment when the instrument, which they believed to be true as the sun, should stand upon the summits, and decide their disputes." Later, during the climb to the summit, he is willing to risk almost anything, including chronic altitude sickness, to insure that the final reading is taken on the summit itself, not "eight or ten hundred feet" below. When he finally reaches the summit and calculates the elevation — "the barometer stood at 18.293, the attached thermometer at 44°; giving for the elevation of this summit 13,570 feet above the gulf of Mexico" — the clear implication is that this reading not only gives us an exact elevation but certifies this elevation to be that of the "highest peak of the Rocky mountains." Although he almost instantly turns around and admits that the summit he has chosen is merely *presumed* to be the highest peak, it is the authority of the barometric reading that allows him to claim, both before and after, that he has *actually* climbed the highest peak. Above all, it is the very fact of this reading — apparently the first ever taken on a summit of the Rocky Mountains — that implicitly refutes Irving's claim that Thompson had already measured the highest peak using "the joint means of the barometer and trigonometric measurement."

Naturally, any time a number appears to be self-evident, it is likely to be self-serving — and in this case, it is also misleading. As a "matter of fact" the accuracy of the barometric reading neither confirms nor contradicts Frémont's claim of having measured the highest peak. With nothing to compare it to (since Frémont neglects to mention any measurements but Long's, and even those were nothing more than a few temperature readings added to the visual inspection of timberlines and snow caps) an elevation of "13,570 feet above the gulf of Mexico" is basically meaningless. All it proves, under the circumstances, is that Frémont has been to the top of a mountain and measured it, a tautological proposition at best. Unfortunately, the very thing that seems to make the measurement so special — its singularity — is precisely what makes it so incomplete. It is not until the last summit of a range is surveyed that the significance of the first one to be surveyed is clear — as we know from the Wind River Range itself, where the summit Frémont measured turns out to be the third highest peak, and from later measurements in Colorado, where twenty-six peaks are now known to be higher.[42]

Not that Frémont was wrong about the measurement. Modern instruments confirm that he was off by exactly 175 feet — an extremely small margin of error for the period (where disputes about how to calculate elevation from barometric readings would last well into the 1870s). Since he arrived at this number using an instrument that had been completely refurbished in the field — and from a material that only a master of bricolage would think to use in the first place — it's a remarkable achievement, all things considered. If Thompson really measured a peak to the north at "twenty-five thousand feet above the level of the sea," he was off by at least eleven thousand feet and probably more.[43]

Reviewing the combined report in 1845, the *Democratic Review* repeatedly focused on barometric data, including the survey of the Great Basin of Utah and Nevada (which Frémont was the first to describe as such) and the profile map of the continent, which "deserves the study of all who wish either to become acquainted with the elevations of our own continent, or to compare it with other continents, or to judge the feasibility of a railroad to Oregon." The review referred to the map, in particular, as having been "made by a scientific and practical man, who has travelled the whole distance, — compass in hand, taking courses;

barometer in hand, measuring elevations; telescope in hand, determining longitudes and latitudes; pencil in hand, sketching the country; pen in hand, writing down the character of the hills and vales, of plains and mountains, of rocks and earths, of trees, grass, and flowers, of rivers, creeks, fountains, lakes, and branches." This tribute to Bacon's prosthetic and steady gaze ended by proclaiming that, "without the aid of scientific assistance" (meaning that the expedition had no official geologist or botanist), Frémont had "so enriched his Report with science as to seem to have been the work of professional *savans*." The obvious implication is that Frémont's singular and manly expertise descended mostly from his flawless use of instruments — of which the measurement on the summit has to be seen as the most noteworthy example.[44]

It is, of course, ironic that the influence of Frémont's undeniably receptive eye can be traced so directly to a measurement that only proved that he had *not* climbed the loftiest peak of the Rockies, much less the Olympian heights of the continent. Still, it was just the beginning of a description in which the summit became emblematic of the nation as a whole. Frémont himself, the man who had "travelled the whole," had already created the conceptual link: "We mounted the barometer in the snow of the summit, and, fixing a ramrod in a crevice, unfurled the national flag to wave in the breeze where never flag waved before." Suddenly the barometric reading of an abstract and imperceptible quantity — elevation — merged with the most conspicuous symbol of the nation. It was a riveting image of vision exceeding the visible. Knowledge and the nation would progress together.

{ THE NATIONAL FLAG }

FRÉMONT WAS HARDLY THE FIRST TO UNFURL A FLAG IN the western winds. Nearly every survey of the West was either led or escorted by the army, and the flag was an important symbol of federal authority. While meeting with a delegation of Lemhi Shoshones, for instance, Meriwether Lewis made a great show of presenting the flag to a village chief — informing him, with a perfectly straight face, that it "was an emblem of peace among whitemen and now that it had been received by him it was to be respected as the bond of union between us." Either encouraging or forcing people to pledge their allegiance to the flag would become an incidental goal of every government expedition to the West, especially as the nation began to claim more and more territory. Since most government expeditions were assisted and supplied by local companies, even trading posts and other private ventures liked to think of themselves as outposts of the nation. When Nathaniel Wyeth completed Fort Hall in Oregon Territory, he opened for business the next day by ceremoniously raising the Stars and Stripes.[45]

Even so, there seemed to be something special about unfurling the flag on the summit of a mountain — especially when that summit had loomed so long on the horizon and was said to be the loftiest peak in the Rocky Mountains. Among other things, it suggests that Frémont's apparently impromptu gesture expressed a new awareness of political symbolism. Long had also carried a flag when he climbed what is now known as Pike's Peak, but he never made patriotism an issue, and the climb itself had nothing like the drama of the *Report* as something either anticipated or achieved. At the time Frémont left for the Wind River Range, however, he and the rest of the nation had just witnessed the so-called Log Cabin Campaign of William Henry Harrison. This was the campaign in which Harrison, a Virginia-born aristocrat who lived in a large house on the banks of the Ohio, chose to associate himself with the rustic simplicity of hard cider and log cabins. "Log cabins were everywhere," Arthur Schlesinger wrote in *The Age of Jackson*, "hung to watch chains and earrings, in parlor pictures and shop windows, mounted on wheels, decorated with coonskins and hauled in magnificent parades." In many respects, this can be seen as the origin of the modern political campaign, and it is hard to believe that anyone as shrewd as Benton or Frémont, who were on the losing side of the election, would have missed the point of it. Both the trajectory of the expedition and the subtle rhetoric of the *Report* (e.g., comparing the elevation of South Pass to "the ascent of the Capitol hill from the avenue") suggest that they didn't. We know for sure that the flag Frémont carried with him had been specially sewn for the expedition, and the illustration that appears in his *Memoirs* shows that it combined the conventional Stars and Stripes with the eagle of the Great Seal of the United States — not one but two powerful images of the nation.[46]

Exactly what Frémont hoped to achieve by unfurling the flag seems fairly clear. Peripherally, anyway, the *Report* implied that he wished to encourage that sense of destiny that many Americans found in the image of Pisgah and the ever-migrating "errand into the wilderness." Bercovitch reminds us that the Great Seal was associated with the persecuted woman in Revelation who is "given two wings of a great eagle, that she might fly into the wilderness" — a popular image during the Revolutionary War period. As Samuel Sherwood declared in "The Church's Flight into the Wilderness," an Election Day address of 1776: "When that God, to whom the earth belongs, and the fulness thereof, brought his church into this wilderness, as on eagles' wings by his kind protecting providence, he gave this good land to her, to her own lot and inheritance forever" — proving that God had, "in this American quarter of the globe, provided for the woman and her seed." After climbing the summit and then retracing his steps to Fort Laramie, Frémont almost imperceptibly draws our attention to this "protecting providence" by casually letting us know that "the fortieth day had been fixed for our return," a disclosure that instantly associates the summit episode with Elijah's trip to the top of Horeb. The specificity of this reference makes the comments about "a stillness the most profound" and the "chasms and fissures" that denote a "terrible convulsion" begin to look like something more than empiricism. Certainly, they evoke the verses in 1 Kings 19:7–19 in which Elijah looks for God in a great and strong wind, and an earthquake, and a raging fire — "and after the fire a still small voice."[47]

And yet the Great Seal also contains the motto *Novus ordo seclorum* — usually translated as "A new order of the ages" — connoting both a new era in the American quarter of the globe and a commitment to science, reason, and progress. It seems significant, then, that the only noise Frémont hears on the summit is "the explosion of our pistols," which, he carefully notes, "had the usual degree of loudness, but was not in the least prolonged, expiring almost instantaneously." This meticulous observation brings us back to the empiricism that is characteristic of the *Report*, suggesting that the various biblical references tend to be incidental and operate within a larger and more precise context. There is little question that Frémont's decisive "errand" into the western wilderness is scientific knowledge. If the flag now waves in a rarefied breeze "where never flag waved before," it is mainly because he has come to the mountaintop to give it "authentically to science." By juxtaposing two singular and secular icons in a single sentence — the barometer in one hand, the flag in the other — Frémont implicitly ties the expansion of the nation to the steady progress of knowledge. It is here, on the summit, that the *Report* begins to suggest that both history and nature share a horizon of indefinite perfectibility.

. . .

FRÉMONT'S TALENTS AND TRAINING MAKE IT SEEM ALMOST inevitable that he would assign a number to the nation, identifying its noblest aspirations with the elevation of its loftiest peak. Strictly speaking, the barometric reading was just the most unique or unusual number to emerge from a report that was dominated by instruments, maps, astronomical observations, meteorological observations, tables of latitude and longitude, tables of distances from point to point. But wrapping this number in the flag showed the underlying shrewdness of the *Report*. Statistics and quantification had long been associated with progress and the state of republican government in America. Benton had relied on much the same approach when he calculated that a population that doubled every twenty-five years would take more than a century before "the product of more than a thousand millions of acres" would be "insufficient to fill the mouths which feed upon them." So had Jefferson when he implied that the nation would be weakened by a population whose density exceeded ten per square mile.

Patricia Cohen has argued that as political parties began to emerge in the 1790s, many Americans found it hard to define the common good for such a large and diverse country and thus turned to statistics: "Statistical thought offered a way to mediate between political ideas based on a homogeneous social order and economic realities that were fast undermining homogeneity. Inventories of descriptive facts about society were touted as providing an authentic, objective basis for ascertaining the common good." In other words, "knowing the exact dimensions of heterogeneity would compensate for the lack of homogeneity." By 1820 or so, as the "benefits of republicanism" were "most readily demonstrated by appeals to quantifiable facts, notably of a demographic or economic character," progress and growth became the surest measure of the common good. The basic assumption was that "*more* meant *better*": "more people, more trade, more daily newspapers, more gallons of lamp oil" — and for many, anyway, more land. As John O'Sullivan would put it so ecstatically in the *New York Morning News* in 1845: "Yes, more, more, more! . . . till our national destiny is fulfilled . . . and the whole boundless continent is ours." Works such as Adam Seybert's *Statistical Annals* openly promoted this version of republicanism. "It is to the condition of the people," he wrote, "in relation to their increase, their moral and physical circumstances, their happiness and comfort, their genius and industry, that we must look for the proofs of a mild and free, or of a cruel and despotic government."[48]

The greater background to Frémont's measurement and the popularity of statistics was an interest in "increase" as a figure of progress. Progress was an especially potent and pragmatic version of millennialism — a way for those who had declared the United States to be the ultimate in geography or history to replace their "faith in prophecy with an even more ardent faith" in practical reform. For Jonathan Edwards it represented what Anders Stephanson has called a "meliorism" — "a gradualist ideology of improvement, an emphasis on constructing the millennium by orderly progress" rather than apocalypse. Stephanson seems to see this as fairly typical, since he argues that throughout the revolutionary period, the "many poetic odes to the 'rising glory' of America" began to combine "science and commerce, empire and millennium, into a final version of 'endless peace' under universal U.S. benevolence." During the 1780s and 1790s, Dr. Samuel Cooper was just one of many to declare that

"Conquest is not . . . the aim of these rising States"; rather, it is "to make a large portion of this globe a seat of knowledge and liberty." A similarly self-serving sentiment would be expressed by Theodore Parker over sixty years later during an actual episode of conquest. Acknowledging the Mexican War to be nasty, "mean and wicked," while also admitting the nation would "possess the whole of the continent" in any case, Parker rather hopefully concluded: "But this may be had fairly; with no injustice to any one; by the steady advance of a superior race, with superior ideas and a better civilization." Of course, nearly all these expressions of rising, universal benevolence derived from a long-standing belief in American exceptionalism—which was now inseparable from the ideology of progress. As John Gardiner put it in a July Fourth oration in 1785, "For times of greater freedom, of nobler improvement, and of more perfect knowledge was reserved the particular discovery of *this happy land*, the place of our nativity."[49]

It is precisely this nexus of progress, discovery, and "more perfect knowledge" that Frémont wished to evoke on the summit of the Wind River Range. If his barometric reading was more accurate and higher than any measure of elevation in Jefferson's *Notes*, the journals of Lewis and Clark, or the various expedition reports that began with Zebulon Pike, it was also a symbol of that entire sphere in which the growth and progress of the nation were inscribed within the more or less indefinite metrics of industry and science. As Frémont surely understood, the great advantage of this strategy was that it sidestepped the impasse of progress that had separated Democrats and Whigs for at least a decade. By equating the future of the nation with the future of industry and science, the *Report* implied not only a horizon of perfectibility beyond an eternal present but a domain of civic endeavor beyond the Mississippi. Instead of being a miserable retreat *to* barbarism, as Whigs saw it, the West now represented the latest in scientific data and the indefinite prospect of even greater knowledge and use. Instead of being a static retreat *from* barbarism, as Democrats saw it, the West now signified a steadily improving future driven by individual initiative and free trade. Indeed, Yonatan Eyal has argued that an "*ethos* of perfectibility" began to emerge among younger Democrats in the late 1840s and early 1850s — and because nothing marked them "as a forward-looking movement" more than their "commitment to technological growth," this ethos was undoubtedly one of the reasons Whigs and Democrats momentarily converged during the period.[50]

Essentially ignoring or superseding the issues of opulence and over-population, the *Report* combined quantitative expansion into space with qualitative change through time, making each a means to the other. Taken as a whole, it suggested that the ultimate yet indefinite future of the nation lay within very definite boundaries yet to be seized and improved. By extension, anyway, the Wind River Range was just the spine of a "great nation of futurity" stretching from sea to sea. But if the barometric reading and the planting of the national flag can be seen as the elements that activated this progressive and patriotic landscape, Frémont turned to a higher law by including the symbolic figure of a bee.

{ *BROMUS*, THE HUMBLE BEE }

FRÉMONT'S DESCRIPTION OF *BROMUS* SEEMED TO STRIKE A deeply resonant chord in nineteenth-century Americans, and it emerged as one of the *Report's* most celebrated and revered episodes. In *Signal Fires on the Trail of the Pathfinder*, a series of poems published during Frémont's campaign for the presidency in 1856, George Shepard Burleigh predictably composed a poem entitled "Frémont's Peak" but added a completely separate poem entitled "To 'Bromus,' on Frémont's Peak." Reading the *Report* as a boy, the poet Joaquin Miller was so delighted by Frémont's tale that he evidently refused to accept the bee's fatal end: "It touched my heart when he told how a weary little brown bee tried to make its way from a valley of flowers far below across a spur of snow, where he sat resting for a moment with his men; how the bee rested on his knee till it was strong enough to go on to another field of flowers beyond the snow; and how he waited a bit for it to go at its will." We might see this oversight as fairly representative, since Burleigh's poem shares Miller's optimistic blindness.[51]

Although the *bromus* interlude may be the most whimsical element of the *Report*, what makes it especially notable is that it probably never happened, suggesting that Frémont added it solely for symbolic or aesthetic reasons. Certainly, the incident has the formal perfection of a literary piece. A "solitary bee" — "the first of his species to cross the mountain barrier" — merrily makes its way to the summit of the Wind River Range, lights "on the knee of one of the men," and is summarily, if rather poetically, pressed between "the leaves of a large book, among the flowers we had collected on our way." Even at the time it was written, this shapely sequence of events seems to have provoked doubts about its empirical truth. John Bigelow included a footnote in his campaign biography of Frémont that begins: "The encounter of Col. Frémont with this solitary pioneer of human civilization upon the summit of the highest peak of the Rocky Mountains, is a curious commentary upon the familiar lines which conclude Bryant's poem of the Prairies, and which will already have occurred to many of our readers upon the perusal of the affecting incident so gracefully recorded by Col. Frémont." Knowing that he needed to avoid the more fanciful implications of such a commentary, Bigelow hastily changed course with a long quotation from Alexander von Humboldt's *Aspects of Nature* — a quotation that began: "'To the surprise of the adventurous travellers, the summit of Frémont's Peak was found to be visited by bees. It is probable that these insects, like the butterflies which I found at far higher elevations in the chain of the Andes, and also within the limits of perpetual snows, had been involuntarily drawn thither by ascending currents of air.'"[52]

Clearly, Bigelow hoped to use Humboldt's authority as an expert witness to dispel any doubts about Frémont's authority as an expert witness. But Humboldt does not say that he has found bees at a similar elevation in the Rocky Mountains, merely that he has found butterflies at even higher elevations in the Andes. So it is hard to see this as anything more than a kind of innocence or expertise by association. Moreover, when we turn to Preuss's journal — the only source we have that directly and independently confirms the details of Frémont's account — there is no mention of a bee. In fact, of all the things Frémont describes on the summit, the only significant detail *not* corroborated by Preuss's journal is *bromus*, the humble bee. The obvious conclusion is that it never happened — at least not on the summit.

Assuming it's not a complete fabrication, the most likely explanation is that something similar happened on the way up or down the mountain and that Frémont merely transformed a routine instance of collecting plant and animal specimens into a symbolic figure of progress. Bumblebees (which are actually of the genus *Bombus*, not *Bromus*) are not uncommon in the Rocky Mountains, and some may be carried there by "ascending currents of air." Although the Linnaean mislabeling suggests that Frémont would not have been able to tell whether a bumblebee was native to the East or to the West and therefore which direction it might have come from if carried up from the plains, it is not unreasonable to assume that he or one of his party actually encountered a bee at some point, seized it, and pressed it into a notebook, acting as the factual basis for what turned out to be an exercise in poetic license. Preuss's journal makes it clear that even where Frémont's facts were accurate, he sometimes played fast and loose with their chronology. On the other hand, the very uncertainty of this speculation suggests that it is just as sensible — and even more interesting, in certain respects — to assume that Frémont simply made the incident up. As it stands, the only thing we know for sure is that he chose to exploit a figure that had been associated with emigration and civilization ever since the Puritans.[53]

. . .

IN ONE OF THE MANY TRACTS WRITTEN DURING THE 1620S and 1630s justifying "removeall" to New England, the Reverend John Cotton poses the following question: "But how shall I know whether God hath appointed me such a place, if I be well where I am?" Among the "foure or five good things, for procurement of any of which I may remove," number three on Cotton's list is "to plant a Colony, that is, a company that agree together to remove out of their owne Country, and settle a Citty or commonwealth elsewhere. Of such a Colony wee reade in *Acts* 16. 12. which God blessed and prospered exceedingly, and made it a glorious Church. Nature teacheth Bees to doe so, when as the hive is too full, they seeke abroad for new dwellings: So when the hive of the Common wealth is so full, that Tradesmen cannot live one by another, but eate up one another, in this case it is lawfull to remove." Two hundred years later, and at least a thousand miles west of New England, Cooper would resort to exactly the same metaphor in *The Prairie*. Arguing that those who remained in the Old World were "wont to claim the empty distinction of antiquity," while the "American borderer" should be "likened to those who have paved the way for the intellectual progress of nations," Cooper pointedly rejects the hive that "has remained stationary" in favor of "the numerous and vigorous swarms that are culling the fresher sweets of a virgin world." Around the same time, and the same longitude, Timothy Flint would also evoke an image of apian progress, noting that "on the edge" of some fields "but recently won" from the wilderness, "six cabins were occupied by a family, its servants, and establishments, which, seen in the distance, had the appearance of so many bee-hives."[54]

As Americans moved farther and farther west of the Mississippi, they increasingly viewed the bee as a herald of things to come — in Frémont's words, "a solitary pioneer to foretell the advance of civilization." Once again, it looks as if this image can be traced most immediately to a comment in Long's report. It appears near the end of the report as the party is moving east through the prairies of the lower Arkansas, anticipating the settlements along the Mississippi: "At evening we returned to the valley of the river, and placed our camp under a small cotton-wood tree, upon one of whose branches a swarm of bees were hanging. These useful insects reminded us of the comforts and luxuries of a life among men, and at the same time gave us the assurance that we were drawing near the abodes of civilization. Bees, it is said by the hunters and the Indians, are rarely if ever seen more than two hundred and fifty or three hundred miles in advance of the white settlements." Whether or not this remark is truly its point of origin, there is a direct and economical line—a beeline, if you will—joining this specific image of Long's report to a series of works that includes Cooper's *Prairie*, William Cullen Bryant's poem "The Prairies," Irving's *A Tour on the Prairies*, and Frémont's account of the great "ocean of prairie." In each of these works, the bee represents a distinct view of republican progress.[55]

Naturally, the most slavish acolyte of Long's report is Cooper, although this is not apparent at first, since he has likened the "numerous and vigorous swarms" of "Anglo-Americans" to "those who have paved the way for the intellectual progress of nations." One of the principal characters in the novel is a bee hunter named Paul Hover, and when Cooper describes Hover's efforts to locate a beehive on the open prairie, we are even treated to a lucid explanation of where the word "beeline" comes from. "When the bees are seen sucking the flowers, their pursuer contrives to capture one or two. He then chooses a proper spot, and suffering one to escape, the insect invariably takes its flight toward the hive. Changing his ground to a greater or lesser distance, according to circumstances, the bee-hunter then permits another to escape. Having watched the course of the bees, which is technically called 'lining,' he is enabled to calculate the intersecting angle of the two lines, which is the hive." However, just as Pike's report contained many sensitive and precise descriptions of the local terrain yet ended as a large-scale one-liner, so does *The Prairie* turn the homing instinct of bees into the triangulation of a nation headed in the opposite direction. Despite his vision of "the fresher sweets" to be found "in a virgin world," Cooper is always looking east, not west, for the signs of progress and civilization. Thus we find that by the end of the novel every Anglo-American who hasn't died on the prairie has returned east. Hover, in particular, returns to his native Kentucky to become "a landholder, then a prosperous cultivator of the soil, and shortly after a town-officer."[56]

Written several years later, either during or after a trip through the prairies of Illinois, William Cullen Bryant's well-known poem takes a completely contrary tack, ending with a vision of the nation in which the westward course of empire seems as inevitable as nature itself:

> The bee,
> A more adventurous colonist than man,
> With whom he came across the eastern deep,
> Fills the savannas with his murmurings,
> And hides his sweets, as in the golden age,
> Within the hollow oak. I listen long
> To his domestic hum, and think I hear
> The sound of that advancing multitude
> Which soon shall fill these deserts.

This is a far more open-ended and Democratic perspective than Cooper's, which is probably why it became the iconic image of the bee as pioneer or as advance scout—evident in Bigelow's remark about the *Report*'s "curious commentary upon the familiar lines" of the poem and even more remarkable in Miller's and Burleigh's blindness to the bee's fate. But it is also a decidedly isolated perspective, in that Bryant's reverie of an "advancing multitude" suddenly ends with him "in the wilderness alone"—and thus the image of the *solitary* pioneer that is an element of Bryant's account but not of either Cooper's or Long's.[57]

The ideology of Bryant's "Prairies" might have remained relatively uncontested during an era so influenced by Jackson, but in yet another turn of events Irving used much the same imagery as Bryant to argue *against* an extended republic. Returning to the relentless pessimism of Cooper's *Prairie*, Irving devoted a short chapter in *Tour*—innocently entitled "A Bee Hunt"—to one of the nineteenth century's most graphic, concise, and wrenching episodes of social degeneration. As an obvious point of comparison, the episode takes place among the forests of the lower Arkansas where Long had found bees a decade earlier. This time, however, Irving and his companions are heading west, not east.[58]

"A Bee Hunt" begins more or less where Bryant's poem ends: "The beautiful forest in which we were encamped abounded in bee trees; that is to say trees in the decayed trunks of which wild bees had established their hives. It is surprising in what countless swarms the bees have over-spread the Far West within but a moderate number of years. The Indians consider them the harbinger of the white man, as the Buffalo is of the red man; and say that, in proportion as the bee advances, the Indian and the Buffalo retire." Irving is even willing to admit that the regions which "skirt and intersect" the prairie "answer literally to the description of the land of promise, 'a land flowing with milk and honey;' for the rich pasturage of the prairies is calculated to sustain herds of cattle as countless as sands upon the sea shore."

However, once the hunters trace several honey-baited bees to the "hollow trunk of a blasted oak," things start to fall apart. At first, the "jarring blows" of the hunters' axes seem "to have no effect in alarming or disturbing this most industrious community," as bees continue to arrive or sally "forth on new expeditions, like so many merchantmen in a money making metropolis, little suspicious of impeding bankruptcy and downfall." Even when the tree comes down with "a tremendous crash, bursting open from end to end, and displaying all the hoarded treasures of the commonwealth," the bees seem oblivious. But the mere sight of the golden lucre sets off a frenzy among Irving's party, as everyone "now fell to, with spoon and hunting knife, to scoop out the flakes of honey comb." Soon "every stark bee hunter was to be seen with a rich morsel in his hand, dripping about his fingers." In the ensuing mayhem, even bees from "rival hives," acting as if they "would carry through the similitude of their habits with those of laborious and gainful men," arrive "on eager wings, to enrich themselves with the ruins of their neighbors." Meanwhile, the "poor proprietors" of the "bankrupt hive" crawl "backwards and forwards, in vacant desolation," wheel about in the air above the fallen tree, "astonished at finding it all a vacuum," and eventually settle down "in clusters" on a nearby tree, buzzing "forth doleful lamentations over the downfall of their republic." When Irving finally "abandons the place," he asks one of the bee hunters what will happen to the remaining honey and is told: "It will be all cleared off by varmint."

Clearly, this is a completely contrary view of the bee — symptomatic of a republic advancing to its doom instead of some new and honeyed golden age. Indeed, Irving seems to be writing as a relatively conventional Whig, worried that the republic will be thrown into chaos by the "jarring" and disruptive forces of a predatory and uncivilized frontier. The bee-hunting party sets out from a "honey camp" that is clearly identified with the frontier, and so are the hunters themselves: "The party was headed by a veteran bee hunter, a tall lank fellow, in homespun garb that hung loosely about his limbs, and a straw hat shaped not unlike a bee hive; a comrade, equally uncouth in garb, and without a hat, straddled along at his heels, with a long rifle on his shoulder." It is precisely these "uncouth" elements who begin to ply "their axes vigorously at the foot of the tree to level it with the ground," setting in motion the catastrophic greed that follows. In effect, the parable of the bee hunt is just the first and most artful version of the "lawless interval" Irving later identifies in *Astoria*.[59]

. . .

APPEARING LESS THAN A DECADE BEFORE THE *REPORT* AND as part of a series of western narratives whose popularity created a serious impediment to a more sympathetic and inclusive view of expansion, Irving's, not Bryant's, image of the bee would have been an obvious and immediate irritant to Frémont. Not only was it the latest and most pessimistic account of the West, it was also the latest and most direct affront to one of the most iconic, endearing figures of western expansion. Although Frémont never says as much, there is a jarring, and otherwise mysterious, element in his own account of the bee which suggests that he had Irving's parable in mind as he was inventing this incident for the *Report*. For what begins as a relatively pastoral evocation of civilization — with a "lover of warm sunshine and flowers" winging its way "from the eastern valley" and landing without fear "on the knee of one of the men" — rapidly turns vulturine and violent: "I believe that a moment's thought would have made us let him continue his way unharmed; but we carried out the law of this country, where all animated nature seems at war; and, seizing him immediately, put him in at least a fit place — in the leaves of a large book, among the flowers we had collected on our way." Coming in the midst of a description dedicated to nationalism and the progress of the human mind and near the end of a *Report* notable for its editorial restraint, such a statement seems especially incongruous. It implies that Frémont felt he had to transcend the fear of savagery and self-interest that so many Americans associated with an expansive republic by simultaneously evoking and deflecting one of the most alarming images of that association. Choosing to do this in an area of the West so clearly identified with the "lawless interval" made Frémont's gesture even more meaningful. And since science was again the means to his end, it was nearly unassailable.

The key to Frémont's feat is the punning image of leaves that also shaped Thoreau's description of the railroad cut in *Walden* and Walt Whitman's *Leaves of Grass*. What each had in mind was Shakespeare's "infinite book of secrecy," Bacon's "book of God's works," Oliver Goldsmith's "book of knowledge," and Andrew Marvell's "mystic book" — that is, the so-called book of nature. As the Reverend Magoon wrote in "Scenery and Mind," "The book of nature, which is the art of God, as Revelation is the word of his divinity, unfolds its innumerable leaves, all illuminated with glorious imagery, to the version of his creature, man." Since the source of this metaphor was the "book of life" mentioned in Ezekiel 2:9 and throughout Revelation, Magoon's frame of reference was both typical and appropriate. Proverbs 30:24–28 can also be seen as relevant, for that is where ants, locusts, spiders, and conies (a small mammal) are singled out as "four things which are little upon the earth," but also "exceedingly wise," proving that God's providential design held true at every scale. The character of this design would be debated for hundreds of years, but by the middle of the seventeenth century the book of life had essentially mutated into a separate and distinct book of nature. Physician Thomas Browne's *Religio medici* seems to be representative of the period: "Thus there are *two Books* from whence I collect my Divinity; besides that written one of God, another of His servant Nature, that universal and publick Manuscript, that lies expans'd unto the Eyes of all."[60]

Any suggestion that nature was "expans'd" enough to be read by "the Eyes of all" also implied that it was *orderly* enough to be read — hardly a controversial idea, since works such as Aristotle's *History of Animals* and Pliny the Elder's encyclopedic *Natural History* had long been taken as confirmation of God's design. In its purest form, this sense of order came to be known as "the great chain of being" — a notion also inherited from Aristotle, in which nature became an infinite yet contiguous series of divisions, a hierarchical scale of perfection, rising from plants to man. In his *Essay on Man*, Alexander Pope would summarize this *scala naturae* as "from Infinite to thee, / From thee to nothing." Locke would be a little more precise in his *Essay Concerning Human Understanding*: "In all the visible corporeal world, we see no chasms or gaps. All quite down from us the descent is by easy steps, and a continued series of things, that in each remove differs very little one from the other. . . . [T]he animal and vegetable kingdoms are so nearly joined, that, if you will take the lowest of one and the highest of the other, there will scarce be perceived any great difference between them."[61]

The point of Frémont's gesture was that both the book of nature and the great chain of being were among the most common metaphors of American political rhetoric during this period. In an editorial inaugurating the *United States Magazine and Democratic Review*, for instance, John O'Sullivan declared that "the eye of man looks naturally forward" and insisted that the "high and holy DEMOCRATIC PRINCIPLE which was designed to be the fundamental element of the new social and political system created by the 'American experiment'" was "borrowed from the example of the perfect self-government of the physical universe, being written in letters of light on every page of the great bible of Nature." At exactly the same point in time, early proponents of a transcontinental railroad claimed that it would represent a "great chain of communications," forming "a permanent and direct link in the great chain of Rail Roads destined to be speedily extended from the extreme eastern point of the Union, across the Mississippi, to the Missouri River; and thence at no very distant day to [the] head of steam boat navigation upon the Oregon." In a less technical but equally expansive vein, Sen. Benjamin Ruggles of Ohio referred to "the great chain of policy that is to elevate the power and wealth of this nation," and Daniel Webster called the Union "the great chain of being" because, in the words of Major Wilson, "it gave stable form to liberty" and "enabled each generation of freemen to relate itself meaningfully" to all other generations, both before and after. Though Webster was a tried-and-true Whig opposed to any expansion that would sunder the contiguity of generations, and congressmen such as Andrew Stevenson of Virginia warned that "the mighty chain of constructive power" was threatening to replace the simple government envisioned in the Constitution, the mere alignment of the United States with the great chain of being and the great bible of nature implied that even expansion would be legitimate if it also appeared to be organic.[62]

So it is that "carrying out the law of this country," seizing a bee, and pressing its carcass into "the leaves of a large book" deliberately evoked the universal and transcendent order of a nation juxtaposed and "nearly joined." To the degree that it did, this concise concatenation of symbols has to be seen as a rather clever reversal of Irving's parable — a negation of his negation. Suddenly, the mere presence of this "solitary pioneer" — "the first of his species to cross the mountain barrier" — encourages us to believe that expansion both fulfills the laws of nature and helps to reveal its providential design. Among other things, it adds to the impression that expansion itself is essentially an organic and orderly process of absolute boundaries morphing into relative ones — with the "highest peak of the Rocky mountains" representing the most elevated coordinate and South Pass the most mundane. The implication is that progress and expansion could never threaten the boundaries or principles of a republic because, in the end, the "laws of this country" are in accordance with "the Laws of Nature and of Nature's God."

What makes this especially striking is that even a war of all against all leaves Frémont himself looking eager and disinterested at the same time. Exploiting the obvious parallel between his own crossing of the mountain barrier and that of the solitary bee, Frémont begins to create a kind of metaphorical aloofness by literally pressing *bromus* into the service of science. The most notable aspect of this indifference is the way he turns a rapacious and impulsive gesture into the diligent and systematic pursuit of science itself. Not only does he reveal his actual measurement of the summit right after he seizes *bromus*, but that measurement is the only way to verify his claim that he has witnessed the "highest known flight of that insect." Both *bromus* and the barometric reading end up as records in a notebook — scientific records and world records of a sort — and there they lie "expans'd" and preserved "unto the Eyes of all." Strictly speaking, it doesn't really matter that Frémont later loses this notebook during the trip down the rapids; nor does it matter that the account may be partially, or completely, imaginary. The point is, *bromus* is a perfect rejoinder to the bee hunt in *Tour*. Whereas Irving's contact with the frontier leads to an outburst of greed, despoliation, and bestiality, Frémont's results in an act of selfless, transparent, and elevated knowledge. It is almost as if the frontier allows his baser nature to be his better nature — as if the bee's instinct to fly higher and farther is matched by Frémont's instinct to measure and record that flight. It is true that the death of *bromus* has been set in motion by Frémont's earlier decision to exceed the "strict order of our instructions." But if this is in some sense equivalent to exceeding the limits of the republic, then the intimation is that knowledge and the nation will converge, not disintegrate, at the frontier. Essentially, Frémont approaches the frontier as a site of impromptu and impartial perception, verified by the latest instruments, and officially documented for both houses of Congress. Nothing could be further from Irving's notion of a "lawless interval."[63]

{ THE FOUR CARDINAL RIVERS }

HENRY TUCKERMAN ONCE WROTE THAT "THE VERY IMMENsity of the prospect" to be seen from American mountains was so expansive and "vague" that "it inspires the imagination more frequently than it satisfies the eye." Doubtless Tuckerman's long stay in Italy had left him more attuned to the Apennines than to any American mountain range, but there was a certain truth in what he said. *Many* of the great vistas in American art and literature can be seen as more satisfying to the imagination than to the eye — a list that includes Jefferson's view from the Blue Ridge, Boone's view "from the top of an eminence," Judge Temple's view from Mount Vision, Leatherstocking's view of "all creation," and Captain Bonneville's view from a summit of the Wind River Range.[64]

The panorama Frémont describes from the loftiest peak of the Rocky Mountains is no exception. Despite the visual clarity he brings to this prospect, Frémont actually provides very few details for the eye itself to focus on. If he has routinely, to this point, either fractured or exaggerated the landscape to help us see it in our mind's eye, what he describes now is almost totally latent. We are effectively asked to visualize an area that exists *beyond the range of visibility*, except as a map or model. As Frémont himself admits: "The day was sunny and bright, but a slight shining mist hung over the lower plains, which interfered with our view of the surrounding country." This is a dazzling inducement to imagine the landscape rather than see it.

To apprehend exactly *what* Frémont is asking us to imagine, it helps to compare his own view from the Wind River Range to the nearly identical view in *Bonneville*—which, as usual, represents what he hopes to negate. Irving's description begins as a sublime reverie, with Bonneville "confounded by the vastness and variety of objects," his eye "lost in an almost immeasurable landscape," convinced that he has "attained that height from which the Blackfoot warrior, after death, first catches a view of the land of souls, and beholds the happy hunting ground spread out before him." Soon, however, this "enthrallment of the mind" gives way to a "long drawn inspiration," and he begins to "analyze the parts of this vast panorama." What follows is a "simple enumeration" of the features visible from the summit of what he calls "one immense mountain, broken into snowy peaks and lateral spurs"—most of it devoted to "the fountain heads, as it were, of the mighty tributaries to the Atlantic and Pacific Oceans." Indeed, Bonneville frames the panorama visible from the summit by literally turning his body in a counterclockwise direction, listing the rivers to be seen south, east, north, northwest, and west. Yet even this more factual view of the Continental Divide ends with an image of restricted space that is as imaginary and ideological as Irving's "lawless interval": "The day was calm and cloudless, and the atmosphere so pure that the objects were discernible at an astonishing distance. The whole of this immense area was enclosed by an outer range of shadowy peaks, some of them faintly marked on the horizon, which seemed to wall it in from the rest of the earth." Just as significantly, this is also where Irving says, "It is to be regretted that Captain Bonneville had no instruments with him with which to ascertain the altitude of this peak," insuring that this trip to the top of the Continental Divide became an utterly overwrought, "immeasurable," frustrating, and obstructive experience. For even if it wasn't "twenty-five thousand feet above the level of the sea," the Continental Divide was still, in Irving's view, a greater barrier than "what was formerly supposed."[65]

Frémont's accurate ascertainment of this altitude sets in motion a description that challenges Irving's ideological view with a perfect, if inchoate, figure of Manifest Destiny. Examining and measuring exactly the same panorama as Irving, Frémont reveals a nation neither limited nor divided by its geography. Not only does he associate the Wind River summit with the "stupendous results of modern science" and the nobility of the national flag, but his exultation at "standing where never human foot had stood before" and his pride in having "accomplished an object of laudable ambition" suggest that he wants to "impart a general impulse to the entire circle of humanity, to rise yet higher than the highest, and to move onward in the path of universal improvement." In short, Frémont chooses to frame the summit description as a *scientific, symbolic,* and *aesthetic* view of the nation that is as open-ended and liberating as Long's image of the Great Desert and Irving's image of the "lawless interval" was restrictive. This description is a consummate example of what Denis Cosgrove has called the "Apollonian gaze," meaning a "divine and mastering view from a single perspective" intended to create a "vision of unity" that is "synoptic," "omniscient," and "intellectually detached."[66]

. . .

BOTH IRVING AND FRÉMONT CAN BE SEEN AS ACCURATE as far as they go, but the summit description in *Bonneville* is far more indebted to the history of Rogers's and Carver's mythical "height of land." Calling the Wind River Range "one immense mountain" can be traced to this history; so can saying that the entire region is "enclosed by an outer range of shadowy peaks, some of them faintly marked on the horizon, which seemed to wall it in from the rest of the earth." Irving even identifies the Columbia River as "the Oregon," harking back to Bryant's "Thanatopsis." Almost none of this makes its way into the *Report*. Although Frémont pointedly reduces the prospect to four rivers instead of Irving's five, deliberately evoking Carver's "four most capital rivers on the Continent," his figurative prototype seems to be Jefferson's schematic image of the Alleghenies and the Blue Ridge. Jefferson's reference to the "great ridge" or great "spine of the country between the Atlantic on one side, and the Missisipi and St. Laurence on the other" is exactly what Frémont seems to mimic in the *Report*. Certainly, he verifies his claim of having reached the loftiest peak of the Rocky Mountains by combining "the description given by Mackenzie of the mountains where he crossed them," the description of "a French officer still farther to the north," and "Colonel Long's measurements to the south." By itself, this appears to locate the summit along a range or chain of summits, suggesting that it is not an "immense mountain" but part of a "great ridge" or cordillera. At the same time, however, he purposely divides our attention between the Colorado and the Yellowstone (one heading west, the other heading east) as well as the Columbia and the Platte (one to the north, the other to the south — but again, the first heading west, the second heading east). Indirectly, at least, this not only adds to the perception of a dividing ridge, a true "division of the waters," but actively undermines the notion of a single, compressed height of land, disgorging rivers in all directions. Reading Irving's description of the summit, it is almost as if we're standing in the midst of a huge reservoir; reading Frémont's, it is more as if we're straddling a "narrow crest." This is a crucial point, for the *Report* can be seen as the next-to-last step in a true account of the Continental Divide.

Notably, neither Irving nor Frémont mentions the headwaters of the Arkansas and the Rio Grande. This is more an accuracy of omission than precision, since neither is able to locate the headwaters. But at least Frémont's account implies that they lie somewhere along the "great ridge" — a notion that may have been suggested to him by Carson, who was familiar with the area, or may have suggested itself when he followed the South Platte to St. Vrain's Fort. Either way, his intuition about the Continental Divide was correct: it needed to be imagined as the lengthy, meandering "spine of the country," not a "common resource region." John L. Allen has shown that Frémont would need two more years to solve this geography but makes it clear that by the end of his second expedition he had "eliminated the mythical Buenaventura [River] from the maps and minds of Americans," determined "scientifically the fact of the Great Basin," and "cleared up the problem of the division of waters by proving that the northern source region" of the Missouri, the Columbia, and the Colorado (Green) "was a completely different area than that region of the Colorado Rockies, some 350 miles to the south, which gave rise to the waters of the South Platte, the Colorado (Grand), the Rio Grande, and the Arkansas." It was a brilliant combination of what Daniel Boorstin has called "affirmative" and "negative" discovery.[67]

. . .

OF COURSE, FRÉMONT NEVER STOPS AT ONE IMPRESSION when he can provoke another, and his decision to limit the hydrology of the summit to the four cardinal rivers is no exception. Almost inevitably, we are reminded of the well-known description in Genesis: "And a river went out of Eden to water the garden; and from thence it was parted, and became into four heads." Like all his other references to the Bible, this association appears to be extremely tangential or offhand, yet it continues to align the continent with "a more goodly country." Just as intentionally, it reminds us that Americans had a fondness for such providential geography and maps. In an editorial written for the *Saint Louis Enquirer* around 1820, Thomas Hart Benton had predicted that the Arkansas, the Platte, and the Yellowstone would be to Americans "what the Euphrates, the Oxus, the Phasis, and the Cyrus were to the ancient Romans, lines of communication with eastern Asia, and channels for that rich commerce which, for forty centuries, has created so much wealth and power wherever it has flowed." An identical, though far more indirect, version of this geography would shape the Reverend Horace Bushnell's sermon, "The Day of Roads," where he speaks of

Switzerland, that "little nation of republicans," as a veritable crossroads of liberty and progress. "Climbing over" its mountain passes, he says at one point: "The traveler is made to feel possibly for the first time in his life what is in a road, how much it means, what victories it signifies; what myrmidons of thought more powerful than armies are pouring over it daily and nightly from nation to nation." Reverend Bushnell is moved to compare the "little nation" to the Forum "in the age of Antonines": "Here again we find four stupendous roads, all virtually new," and "passing at the summit between peaks of eternal ice; smooth, wide, easy of ascent and descent; northern Europe pouring over into southern, Protestantism into Popery, and Popery back in Protestantism; new ideas and old traveling back and forth and passing on their way." Expanding outward, then, from the headwaters of the four cardinal rivers, Frémont is able to suggest a crossroads, a grid, the coordinates of latitude and longitude, the last remaining quadrant of earth, and all four corners of the globe.[68]

Associations of this sort are significant because each helps to reveal or exaggerate the peculiar nature of the summit description itself. If we juxtapose these various associations with the barometric reading, the incident with *bromus*, and the challenge to Rogers's and Carver's height of land, it becomes apparent just how much the summit description disregards the scenic aspects of topographic geology in favor of maps and a geographic point of view. It was not a simple matter to align the axis of the nation with the axis of things — not least of all because at the time he wrote the *Report*, the prevailing image of the Rocky Mountains still corresponded to the "convenient, natural, and everlasting boundary" described in Benton's speech of 1825 and reiterated in Irving's *Bonneville*. But if Frémont could reach past this boundary to equate the Rocky Mountains with the Continental Divide, and the Continental Divide itself with the spine of the country, Americans would have to interpret the natural order of the country quite differently. As Cosgrove has written, the cardinal directions represent a "powerful teleological and anthropological resonance. Constructed in large measure by these conceptual points and lines on the globe, the geographical imagination in the West has expended untold physical energy and passion in rendering them actual across terrestrial space."[69]

Even before he reaches the summit, therefore, Frémont begins to reduce it to a map. In a typical juxtaposition of images and ideas, the paragraph that comes immediately after his description of the barometer repair reads as follows:

> As will be seen on reference to a map, on this short mountain-chain are the head-waters of four great rivers of the continent; namely, the Colorado, Columbia, Missouri, and Platte rivers. It had been my design, after having ascended the mountains, to continue our route on the western side of the range, and, crossing through a pass at the northwestern end of the chain, about thirty miles from our present camp, return along the eastern slope, across the heads of the Yellowstone river, and join on the line to our station of August 7, immediately at the foot of the ridge. In this way, I should be enabled to include the whole chain, and its numerous waters, in my survey; but various considerations induced me, very reluctantly, to abandon this plan.

Despite his obvious disappointment, Frémont does not abandon the cartographic design of this thwarted scheme once he reaches the summit. Rarely has a mountain view been more visibly reduced to elevation, location, and direction. Indeed, one of the most remarkable aspects of the summit description is how little it appeals to the eye. Strictly as a matter of scenery, it must be one of the most meager or perfunctory descriptions ever to have had such a profound effect on the American landscape. Though Jefferson and Irving also examine such things as geography and earth science, the vistas in the *Notes* and *Bonneville* seem ecstatically romantic by comparison — and purposely designed to mimic a sublime painting or panorama. Obviously there are glimmers of this in Frémont's account — the "unstable and precarious slab," the "abyss below," the "terrible convulsion" — as well as the idea that he has reached the loftiest peak of the Rocky Mountains in the first place. By piecing together the entire description, we can even begin to construct a foreground of the unstable crest and the crevice where he mounts the flag; a middle ground that includes the "immense snow-field," which begins at the bottom of the five-hundred-foot precipice; and a background that includes the camp at Island Lake, the camp at Two Hills, and the series of peaks and rivers which quickly exceed the limits of human vision.[70]

But contrary to Jefferson (who points out that "the distant finishing which nature has given to the picture is of a very different character" — "a true contrast" "to the fore-ground") or Irving (who creates a kind of natural cyclorama by enclosing his "immense" view within an "outer range of shadowy peaks"), Frémont seems to resist the idea of a conventional summit view. Instead, he emphasizes the width and "inclination" of the narrow crest; the barometer and thermometer readings that give him the difference in elevation between the summit and the camp at Island Lake; the "bearing" of the camp at Two Hills, "an astronomical station" that, "with a bearing afterward obtained from a fixed position, enabled us to locate the peak"; the bearing of the "*Trois Tetons*"; and the bearing of the Continental Divide itself. The only thing unifying this largely statistical description is the "informative viewability" of a map. It is all about location — fixing the position of the "little crest of the wall on which we stood" within a grid of map coordinates that jumps back and forth in scale from the narrow crest, to the summit peak, to the Wind River Range, to the Continental Divide, to the entire continent, and, by extension, to the world. To quote Cosgrove again, "the Apollonian link between global vision, graphic representation, and the abstract intellectualism that characterizes humanity is forged through geometry."[71]

. . .

THERE ARE SEVERAL REASONS WHY FRÉMONT MIGHT RESORT to such an abstract approach in the *Report*. To begin with, he was still a year away from exploring anything west of the Wind River Range — and for someone who placed such an emphasis on firsthand knowledge and who treated so many of his personal observations and measurements as a revision or refutation of earlier accounts, this would have been a compelling constraint. In his own eyes, anyway, his perfected knowledge of the land to the east and south was more than offset by his ignorance of the land to the north and west. On top of this, he could not be sure that the observations and measurements he *knew* to be right would inspire his readers with the same sense of awe and national purpose that could be expected from any reference to Mount Washington or Niagara Falls. The *Report* as a whole was such a novel version of the Great Desert, and the summit description in particular such a seismic displacement of Rogers's and Carver's height of land, that it was reasonable to conclude Americans might find it hard to imagine a nation symbolized by such alien or refigured terrain alone. Even the laws of nature were bound to seem alien when they differed so much from what the Reverend Magoon would call the "ineffaceable" influences of the East.[72]

A map, on the other hand, was different. As one early twentieth-century historian astutely noted, "Every forward step in American expansion meant a more scientific boundary. Behind every process of rounding out the contours of our political territory lay the geographical motive." More recently, Bruce Harvey has shown that atlases and geographical primers, which began to be popular after the Revolutionary War, had become a staple of American culture by the 1830s and 1840s. "The geographical gaze," Harvey writes, "produced the body of the nation itself, which otherwise could not quite 'see' itself, or only rhetorically so in, for example, July 4th speeches and other self-laudatory occasions." Though this can be viewed as yet another of the textual traditions Edward Said made so much of, Martin Brückner has actually taken Harvey a step further, arguing that even American literacy emerged as a form of geographic literacy. His most compelling example is Noah Webster's *A Grammatical Institute of the English Language* (1783), which not only sought "a national 'standard of pronunciation'" but sought to "mediate among a regionally and socially differentiated people" by utilizing "the discourse of geography, in particular the spelling of place-names." Coincidentally, perhaps, Webster's speller included an exercise that anticipated the way the founders would sign the Constitution four years later—state by state, north to south.[73]

The textual tradition of this geographic gaze—often reflecting the tradition of overreach that began with John Smith's map of Virginia—was especially critical during the era of Manifest Destiny. As Harvey has also pointed out, "The republic lacked a shaping sense of a dense anterior history, and this formlessness was intensified by the belief in Manifest Destiny, which compelled citizens to see the nation in terms of futurity, and of the country's ever dissolving and reconstituting its borders as it advanced westwards." Maps themselves were assumed to be part of this futurity. In a preface to his *Geographical Reader: A System of Modern Geography* (1840), Augustus Mitchell acknowledged that he had revised a number of earlier maps but claimed that the revisions were "introduced as the progress of discovery and science demands"; in a preface to *The World: Geographical, Historical, and Statistical* (1854), Charles Savage declared, "There remains scarce a nook or corner on the entire globe which has not been penetrated, its history obtained, and its resources developed and appropriated to the service of mankind and the benefit of science." Given that Frémont had explicitly "appropriated" the summit of the Wind River Range for "the service of mankind and the benefit of science," it would have been bizarre if he had not also resorted to a geographical gaze to "round out the contours" of a nation he hoped to see stretching from sea to sea.[74]

Oddly enough, it hardly mattered that Frémont was as far away from mapping anything west of the Wind River Range as he was from observing it firsthand. Certainly it did not interfere with his effort to make Americans "see" a continent that was even more unseen and amorphous to them than to him. Among the many advantages of a map was an abstract conciseness that even the best prospect or panorama could never match. On a map of, say, thirty-five miles to the inch, the length of that step that nearly precipitated Frémont onto the immense snowfield would equal the distance from the summit of the Wind River Range to the Gulf of Mexico; on a map of one hundred miles to the inch, the width of the precarious slab would equal the width of the continent. At either scale, the amount of information he included would never come close to what he excluded—boosting by several orders of magnitude the kind of erasures and gaps that helped to make his view of the Great Desert so compelling and eliminating any immediate need for a survey west of the summit. Frémont possessed the kind of geometric imagination that allowed him to equate the inclination of the narrow crest with the gradual ascent of South Pass, the "increased elevation" of eastern Kansas, and the immense inclined plane formed by the trans-Mississippi valley. But once he reaches the summit, he essentially asks us to identify the nation with the all-encompassing design of the continent, not a list of singular or specific features. As Denis Wood and John Fels have pointed out, a map "is not a picture" but "an argument" — and as such, it fundamentally unites "an existence claim and a location." To insist that the nation was *there* on the summit of the Rocky Mountains was also to imply that the nation *was* the Rocky Mountains.[75]

Such a cartographic point of view seems especially significant if we see the summit episode as an implicit leveling of the Rocky Mountains. When Frémont speaks of having "accomplished an object of laudable ambition," he undoubtedly means that his various barometric and astronomical readings have effectively eliminated the loftiest peak of the Rocky Mountains as an impediment to knowledge and national ambition. In itself, this begins to topple that "statue of the fabled god Terminus," which Thomas Hart Benton had erected on the Continental Divide in 1825. But Frémont adds to this impression by locating the headwaters of an elaborate and encompassing system of rivers — rivers that convulsively stretch out in all directions, traversing hundreds, even thousands of miles before joining the waters of the Pacific, the Gulf of California, and the Gulf of Mexico. Not only is this an extensive and unifying map of the continent, but it is compiled from an ideal vantage point that happens to be the *source* of this elaborate system, not an obstacle to it. Meanwhile, the entire trip to the summit is bracketed by two descriptions of South Pass — the most visible "culminating point" of the Oregon Trail but so nondescript that it can hardly be located either on the way to the Wind River summit or on the way back. Clearly, Frémont would like us to believe that no matter where we are on the Continental Divide, it is no longer an obstacle or divide at all — either to the nation or to the progress of the human mind. In fact, he finds so many ways of reaching past or leveling the Continental Divide that the

Report unwittingly reveals the extent of Benton's duplicity in 1825. For as Augustine had recounted in *The City of God* (and as Benton was undoubtedly aware), when Terminus, in the form of a boundary marker, refused to make room for the Temple of Jupiter in Rome, the builders just incorporated him into the temple itself.

The result was a new map of America, redrawn from the alien and distant perspective of the Rockies rather than the Alleghenies of Jefferson's precious maps or the Adirondacks of Cooper's Leatherstocking tales. It was a map that brilliantly transformed a culminating point into a dividing ridge — and the dividing ridge itself into a way to confederate, not limit, the nation. Implicitly, Frémont seemed to understand what Albert Weinberg called the "principle of territorial nexus" — a principle Weinberg defined as positing "the geographical unity of two adjacent regions on the ground of some common feature which appears as a nexus between them." If the Mississippi had not yet become a nexus for the nation, it was only because the Great Desert and the Rockies seemed to create an interval or gap between East and West. But by reaching past the Mississippi and the Great Desert to a map that rendered the troublesome Rockies a "common feature" because it was now "the spine of the country," the *Report* effectively erased this interval once and for all, creating a large-scale nexus, a continental propinquity, of East and West. Within the space of a few sentences, in fact, Frémont has given form to virtually the entire map of Manifest Destiny. Again, it is hard to imagine a more ideal example of the Apollonian or geographical gaze.[76]

· · ·

ALAS, THERE IS ANOTHER ELEMENT OF THE APOLLONIAN gaze that brings to mind George Kateb's theory of "aesthetic cravings." Kateb first proposed this theory in an essay entitled "Aestheticism and Morality: Their Cooperation and Hostility." Observing that people often found themselves caught up "in immorality in an apparently idealistic way," Kateb begins the essay with a list of examples that seem to fit this model. Included are Western religion, with its power to inspire countless believers "to perform acts of war, persecution, and sacrifice of all sorts";

"the readiness of people to preserve or advance a distinctive culture or way of life at any moral cost"; an ideal of masculinity that includes "a passion for adventure, risk, discharge of energy, the exploration of human possibility, or a will to transgress limits" that makes "criminality look like an integral part of it"; the senseless "provocation or inspiration for conflict" that results from politics being treated as an end in itself; and a radical environmentalism that puts "the cause of nature above human ends of any sort." Looking for a common denominator among this eclectic list, Kateb suggests that each of these ideals can be seen as *aesthetic* in one way or another. Where they are not completely aesthetic, they are still motivated to one degree or another by aesthetic cravings—and it is these cravings, "seeking satisfaction or gratification," that "help to swell the amount of unconscious or rationalized immorality in the world" by encouraging us to pursue ideals that are either "loved more than morality, or are so loved that the moral cost does not break into consciousness with any force." Walter Benjamin, for one, was so acutely aware of these cravings that he believed mankind could "experience its own destruction as an aesthetic pleasure of the first order."[77]

Benjamin felt that this pleasure implied a profound "self-alienation," but Kateb makes the far simpler assumption that we all look for beauty in our lives—as when the editor Rufus Wilmot Griswold, calling for a national literature in America, appealed to "the principle of beauty as a law of life." Kateb defines an aesthetic craving as a powerful yearning for such things as contrast, shapeliness, coherence, purity, and novelty, and this is a desire we can all identify with. According to Emma Rothschild, even something as indirect as Adam Smith's notion of the "invisible hand" essentially appealed to people's "love of beautiful and smoothly functioning political schemes," their "love of system." However, Kateb makes a fundamental distinction between aesthetic feelings or attitudes, which "tend to be conscious and associated with works of art," and aesthetic cravings, which seek from experience what we "ordinarily seek and often find in works of art." This is important because it is not just the urgency but the *immorality* of an aesthetic craving that derives from the largely unconscious need to order experience as if it were a work of art. "These are cravings that are satisfied only when we are convinced that the world is one way rather than any other, is beautiful rather than not. And if the world is not yet what it should be, then we insist that it must be made to conform to our determination of it." Both Smith and Condorcet, for instance, seem to trace the *idea* of morality to the craving for a *system* of morality, implying that a love of beauty and order outweighs a love of goodness per se and that a systematic immorality might be just as appealing.[78]

Kateb is quick to dismiss those who judge the quality of a society by the quality of its art, as well as those who "urge that much of social life be *made over* so that it deserves to elicit aesthetic attitudes and feelings" (a model of social purity that embraces Hitler's concentration camps as comfortably as Le Corbusier's "Radiant City"). But he also presents a more modest and emancipated version of beauty—something he calls "democratic aestheticism"—that deliberately evokes a kind of disorderly, hybrid, open-ended virtue that he associates with Emerson, Thoreau, and Whitman, among others. Citing the philosopher George Santayana, Kateb seems to see this aestheticism playing out as a heightened and modified *alertness* to social reality: "The mission is to make the unpromising world worthy of attention; to grant standing to what seems not to merit it; and to hear the often silent or distorted appeal of everyone and everything for perception, interpretation, and contemplation." Democratic aestheticism assumes that there is far more beauty in the world than conventional taste will allow and that even objects or conditions which seem to *lack* beauty are "worthy of the aesthetic feelings that may grow by means of attention." Whitman and Thoreau were particularly alert to "the ugly or what often passes as the ugly—the impure, the incomplete or inconclusive, the hybrid, the uncomposed composite, the definitively undefinable, the ill defined, the unstable, the heterogeneous, the random, the disorderly, the out of place." Certainly Whitman's *Leaves of Grass* is a messy anthem to the "divine average," and Thoreau's "Walking" reveals the "wildness" to be found in even the most pedestrian landscape. And because democratic aestheticism explicitly aligns itself with morality, hoping to enlarge the imagination of moral conduct as well as that of beauty, its eager and inclusive eye becomes a corollary of political and moral tolerance. Near the end of the article Kateb says: "Everyone and everything deserves patient attention, a look, a gaze, but not to be followed by an attempt to remedy or control or to make over." By making everyone and everything *worthy* of beauty, democratic aestheticism happily "checks the tendency to condemnation and punishment."

That the *Report* is also shaped by a dialectic of "democratic aestheticism" should be evident. Frémont completed the *Report* before most of the works Kateb identifies with democratic aestheticism were published, but as we have seen, nearly everything he describes on his way to the summit is governed by a desire to make an unpromising world worthy of attention. Where others looked at the great ocean of prairie and saw a menacing, measureless, infertile void, Frémont looked at the same landscape as if it merited aesthetic attitudes and feelings. Again, Preuss's journal entry comes to mind: "Eternal prairie and grass, with occasional groups of trees. Frémont prefers this to every other landscape." The double negative that emerges in the pages of the *Report* can be seen as one of the earliest and most radical versions of democratic aestheticism.

On the other hand, the aesthetic attitudes and feelings that helped to draw Americans west and encouraged them to emulate the descriptions in the *Report* coincided with a more abstract set of cravings that could not be satisfied by anything as disinterested or self-contained as a work of art, even as they upheld the "largely unacknowledged need to order experience *as if* it were a work of art." Since it is the very urgency of this unconscious need that often transforms the elevated and impulsive search for beauty into destructive or immoral behavior, the actual history of western expansion played out as the history of Indian removal, war with Mexico, California-or-bust gold fever, "hell-on-wheels" railroad towns, and every other febrile enterprise meant to explore, lay claim to, and settle the West under the aegis of Manifest Destiny. Whatever else the West stands for, it undoubtedly represents the most prolonged and tangible struggle between idealism and outright ruin in American history.

The *Report* is an important part of this history. With all its contributions to a democratic view of landscape, the *Report* is basically a republican blueprint for expansion at any cost. And nowhere is this clearer than on the summit of the loftiest peak of the Rocky Mountains. The summit represents the point at which Frémont's artful descriptions cease to satisfy our most passionate need for beauty — or the point at which his eagerness to *educate* our sense of beauty ceases to serve a purely moral and democratic end. It is as if Frémont has known all along that the American people might be hesitant to pursue his idealistic horizon without a more urgent and encompassing image of the nation — the kind of image that would insistently goad their readiness to "advance a distinctive culture or way of life at any moral cost." And thus his decision to substitute an imaginary and providential map for the kind of scenic description that would later become a staple of western art and literature.

Of course, Americans had often associated expansionism with the beauty of maps. In the *Geographical Description* (1816) that accompanied his still sketchy and uninformed map of the United States (see fig. 3), John Melish wrote that it "shows at a glance the whole extent of the United States territory from sea to sea; and, in tracing the probable expansion of the human race from east to west, the mind finds an agreeable resting place on its western limits. The view is complete, and leaves nothing to be wished for. It also adds to the beauty and symmetry of the map." Indeed, Melish specifically noted that to have a map of the United States "end with the Rocky Mountains" would violate the vaunted principles of beauty and symmetry; "adding the two western sheets, so as to carry it to the Pacific Ocean," was simply a matter of "propriety." Though sentiments of this sort would appear over and over again in the decades prior to the *Report*, nothing was blunter than an essay published in 1821 and later reprinted in such magazines as the *North American Review*. Responding to British critics who had cynically accused the United States of imperialism during the frontier wars against the Cherokee, Choctaw, and Chickasaw nations, the author of the essay declared that "Americans are far from being pleased with the irregular figure which the Republic exhibits upon the map. This and that corner of the continent must be *bought* (or conquered if it cannot be bought) in order to give a more handsome sweep to their periphery." It was precisely because cartography was such a "seductive article" — such a "mischievous *familiar* of ambition" — that Americans were so shocked when the Great Desert first appeared on a map two years later, sundering the figure of a republic stretching "from sea to sea." Thus one of Frémont's greatest tasks in the *Report* was to revive a providential aesthetic that encompassed "a more handsome sweep."[79]

On a more practical level, the *Report* also followed the tradition of treating maps as an a priori claim to territory that might otherwise be invisible or belong to others. The origin of this practice may have been the royal land charters of the early 1600s, which had commonly (if only out of ignorance) granted land from "sea to sea" and were therefore, as D. Graham Burnett has argued, less "a territorial claim" than "a cartographic statement of belief." But a more relevant example was the republican grid of the late 1700s, which had first staked a theoretical claim to everything west of the Ohio River valley and was steadily making good on that claim with each passing year. Over the course of two and a half centuries, Americans had repeatedly sought to define their nation by sending out long lines of latitude and longitude, assuming that even the sketchiest of maps represented something more than an empty promise. It didn't hurt that maps were so easy to make and market. In 1803 the New York State Senate passed a resolution calling on the governor "to furnish the executive of each State, for the use thereof, with a map of this State lately made by the Surveyor-General" — a practice that would become quite common in the nineteenth century, as even counties, cities, towns, and railroad companies began to promote themselves in this way. The writer Caroline Kirkland offers a fine example of this practice, noting that the name of the town she and her husband were about to found in Michigan had to "be decided at once. The village plot was to be drawn instanter — lithographed and circulated through the United States." Later, she would see such maps in a more ironic light, writing that when the lots of a nonexistent town named "Grand Junction" were to be sold, "the whole fair dream was splendidly emblazoned on a sheet of super-royal size; things which only floated before the mind's eye of the most sanguine, were portrayed with bewitching minuteness for the delectation of the ordinary observer." It would be many years before the majority of the property lines shown in these maps existed anywhere but on paper. But almost as a matter of course they became a self-fulfilling prophecy.[80]

By turning the summit description into a composite of the providential and practical map, Frémont offers not only an image of the nation that spans the entire continent but an image that, to be realized in all its glory, would require Americans to advance their way of life no matter who or what they had to eclipse. In Kateb's words again: "If the world is not yet what it should be, then we insist that it must be made to conform to our determination of it." Both as a means and an end, this sketchy map of the western drainage system is a thoroughly idealistic entreaty to immorality—an immensely expedited land grab presented as the consummation of a long-delayed destiny. Along with every other element of the summit description, it adds to an image of nationhood that is comprehensive, elevated, shapely, abstract, progressive, and profoundly indifferent to any moral complications. Frémont's dazzling eye for detail has always implied a way of life as well as a work of art, and the summit description proves Kateb's point that the "greater aesthetic urgency" is always directed to life, not art. No work of art could compete with the beauty of a continent measured and mapped—a truth Thoreau would discover after mapping Walden Pond, as he found that "the line of greatest length intersected the line of greatest breadth *exactly* at the point of greatest depth." Frémont would agree with Thoreau that "the rule of the two diameters" always "guides us toward the sun in the system and the heart in man," but he also makes it clear that the length and breadth of the nation intersected a receding horizon. Once Frémont finds himself on the loftiest peak of the Rocky Mountains, all that has come before in the *Report* suddenly becomes a *longing* for beauty rather than beauty itself. Much of this is because the summit description equates the nation with a more distant geographic area than before, postponing the fulfillment of a republic still in search of its natural limits.[81]

. . .

HAVING POINTED TO WHAT ONE WESTERN PROMOTER WOULD call "the *untransacted* destiny of the American people," the remaining pages of the *Report* leave us dangling, more or less, in a state of suspended animation. Despite the formal elegance of a narrative that reaches its peak on the summit of the Wind River Range and then ends exactly where it began at the mouth of the Kansas, Frémont clearly intended the *Report* to be read asymmetrically — inciting a fear of falling short rather than fulfillment. Evidently he felt that a nation still huddled east of the Mississippi would be reluctant to pursue the destiny he maps out on the summit unless the *Report* also exaggerated its lack of completion. As with any aesthetic craving, beauty delayed is beauty denied — and Frémont wanted the craving for expansion and progress to be experienced as a kind of anguish as well as anticipation.[82]

So after feeling "the exultation of the first explorers" and "standing where never human foot had stood before," Frémont brings the narrative to a close with (1) an oddly mournful visit to Independence Rock, where he adds "the impression of a large cross" to "the names of many who have long since found their way to the grave, and for whom the huge rock is a gravestone"; (2) a nearly fatal attempt to shoot the rapids of the upper Platte, during which he destroys his India-rubber boat, manages to save the men, but loses everything else except a single notebook, a single instrument, a few scattered notes, and a few blankets; and (3) an utterly exasperating effort to navigate the shallows of the lower Platte in a bull-boat. His description of this final incident — a last attempt "to descend the Platte by water" — is especially tight-lipped:

> Men were sent out on the evening of our arrival, the necessary num-
> ber of bulls killed, and their skins brought to the camp. Four of the
> best of them were strongly sewed together with buffalo sinew, and
> stretched over a basket frame of willow. The seams were then covered
> with ashes and tallow, and the boat left exposed to the sun for the
> greater part of one day, which was sufficient to dry and contract the

skin, and make the whole work solid and strong. It had a rounded bow, was eight feet long and five broad, and drew with four men about four inches of water. On the morning of the 15th we embarked in our hide-boat, Mr. Preuss and myself, with two men. We dragged her over the sands for three or four miles, and then left her on a bar, and abandoned entirely all further attempts to navigate this river.

Considering everything that happens after the summit description, it is hard to avoid the thought that Frémont at least instinctively hoped the *Report* would evoke the tradition of the jeremiad. Sermons such as Reverend Cotton's "Gods Promise to His Plantations" were among the earliest and most perfect examples of an aesthetic craving for expansion, and they would be cited and modified many times over the centuries as the nation delved ever deeper into the wilderness. Bercovitch has called America's version of the jeremiad "the ritual of a culture on an errand—which is to say, a culture based on a faith in progress." But as he goes on to argue, if the function of the European jeremiad was "to make social practice conform to a completed and perfected social ideal," the function of its American counterpart was "to create a climate of anxiety that helped release the restless 'progressivist' energies required for the success of the venture." In fact, "it made anxiety its end as well as its means. Crisis was the social norm it sought to inculcate. The very concept of errand, after all, implied a state of *un*fulfillment."[83]

The summit description materially reconfigures this state of unfulfillment by translating the Puritan search for salvation into the geography of Manifest Destiny. Soon the entire nation would yield to the "subtle magnetism in Nature" that led Thoreau to declare: "Eastward I go only by force; but westward I go free." Yet as Frémont rapidly ends the expedition with a melancholy trip to Independence Rock and two disheartening trips down the Platte, the final pages of the *Report* effectively push that horizon of freedom further and further into the future. The barometric reading and the India-rubber boat may represent the latest in scientific exploration, but the disparity in their results seems to represent a step backward. Moreover, as Frémont gradually follows the Platte downriver he regresses to a method of boat building that had been around since the ancient Assyrians. By the time he wakes up to the "tinkling of cow-bells at the settlements on the opposite side of the Missouri" — an image of pastoralism as old as Hesiod and Virgil — the summit description seems little more than a disturbing and insistent dream. Frémont appears to want the longing he has unleashed on the summit to seem so "untransacted" as to be almost unbearable.[84]

Thus we find that the *Report* deliberately arouses both the aesthetic enterprise of Manifest Destiny and the anxiety that "helped to release the restless 'progressivist' energies required for the success of the venture." Essentially, it is an instrument of unfulfillment — the first of many to emerge in the era of Manifest Destiny. When Senator Linn stood before his still dubious colleagues, calling for a thousand extra copies of the *Report* to be printed, he brandished an elliptical and juxtaposed logic that would be emblematic of Manifest Destiny: "This report proves conclusively that the country for several hundred miles from the frontier of Missouri is exceedingly beautiful and fertile; alternate woodland and prairie, and certain portions well supplied with water. It also proves that the valley of the River Platte has a very rich soil, affording great facilities for emigrants to the west of the Rocky Mountains." Only someone driven to satisfy some larger and still frustrated sense of beauty would see the exceedingly fertile country of the Platte as the means of leaving it behind. Doubtless it was this, as much as the need for beauty itself, which led to a sudden spike in emigration less than two months after the *Report* was published — prompting the *Niles National Register* to report that "Oregon fever is raging in almost every part of the union." It was also this which helped to push the Oregon and California fever ever higher, unabated, as the nation continued to pursue its democratic and progressive way of life using an ever-expanding immorality of means. Unfulfilled beauty always implied a state of agony, and anything that added to it created a kind of frenzy for gratification.[85]

To the Pacific and Beyond

THE DECADE FOLLOWING THE *REPORT* WOULD EMERGE AS
one of the most frenzied and expansive in the nation's history. Between
1843 and 1853, when the Gadsden Purchase was completed, the United
States government surveyed and mapped a number of overland trails
to the Pacific coast, aggressively waged and won the Mexican War, took
possession of all Mexican claims to Wyoming, Colorado, New Mexico,
Nevada, Utah, Arizona, and California, negotiated a treaty with Britain
that ended joint occupation of Oregon Territory, secured the northern and
southern boundaries of what would become the forty-eight coterminus
states, admitted the states of Texas and California, and guaranteed that
a railroad to the Pacific could be built anywhere from the forty-ninth to
the thirty-second parallel. Thomas Hart Benton was so elated by these
events that he stood before his colleagues in the Senate and announced:
"We now own the country from sea to sea—from the Atlantic to the
Pacific—and upon a breadth equal to the length of the Mississippi and
embracing the whole temperate zone."[86]

Frémont's contribution to the landscape of Manifest Destiny was
both singular and far-flung. He was directly involved in every aspect of
Manifest Destiny except the annexation of Texas. On his first expedition he shattered the monolithic image of the Great Desert, mapped
the first half of the Oregon Trail, leveled the Rockies, and proved the
navigability of western rivers to be, in Edwin Bryant's words, a "nullity."
On his second expedition he completed his map of the Oregon Trail,
headed south before crossing the Sierra Nevada into California, introduced the nation to the "frank and cordial" Captain Sutter, described
the fertility of California's Central Valley, made it clear that the Rockies
were a continental divide rather than a "height of land," and identified

FIG. 20. *Planting the American Flag upon the Summit of the Rocky Mountains*, 1856. Woodcut from Samuel M. Smucker, *The Life of Col. John Charles Fremont*. Image courtesy of Bob Graham.

the area lying between the Rockies and the Sierra Nevada as an isolated basin with no river outlets to the Pacific or the Gulf of California. On his third expedition he supported the Bear Flag uprising in northern California, massacred a Klamath Indian village in southern Oregon, named the entrance to San Francisco Bay the "*Chrysopylae*, or GOLDEN GATE," led the so-called California Battalion in various battles against the Mexican army, and eventually negotiated the Treaty of Cahuenga with Gen. Andrés Pico, ending the Mexican War in California. Later, on his fourth and fifth expeditions, he tried to find a route through the Rockies that would allow the Pacific railroad to follow a line of latitude that bisected Benton's home state of Missouri.

Virtually the entire enterprise of Manifest Destiny can be perceived in the arc of Frémont's expeditions to the Far West — everything from its idealistic image of science and republican progress to the often horrifying, rapacious, expedient, immoral, and technical pursuit of that end.

FIG. 21. *Fremont Plants the American Flag on the Highest Peak of the Rocky Mountains*, 1856. Etching from John Bigelow, *Memoir of the Life and Public Services of John Charles Frémont*. Image courtesy of Bob Graham.

But easily the most emblematic image of this enterprise was Frémont's trip to the summit. When three separate campaign biographies appeared during his run for the presidency in 1856, each included an illustration showing Frémont planting the American flag on the highest peak of the Rocky Mountains (figs. 20, 21, 22). It was the only illustration common to the three works (indeed, the only illustration at all in one of them),

FIG. 22. *Hoisting the American Flag on the Highest Peak of the Rocky Mountains,*
1856. Etching from Charles Wentworth Upham, *Life, Explorations and Public
Services of John Charles Fremont*. Image courtesy of Bob Graham.

COL. FREMONT
PLANTING THE AMERICAN STANDARD ON THE ROCKY MOUNTAINS.

FIG. 23. *Col. Fremont Planting the American Standard on the Rocky Mountains*, 1856. Woodcut engraving with letterpress, Baker & Godwin. Library of Congress Prints and Photographs Division, Washington DC.

and though the renderings of the famous scene ranged from low-key to jingoistic, each chose to commemorate that iconic moment when nationhood and progress converged on the Continental Divide, symbolically incorporating the entire "nervous, rocky West." Yet another version of the moment was used as a poster for the campaign (fig. 23).

So compelling was the yearning for beauty Frémont had unleashed that thousands of Americans began to make their way to Oregon and California—and the trip itself was generally written into their diaries and letters as a testament to a new landscape and a new way of life. Among these was Brigham Young, who was so struck by the incongruous image of "a large salt lake in the interior of our continent, in the middle of a great fertile plain" that he decided to move the entire Mormon community to Utah. That he and so many other Americans chose to embrace the

West sight unseen — often risking their lives on the strength of Frémont's maps and descriptions alone — suggests that the *Report* was one of the most impressive and influential documents in American history. Jessie Benton Frémont was neither exaggerating nor indulging in hagiography when she later wrote of her husband: "Railroads followed the lines of his journeyings — a nation followed his maps to their resting place — and cities have risen on the ashes of his lonely campfires."[87]

. . .

ALL OF THIS OUGHT TO MAKE US WONDER WHY FRÉMONT'S reputation has become so stunted over the past century or so — or why his influence has been so freely and widely acknowledged but so slightly or narrowly understood. It would appear that Allan Nevins, the first of several twentieth-century biographers, charted the essential boundaries of this influence when he wrote that Frémont's "careful mapping of old paths" had done little more than dispel "the myth of a wide desert in the Platte country" and provide "encouragement to well-planned emigration" — a judgment that took into account Frémont's practical contributions to expansion and Manifest Destiny while ignoring his contributions to its ideology. Nevins's account of Frémont's actions during the Bear Flag uprising and the course of the Mexican War was no less event-driven or limited to practical concerns, nor was his account of the various railroad surveys Frémont carried out. More recent biographies may include more detail and speculation about these actions and events, but they similarly underestimate Frémont's effect on the nation's basic understanding of itself as an historical entity. The surest sign of this is that studies strictly confined to Manifest Destiny — studies that have become more sensitive to gender, race, ethnicity, and class while retaining a focus on the disputes of the 1840s and early 1850s, which usually bracket Manifest Destiny as an historical phenomenon — barely mention Frémont or ignore him completely. Yet there is reason to believe Frémont had more than a passing influence on John O'Sullivan's famous declaration that America's claim to Oregon and Texas was "by the right of our manifest destiny to overspread and to possess the whole of the continent." And by helping to shape the debate over a transcontinental railroad, he undoubtedly affected the way Americans began to rationalize their right to "overspread and possess" the entire world. Significantly, it was a right that radiated out from the center of the continent; and instead of representing the culmination or end of history, it signaled the dawn of a new and boundless age.[88]

. . .

EDWARD WIDMER HAS SHOWN THAT O'SULLIVAN WAS ONE of a coterie of New York Democrats who shared an ideology most concisely elaborated by Emerson's "The Young American" (1844), a lecture in which the famous transcendentalist had declared that "this land too is as old as the Flood, and wants no ornament or privilege which nature could bestow. Here stars, here woods, here hills, here animals, here men abound, and the vast tendencies concur of a new order." "Looking backward and forward at the same time," Widmer argues, "young Democrats peered through history to Jefferson and Paine, and also projected themselves into the future as role models for the rest of humanity. Many admired the French Revolution (hardly a popular sentiment in Whig circles), and distrusted England as the aristocratic enemy. All expressed Talmudic reverence for the Declaration of Independence, the living document that marked 'the new order of things.'" As O'Sullivan would say in the inaugural issue of the *Democratic Review*, "All old subjects of thought and all new questions arising, connected more or less directly with human existence, have to be taken up again and re-examined" in light of "the democratic principle." Paralleling this, however, was an almost Whiggish effort to combat the growing polarization and fragmentation of the country by emphasizing the need for a national literature and politics. Fearing the centrifugal forces of society, the young Democrats looked to the centripetal influences of a distinctly "American" culture able to transcend sectionalism, often finding confirmation for their ideas in the topographic geology of the nation. Implicitly recalling Jefferson's description of the Blue Ridge as "the spine of the country," the lawyer David Dudley Field went before the New-York Historical Society in

1845 and announced that the Allegheny Mountains, ranging both north and south of the Blue Ridge, bound "the country together, as with a band of iron."[89]

This dialectic between unity and progress would fundamentally shape the trajectory and ideology of Manifest Destiny. Widmer notes that O'Sullivan and his circle were so "sensitive to the fragility of the national coalition and the need to accommodate the South and West" that their effort to reach forward in time inevitably forced them to reach forward in space as well — suggesting that "the national culture they sought to promote" was essentially "panoramic." Again, "The Young American" was a precedent, since the essay joyously declared "the nervous, rocky West" to be "intruding a new and continental element into the national mind" while linking this "continental element" to the appearance of "an American genius" yet to come. Throughout the essay, in fact, Emerson speaks of time "given a new celerity" and "distance annihilated," and his perspective is inherently of a scale proportionate "to the majesty of nature." Thus the new order he envisions is that of "a heterogeneous population crowding on all ships from all corners of the world to the great gates of North America, namely Boston, New York, and New Orleans, and thence proceeding inward to the prairie and the mountains, and quickly contributing their private thought to the public opinion." These sentiments would find a more practical outlet in the *Young American*, a newspaper founded later that year by the Democrat George Henry Evans, who called on the federal government to distribute western lands to settlers.[90]

Emerson delivered "The Young American" less than a year after the *Report* was published. It isn't clear that Frémont influenced the lecture, but 1844 seems to be the moment the nervous, rocky West first intruded a "new and continental element" into Emerson's own mind, and the arc of emigration he describes — "inward to the prairie and the mountains" — mimics the trajectory of the *Report* by stopping at the Rockies and leaving the rest of the continent implied. Certainly Emerson read and admired Frémont, for whenever a friend or colleague wanted to know about the West, he told them to begin with Frémont's reports. Thoreau may have been one of those to take Emerson's advice, since he was reading some version of the reports just before his first trip to Maine, and it could be argued that the essay he wrote afterward, "Ktaadn," also mimics the trajectory of an expedition that journeyed to the top of a mountain and back. But such admiration was generally true of the nation—with the *Democratic Review*, we might recall, publishing an article on California in which it cited several passages from Captain Beechy, and several from Captain Wilkes, while neglecting to quote from Frémont's reports, "as it is probably in the hands of all who pursue this communication, and because it is very difficult to *select* from so large a mass of highly important and favorable testimony."[91]

A similar influence may be inferred, if not proved, by the disparity between O'Sullivan's two editorials "The Great Nation of Futurity" (where he argued that "the far-reaching, the boundless future will be the era of American greatness") and "Annexation" (where he argued that "Texas is now ours" and bemoaned the "spirit of hostile interference against us, for the avowed object of thwarting our policy and hampering our power, limiting our greatness and checking the fulfillment of our manifest destiny to overspread the continent allotted by Providence to the free development of our yearly multiplying millions"). Written midway between the two editorials, it is hard to imagine the *Report* did not have a significant effect on O'Sullivan's thinking—especially when it was augmented by his second report. Surely it is not just coincidence that the issue of the *Democratic Review* which included "Annexation" also included the long and admiring review entitled "Frémont's Expeditions."

In the earlier essay, O'Sullivan had openly argued that because the Declaration of Independence was "entirely based on the great principle of human equality, these facts demonstrate at once our disconnected position as regards any other nation." He had also argued that America was "destined to be *the great nation of futurity*" because (as Montesquieu might have said) "the principle upon which a nation is organized fixes its destiny, and that of equality is perfect, is universal." Although he claimed that "our national birth was the beginning of a new history, the formation and progress of an untried political system," his typology of equality made it clear that the nation had no need to progress as such, because it was already perfect and had already brought forth the "personal enfranchisement" that embodied "freedom of conscience, freedom of person, freedom of trade and business pursuits, universality of freedom and equality." At that point (and for several years afterward, since he initially opposed the annexation of both Texas and Oregon), O'Sullivan did not even equate the "untrodden space" of the future with the untrodden space of the continent. He simply believed that America was "destined to manifest to mankind the excellence of divine principles" — a notion that had nothing to do with the continent as such. Indeed, he stipulates that "American patriotism is not of soil, we are not aborigines, nor of ancestry, for we are of all nations; but it is essentially personal enfranchisement, for 'where liberty dwells,' said Franklin, the sage of the Revolution, 'there is my country.'"[92]

Frémont's two reports, on the other hand, focused almost exclusively on the material space of the continent, transforming the abstract map of the summit view into the topographic geology of a continent seen and explored in full. As the review of "Frémont's Expeditions" put it, "The result of the combined objects is an immense collection of geographical, botanical, geological, and meteorological information, mixed up with the details which would enable a general to march an army, or an emigrant to move his family to Oregon; and from which a statesman might judge the value of the country, and a farmer choose a residence in it." It is in exactly the same spirit that O'Sullivan seems to approach the later editorial. Echoing the symbolism of Frémont's double-edged gesture on the summit — first measuring its elevation to authenticate its physical reality and then planting a custom-made flag to stake the nation's claim to this reality — O'Sullivan says of Texas: "Her star and her stripe may already be said to have taken their place in the glorious blazon of our common nationality; and the sweep of our eagle's wing already includes within its circuit the wide extent of her fair and fertile land. She is no longer to us a mere geographical space — a certain combination of coast, plain, mountain, valley, forest and stream. She is no longer to us a mere country on the map. She comes within the dear and sacred designation of Our Country."

To be sure, O'Sullivan's most immediate concerns at the time were an enduring fear of poverty and hunger and a more temporary fear of Mexican and British designs on the continent. But to justify a trajectory of annexation that had quickly surpassed Texas to include California, O'Sullivan also invokes a principle of propinquity or territorial nexus that was largely missing before the *Report*—both practically and as a matter of republican ideology (since even Jefferson's claim that "a government by representation is capable of extension over a greater surface of country than one of any other form" had run afoul of the Great Desert and the Rocky Mountains). Indeed, O'Sullivan begins by suggesting that a *lack* of propinquity, magnified by the wrong sort of government, is precisely what set California apart from Mexico. "California probably, will next fall away from the loose adhesion which, in such a country as Mexico, holds a remote province in a slight equivocal kind of dependence on the metropolis. Imbecile and distracted, Mexico never can exert any real governmental authority over such a country. The impotence of one and the distance of the other, must make the relation one of virtual independence." That California was actually *part* of Mexico and over fifteen hundred miles from the United States was not a problem because "the Anglo-Saxon foot" was "already on its borders" and a population would "soon be in actual occupation of California, over which it will be idle for Mexico to dream of domination." Not only that, but it would happen "without the agency of our government, without responsibility of our people—in the natural flow of events, the spontaneous working of principles."

Obviously, the most pressing of these principles was the need for a contiguity with the existing republic. O'Sullivan allows that the question of whether Californians "will then attach themselves to our Union or not, is not to be predicted with any certainty," but immediately sets his sights on a mechanism of contiguity that would guarantee it: Asa Whitney's "projected railroad across the continent to the Pacific." Although he argues that even if it weren't built, "the day is not distant when the Empires of the Atlantic and Pacific would again flow together into one, as soon as their inland border should approach each other," he feels that the railroad "cannot remain long unbuilt" because it would bind and hold "together in its iron clasp our fast-settling Pacific region with that of the Mississippi valley," insuring that "the conveyance" of "representatives from Oregon and California to Washington" would take "less time than a few years ago was devoted to a similar journey by those from Ohio."

This alone may be the clearest indication of Frémont's influence. O'Sullivan had a long-standing interest in Central and South America, and he once confessed to Martin Van Buren that his interest in building a canal across the isthmus of Panama bordered on "monomania." For him to conceive of Manifest Destiny within the context of Asa Whitney's plan for a railroad to the Pacific while ignoring those proposals that found the isthmus to be a more desirable route was a significant development. Yonatan Eyal, in his own study of O'Sullivan and the Young Americans, has shown that an overwhelming support for railroads not only ameliorated Democratic opposition to federal powers but emerged as an important aspect of their foreign policy. "Unlike projects such as the Cumberland Road or various river and harbor bills," Eyal writes, the railroad "usually involved the United States in foreign policy decisions that had not formed a major part of the Democratic platform until this time." More to the point, Eyal contends that "by granting the West access to established population centers," by spreading "democracy and the values of an ordered, settled society," and by being part of "one grand futuristic vision," "no agent of Manifest Destiny appeared as important" to O'Sullivan and the Young Americans "as the railroad." Since Whitney's plan for a railroad to the Pacific was basically a mechanized version of the *Report*, and the *Report* itself implicitly repositioned the center of the nation as the center of the world, Frémont's contribution to the ideology of Manifest Destiny seems undeniable.[93]

· · ·

WHITNEY WAS A MACHINIST, A MERCHANT, AND A FORMER superintendent of the Mohawk & Hudson Rail-Road Company. Such a background helps to verify the claim, made by Richard Francaviglia and Jimmy Bryan Jr., that his remarkable proposal had its roots in a discourse that began at least as early as 1820 with Robert Mills's plan for a system of canals and railroads intended to "connect the Schuylkill, Susquehanna, Allegheny, Ohio, Missouri, and Columbia rivers." Sadly, like every other proposal that had appeared before the *Report*, Mills's vast and visionary project had eventually foundered on a series of geographical calculations that proved to be either ignorant, partial, or faulty. Many of these proposals had also foundered on the issue of sovereignty, since they planned to run the railroad through territory still owned by Mexico. It was not until Whitney sat down to write a "memorial" asking Congress to grant him a strip of land sixty miles wide and over fifteen hundred miles long—a memorial introduced by Rep. Zadock Pratt of New York early in 1845—that this situation took a turn for the better.[94]

Note the cartography of Pratt's address "To the People of the United States": "Mr. Whitney proposes to start his road somewhere on Lake Michigan, where he can find the lands unoccupied, and thence across the Mississippi, near Prairie du Chien, in the parallel of about 43 deg.; and thence over to the Missouri, between Council Bluffs and the Big Sioux; thence to the Pass, on the parallel of about 42½ deg.; thence to the best point on the Pacific." Knowing that Mexico claimed everything south and west of what is now Cheyenne, Wyoming, Pratt was extremely careful to include the lines of latitude the route would follow, especially the latitude of South Pass, to assure everyone that it would cross the Continental Divide within American territory. Whitney himself would be even more specific, explaining that if the route of the railroad paralleled the Oregon Trail more or less, it would fall entirely within territory either owned by the United States or shared jointly with Britain. Of course, the only reason either man could be sure of such a route was that Frémont, who had completed his second expedition by this time, had already surveyed it from the Missouri to the mouth of the Columbia. In fact, it is hard to ignore the conclusion that Whitney's project became such a bellwether during the late 1840s—even after the nation won the Mexican War and took sole possession of Oregon—because it was the only proposal linked to a map *known* to be accurate and precise and *universally accepted* as accurate and precise. Why else would Congress later commission four additional surveys to settle the sectional differences that had arisen over the railroad?[95]

It was mostly because of Frémont that a *railroad* to the Pacific suddenly became the focus of attention. Until the *Report* appeared, one explorer after another had headed up the rivers of North America expecting to find Hakluyt's Northwest Passage. The Lewis and Clark expedition was specifically driven by Jefferson's orders "to explore the Missouri river, & such principal stream of it, as, by it's course & communication with the water of the Pacific Ocean may offer the most direct & practicable water communication across this continent" — and every subsequent expedition, including Frémont's, set out to survey and map the great east–west arteries. Steamboats were already operating on the Mississippi and Missouri Rivers, and it was assumed they would eventually link the Atlantic and Pacific coasts. As early as 1826 Timothy Flint had written that "the distant points of the Ohio and Mississippi used to be separated from New Orleans" by the "internal obstruction" of river navigation — only to be "brought into *juxtaposition*" by the "energy and power" of the steamboat. What Frémont's various experiments in navigation proved, however, was that the rivers west of the Mississippi and Missouri were either too fast (as in the case of the upper Platte, where his India-rubber boat is wrecked) or too slow (as in the case of the lower Platte, where his bull-boat founders) to act as inland waterways. Although it would take a few more years to prove that the rivers west of the Continental Divide were equally impractical, the implication was clear. If the continent were to be crossed quickly — in the time needed to transport goods and maintain a representative government — only a railroad would do.[96]

Frémont is repeatedly cited as an expert witness in *A Project for a Railroad to the Pacific*, Whitney's most detailed and comprehensive version of his plan, published in 1849. Whitney does include letters from Stephen Long and Pierre Chouteau Jr. to prove that the Missouri, in particular, is not a reliable means of transportation; he also mentions Thomas Fitzpatrick, the man who led the Oregon party three weeks ahead of Frémont on the trail, to prove that snow would not be an issue along the route; and he refers to surveys by Gen. Stephen Kearny and Lt. William Emory to prove that other routes were longer or less feasible. But his ultimate authority is always Frémont, whom he seems to have consulted personally. Very early in *A Project* he writes that "Col. Frémont in person, and accounts from others, had satisfied me of the feasibility of the whole route." Then, as he begins to discuss the route, Frémont's influence becomes more and more crucial, supplying distances, grades, elevations, the state of the country to be crossed, and practicality. Assessments such as the following are common: (1) "thence to 'the South Pass,' the grade would be very light—by Col. Frémont's elevations would not exceed 6 feet to the mile, and 'the inequalities now existing,' he says, 'may be much improved at small expense'"; and (2) "from 'the South Pass' the route is more difficult, though perfectly feasible, as may be seen by the report of Col. Frémont, who has taken the elevations from the Missouri River to the Pacific, at several different times" and "says that 'impracticability is not to be named with the subject.'" Frémont would be written so completely into the record that, at least until the end of the decade, virtually every Senate and House report on the transcontinental railroad, not to mention every article on the railroad in the *Democratic Review* and the *American Review*, would include language echoing that of Illinois senator Sidney Breese: "The committee rely with confidence upon the testimony of that scientific and high meritorious officer, Colonel Frémont, and submit his own words, bearing directly upon the point under consideration."[97]

. . .

THAT FRÉMONT'S INFLUENCE WAS SOMETHING MORE THAN factual is suggested by the rhetoric that began to envelop the railroad from the moment of Whitney's first memorial. Like many other moments when the country changed direction or priorities, there are glimpses of Columbus's Passage to India, Morton's "golden meane," the Puritans' errand into the wilderness, Berkeley's westward course of empire, Montesquieu's republic, Smith's wealth of nations, Malthus's principle of population, and Condorcet's indefinite progress. As Bruce Harvey has observed, to read the texts of such popular geographies as Samuel Goodrich's *Parley's Geography for Beginners* (1830) and Arnold Guyot's *The Earth and Man* (1849) was to encounter "the central role that the United States had in helping the world progress into futurity." Asa Whitney always included *two* maps of the world in his public lectures on the railroad, one with "Europe, Asia and Africa placed together, and our continent [to] one side of all, as if of no importance," the other with North America "in the center of all." Although earlier calls for a continental railroad had indulged in the wonder of it all—with Robert Mills exclaiming, "What a sublime field for contemplation opens to the mind on this view of the subject!"—the rhetoric associated with Whitney's proposal implied a far more advanced and specific geography.[98]

Frémont's contribution to this geographical gaze cannot be reduced to his "careful mapping of old paths." One of the more conventional distinctions between art and science is the notion that artists *invent* aesthetic forms that are subjective and uniquely their own (such that only Christopher Marlowe could have written *The Tragical History of Doctor Faustus* and only Johann Wolfgang von Goethe could have written *Faust*), while scientists *discover* physical or mathematical laws that exist outside themselves and are often predicted or perceived by more than one person at a time (a view that accounts for the long history of independent discovery in science). At first glance this might suggest that Frémont's influence was purely circumstantial. Since Nicollet also had the training to calculate the latitude and longitude of South Pass and compile a detailed map of the Oregon Trail, it could have been *his* report that Whitney and members of Congress repeatedly cited during the Pacific railroad debates. But the greater truth is that Frémont helped to influence history mostly by offering an artful and compelling view of data that others might have described (or, in the case of Pike and Long, had already described) without the benefit of his foresight, his symbolism, and his distinctly picturesque eye. Essentially, this was a matter of style as much as accuracy. And as Gunther Stent has pointed out, even science has to acknowledge the elements of style. Francis Crick and James Watson may have discovered the structure of DNA mere months before other scientists, but it was the remarkable completeness and elegance of their explanation, not to mention the now-classic illustration (drawn by Crick's wife, Odile) which accompanied their understated paper in *Nature*, that quickly convinced the world they were right.[99]

Similarly, one of the most important elements of the *Report* is that it culminates in a map that depicts the nation not only *from* the very heart of the continent but *as* the very heart of the continent. Standing on the "loftiest peak of the Rocky mountains," undeterred by the "slight shining mist" that hangs over the lower plains, Frémont offers a view of the "surrounding country" which stretches far beyond anything he can actually see. Essentially, it is a double view, shaped by the Continental Divide, in which the Colorado and the Columbia run west to the Gulf of California and the Pacific, and the Missouri and the Platte run east to the Mississippi and the Gulf of Mexico, such that the continent as a whole is "brought into juxtaposition." More than just a view of continental or national unity, it is an image of the nation reaching east and west at the same time, not simply advancing east to west. In the context of the entire *Report*, it leaves little doubt that the nation needed to develop from the inside out as well as the outside in. Certainly it implies that the great "inland border" of the continent is where "the Empires of the Atlantic and Pacific would again flow together into one." And by indicating a way across the continent — charting the providential divide that now united the continent — it also implies that the center of the United States would be crucial to a more central role in world history. Nothing to date had so closely aligned the geographical destination of the country with the lay of the land. Atlases produced before 1840 had never sought the nation's destiny in the center of the continent, and even the proposals for a continental railroad had sought to ignore the region, not elevate it to the pinnacle of their vision. Both empirically and stylistically, then, the *Report* was a turning point.

THE LECTURE THAT THE REVEREND CALVIN COLTON DELIV-
ered "at the Request of Numerous Members of Both Houses of Congress"
is typical of the way Frémont's influence took hold during the debate
over a railroad to the Pacific. Like many others at the time, Colton was
lobbying for Whitney's route as well as the sixty-mile corridor of land
that would be needed to build it. Although his argument is both literally and metaphorically all over the map and includes a laudable appeal
to "science, and art, and invention, allied to the provisions of nature,"
Colton essentially treats the route as both a Passage to India and a kind
of golden mean that is also a means to human progress. Beginning with
the continent of America, he announces: "It happens, fortunately, that
the only route where the lands lie that will build the road, is directly on
that line which is most fair for all parts of the Union in its broad extent."
Elaborating a bit, he goes on to say that "providence has placed and left
the lands, necessary as capital to build the road with, precisely where the
road should be, and the committees of Congress have undertaken to
show, that, if the opportunity is neglected, the road can never be made
for want of *means*." Then, stepping back to consider America's position in
the world, his point of view becomes even more explicitly cartographic:

> Take a terrestrial globe—for I do not know of any common map
> that will answer this purpose—take, then, the globe in your hands,
> and find thereon, our relative position to Europe and Asia, and to
> the great masses of mankind; see how near and how easy of access all
> the great industrial and producing nations will be to us, with a great
> highway across this continent, on the line proposed; and there you
> will find the *great future bond* of nations, commercial, social, politi-
> cal, and religious; there you will see that the intercourse of nations
> is inevitably destined to follow this route.[100]

Frémont's contribution to this trajectory seems especially significant
if we recall that the summit episode emerges as a figurative leveling of the
Rocky Mountains. By eliminating rivers as a way across the continent,

Frémont had actually cast the Continental Divide into even higher relief as a latent obstacle. Obviously, those who wished to build a railroad to the Pacific had to take this into account — which meant that the Rockies were almost as emblematic in the articles and orations promoting the railroad as they were in the pages of the *Report*. Time and again they rise up as a natural barrier or separation, only to be leveled by the mechanism of the railroad itself. An essay in the *Democratic Review* called the Rocky Mountains "a geographical and commercial division of the whole world" — and then instantly overruled this image by claiming that "the people of the whole country have decided that we shall undertake this great change in nature's arrangement, by opening a great highway up through the Rocky Mountains, by which the Atlantic slope, the depot for the commerce of the country with Europe, shall be united with the Pacific slope, the depot for that with Asia." The *American Review* was equally dualistic: "The great Rocky Mountains, and the deserts said to lie between the two sides of the nation, will form a barrier to prevent the sense of oneness, the preservation of national feeling, and of true social and political union. But let the stupendous results of modern science be applied, let the great projected lines of railroad communication connect the two sides of the continent; let the telegraphic wires electrically unite them; and how different the case": "The Rocky Mountains, as to all practical effect, will sink down"; "the barriers of time and space will be annihilated"; and "the tide of emigration, setting in from all parts of the country," will "roll through the mountain passes."[101]

So it is that Frémont's point of view began to level the hardened barriers of party affiliation along with the Continental Divide, as even those who remained fearful of large republics understood the implications of a graded globe. Almost as a matter of course, both Democrats and Whigs were reminded of the Roman Empire. An essay in the *Democratic Review* declared:

> Since the breaking up of the great Roman Empire, there has never been embraced under a single government so great an extent of continuous territory — peopled by an active, intelligent people — as is now

subject to the laws of the federal government. The immense territory, which, subjected by the Roman legions, gradually fell under the sway of the "eternal city," was cemented and held in subjection only by the prompt construction of those wonderful highways, whose firmness has withstood the efforts of fifteen centuries. . . . These roads were the arteries that gave vitality to the government; and if in those days, they were important to facilitate the movement of troops — which were the instruments of territorial aggrandizement — how much more so are they in our country in the 19th century, when industrial enterprise is the agent of annexation, and commercial intercourse the means of consolidation?

Surprisingly, the *American Review* was even more effusive, noting:

Representatives from Oregon and California can reach their seats in the Capitol more quickly and more easily than representatives came from New Hampshire once. Add to this the communication of thought, passing literally with the speed of lightning to and fro across the continent, and from the central seat of government to the remotest points in the circuit of the nation; and how different is the problem of binding together in a central union immense and remote states, from what it was in the time of the Roman Empire.

Apparently, the way to extend the reach of Montesquieu's republic was by exceeding his preindustrial grasp of history — an insight that gave new meaning to James Madison's claim that "the natural limit of a republic is that distance from the center which will barely allow the representatives of the people to meet as often as may be necessary for the administration of public affairs." Rather than advancing into space to delay the effects of time or holding on to space to accelerate the effects of time, the railroad promised to "annihilate" space and time, opening up more and more territory to settlers and local interests while building out the infrastructure of a consolidating and improved republic. What better way to fulfill Jefferson's notion of "an empire for liberty."[102]

Arising from all this was a nation far more devoted to longitude than latitude. Prior to 1840, latitude was generally the guiding principle of American history: Columbus sought the Passage to India by sailing due west; Hakluyt located the Northwest Passage along the fortieth parallel; Morton's "golden meane" lay "betwixt two extreames" of latitude; the royal charters stipulated latitude while leaving longitude open-ended; the nation generally divided itself by such geographical boundaries as the Mason-Dixon Line and the line of 36°30' North written into the Missouri Compromise; and the populace generally migrated due west, following the climate and attitudes of their birth. Indeed, latitude would remain a determining factor long after the Civil War ended. But it was during the 1840s that Americans also began to think of their nation as a "golden meane betwixt two extreames" of *longitude*, signified in the short term by the Atlantic and Pacific coasts and in the long term by the continents of Europe and Asia. Aside from its geographical realignment, this had a tremendous impact on American views of progress and Manifest Destiny.

Evidence of a realignment inward would emerge in various forms over the next several decades. A peripheral member of Frémont's second expedition, William Gilpin (no relation to the eighteenth-century aesthetician), wrote a work entitled *The Central Gold Region* (1859), which points to 1842, the year of Frémont's first expedition, as the moment when "the energetic geographical movement" began "to agitate itself throughout America" and "reorganize the column of central progress artificially stagnated in Missouri since 1820." Referring to the Great Desert as a "dogmatic *mirage*" and South Pass as "the gateway of the American people," Gilpin eventually turns his attention to the "Basin of the Mississippi," calling it "the most obviously remarkable physical feature of America and of the inhabited globe." Although it is "all within the *Temperate Zone*" and is "exactly *central* to the continent" and to the "centre of the American Union," what makes it so remarkable is its shape. Whereas Europe "culminates in its centre into the icy masses of the Alps" and Asia in "the stupendous central barrier of the Himalayas," the "interior of North America presents towards heaven an expanded, *concave* bowl, to receive and fuse into harmony whatsoever enters within its rim." In

FIG. 24. Emanuel Gottlieb Leutze, study for *Westward the Course of Empire Takes Its Way*, 1861. Mural study, U.S. Capitol. Oil on canvas, 33¼ x 43⅜ in. Smithsonian American Art Museum, Washington DC/Art Resource, New York.

effect, America emerges as "a sublime *amphitheatre*, of gorgeous fertility and transcendent proportions." And from this essentially paradoxical version of Montesquieu's geography—both expansive and centripetal at the same time—Gilpin reasons that "the American Republic is then *predestined* to expand and fit itself to the continent."[103]

An equally expansive view of the center can be found in one of the images most closely associated with Manifest Destiny: Emanuel Leutze's *Westward the Course of Empire Takes Its Way* (fig. 24). Prior to Frémont's first expedition (and even after it, since many Americans still had their eyes fixed on Europe and the Atlantic coast), images of progress usually emulated the trajectory described by Jefferson in a letter to William Ludlow. Proposing a kind of thought experiment, Jefferson asks Ludlow to imagine a "philosophic observer" journeying "eastwardly" from "the savages of the Rocky Mountains" to the "most improved state of our seaport towns"—a fanciful odyssey that could be seen as "equivalent to

FIG. 25. George Inness, *The Lackawanna Valley*, ca. 1856. Oil on canvas, 33⅞ x 50³⁄₁₆ in. National Gallery of Art, Washington DC. Gift of Mrs. Huttleston Rogers. Image courtesy of the Board of Trustees, National Gallery of Art, Washington DC.

a survey, in time, of the progress of man from the infancy of creation to the present day." Clearly, this convention accounts for some of the best-known paintings of the period — a list that includes Asher B. Durand's *Progress* (1853), George Inness's *The Lackawanna Valley* (ca. 1856), and Jasper F. Cropsey's *Starrucca Viaduct, Pennsylvania* (1865) — not to mention many of the panoramas popular during this period (figs. 25, 26). Each has a foreground of relatively primitive woods or wilderness (either littered with cut or blasted trees, or actually cleared of trees, except for the remaining stumps), while in the distance is a steadily improving landscape that culminates in a line of railroad cars and the rising smoke of an industrial or urban setting. In mimicking Jefferson's linear view of history, American artists also seemed to be duplicating the eastwardly direction of his gaze.[104]

Leutze does not follow this example. Instead, he chooses the perspective of a nation needing to unify and define itself from the inside out. Not

FIG. 26. Jasper F. Cropsey, *Starrucca Viaduct, Pennsylvania*, 1865. Oil on canvas, 22⅜ x 36⅜ in. Toledo Museum of Art, Toledo OH/Photo Incorporated, Toledo. Purchased with funds from the Florence Scott Libbey Bequest in Memory of her father, Maurice A. Scott (1947.58). Photo credit: Photography Incorporated, Toledo.

only does his historical panorama take place on the Continental Divide, but it features a vignette that appears to be lifted from an illustration of Frémont on the summit of the Wind River Range — maybe the one in John Bigelow's campaign biography or the one on a Baker & Godwin poster, both published during Frémont's historic run for the presidency four years earlier (see figs. 21, 23). In the Bigelow illustration, a flagrantly sublime conceit in which the summit appears as a sharp and precipitous pinnacle of rock and Frémont himself is silhouetted against a melodramatic gathering of clouds, the intrepid explorer is shown holding the sacred symbol of the nation in one hand, the perpendicular summit in the other, while roundly cheered by his jubilant, hat-waving men below. Although Leutze juggles and tones this imagery down a little in the vignette that includes the Frémont-like figure celebrating on a naked crest of rock and the figure struggling to join him, the effect is much the same. Certainly the mural emphasizes the Continental Divide as both a "culminating point" and a symbol of the nation's exuberant future. It is almost as if the nation exists nowhere else. True, the rather motley collection of trappers, adventurers, and emigrants is moving in a cluttered, ramshackle way from east to west. But what they leave behind is not the "improved state" of the Atlantic seaboard or even the "progress of man" that might be found in between; rather, it is a primitive, chaotic terrain that Leutze, evoking John Bunyan's *Pilgrim's Progress*, calls "the valley of darkness." Moreover, the region that lies ahead, though suffused with the enticing and glorious light of a "promised land" or "Eldorado," is just as rocky and rough. Thus everything signifying the agency of improvement is confined to the center of the continent — an impression reinforced by the composition itself, which forces our eye upward to the Frémont-like figure, standing midway between east and west. It could be said that Leutze creates a mobile axis of civilization, represented by the fixed point of the covered wagons, and then inflates it to a view of the nation.[105]

Of course, Leutze's unruly oxen-drawn train is ultimately just a proxy for the steam-powered train that would soon take its place. Both of the most popular images of Manifest Destiny after 1860 — Frances Palmer's *Across the Continent: Westward the Course of Empire Takes Its Way* (1868) and John Gast's *American Progress* (1872) — depict the nation as a continent united by the railroad (fig. 27). This historical vector ought to make it clear that the earliest verification of Frémont's inside-out perspective was actually Whitney's plan for a transcontinental railroad. For a variety of reasons, Whitney found Frémont's point of view as convenient as the route he had surveyed, and *A Project for a Railroad to the Pacific* is largely an argument about the center of the continent and the center of the globe. Whitney had reasoned all along that a railroad would "change the route for the commerce and intercourse of Europe with Asia," creating "a means of transit so convenient and cheap" that the Mississippi valley would reach a market that included "all the Atlantic coast and Europe" as well as "all Asia"; he had also reasoned that the railroad would establish a "direct and rapid communication with our possessions on the Pacific coast, and thereby bind them to us by interest and affection." Much of this recalled Jefferson's "direct & practicable

FIG. 27. Frances Palmer, *Across the Continent: Westward the Course of Empire Takes Its Way*, 1868. Currier & Ives color lithograph. Museum of the City of New York. Scala/Art Resource, New York.

water communication across this continent." But it was elaborated as a rhetoric of bifurcated, inside-out unity that more closely echoed Frémont's figure of the Continental Divide. And in acknowledging that it would have to follow a route "more than 2,000 miles of which is a howling, savage, waste wilderness," Whitney went a step further, making it clear that a "grand highway" through the center of the continent would also make America the center of the world. "This road," he wrote,

> would give to every man, woman, and child on the earth means to live and be comfortable, if they would but work. It would raise up a competition between all the Atlantic States and cities, and force the means for the completion of all the roads now commenced from New Orleans to Maine, because all could join it to equal advantage, near to where it would cross the Mississippi River. Then the grand centre of this continent and of all the world would be near the Missouri River; and at 30 miles per hour, it would require but 2½ days to any Atlantic city—but 2½ days to the Pacific; and at the present speed of steamers, but 25 days to any important city on the globe. Thus we

could be brought together as one family, at the grand centre, in 2½ days; and the whole world, as one nation, to the same centre, in 25 days.

Such numerical reasoning must have seemed as modern as the railroad itself—already on its way to being the "well conducted institution," able to "regulate a whole country," that so impressed Thoreau in *Walden*. But Whitney's tract also reinforced Americans' more ancient belief in latitude and longitude and the providence of design. *No* nation could resist seeing itself as the center of the world. *A Project for a Railroad to the Pacific* simply suggested that no *other* nation could claim this as the truth anymore. Like Frémont's restructuring of the picturesque, it was a new beginning, a new ground zero.[106]

. . .

IT IS WORTH REMEMBERING THAT BEFORE THE *REPORT* appeared the very idea of America's frontier was largely a residue of European exploration and colonialism. As a model of the asymmetrical relationship between a civilized, safe, Anglo-Saxon center and a hazardous, hybrid, essentially unpredictable periphery, the frontier merely extended that conjunction of Old and New Worlds which had emerged with the first landfalls. Once Frémont began to treat the frontier as the true heart of the country, however, this dialectic had to unravel—which is exactly what happened as both Democrats and Whigs began to equate the nation as a whole with the immeasurable resources of the trans-Mississippi valley. Ever the voice of free land and free trade, the *Democratic Review* was quick to note that "the natural resources of the Mississippi valley are such as to designate it as the inevitable, *ultimate seat of manufactures for the world*. Nations and sections may struggle by means of protective laws, and all sorts of idle absurdities, . . . but the laws of trade are inviolable": "There will be but *one* transportation, that of goods *from* the great valley." In the short run, anyway, it was this development which provoked Whitman to observe that the great interior of the country was "rapidly concentrating the political power of the American Union" and that Americans, generally, had become a "central inland race." "We stand self-pois'd in the middle," he wrote, "branching thence over the world."[107]

The greater effect of this realignment was a more abstract and far-sighted view of the nation, a view that steadily advanced many of the themes that had preoccupied Democrats and Whigs for over a decade while adding to a trajectory of history in which the former colony would become an imperial power. Pratt's "To the People of the United States" put it this way:

> When we look at the past, and see how civilization has travelled west, bringing commerce and the useful arts with it — when we see that civil and religious liberty was driven to this continent, as its apparent last resting place — when we see the progress and even strides of these United States in wealth and greatness — when we see this vast, this rich continent, ... more congenial to grow the whole man than any other part of the globe, placed directly in the centre of the earth — Europe, with more than 250,000,000 of souls on the one side, with the Atlantic 3,000 miles wide between us, and on the other side all Asia, with 700,000,000 souls, and the Pacific a little more than 5,000 miles between us; and when we know that the earth does not produce enough to sustain the vast multitudes on either side, and nowhere for them to go but to us; and when we know that the building of this great road will open to settlement, production, and intercourse with all the parts of the globe this vast wilderness of 2,500 miles in extent, can we doubt that it is our destiny and paramount duty to go forward and accomplish it?

Though Whigs had generally opposed the annexation of Texas and Oregon and continued to refer to the Mexican War as an act of aggression, by 1849 even the *American Review* would include an article entitled "California," which proposed "to show the immense results that seem destined to follow from our new territorial acquisitions on the Pacific":

> It is no ordinary position, that in which these acquisitions have placed us. It is a position of the deepest world-wide historical significance. ... Its significance is not so much in what we actually see to-day, as in what we know must come to pass, as the stream of the world's his-

tory goes broadening and deepening on in the ages to come. . . . We do not say we can predict with absolute certainty when and how far this is to be; but we say that, in the present condition of the world, its civilization, its science, its arts, its commerce, its means of communication — there are the conditions, the forces, which have but to work naturally forward in the direction they are now working, and, in all human likelihood, this stupendous result must in due time come to be accomplished — a new historical centralization of the nations, and America the mediator between both sides of the old world.[108]

Reading these excerpts one after the other makes it apparent just how thoroughly the Pacific railroad had begun to transform Berkeley's westward course of empire into a version of Condorcet's limitless progress. All of a sudden the continent of America ceased to be the "uttermost parts of the earth"; its Pacific coast ceased to be what the poet Eugene Lies had called the "utmost West"; it finished "the great circle" Crèvecoeur had spoken of not by terminating the flow of civilization but by actually completing the circuit between Europe and Asia; and if it represented the fifth and final act of human progress, Americans still found it hard to "predict with absolute certainty when and how far this is to be" because "the stream of the world's history" would be "broadening and deepening on in the ages to come." The "stupendous" conditions and forces already annihilating "the barriers of time and space" seemed to offer a way past Malthus as well as Montesquieu, and they certainly overstepped the boundaries of freedom and progress that had separated Democrats and Whigs. In many respects, space and time ceased to have any boundaries at all. Instead, they became the more or less indefinite sphere of a rapidly consolidating nation and a rapidly expanding level of knowledge and commerce.[109]

Even the errand into the wilderness was renewed by a mission that exceeded the latter days of earth's last remaining quadrant. Whitney had righteously said of the railroad: "I need not declare what must be its inevitable results morally, religiously, commercially, and politically. It would carry with it from ocean to ocean, 3,000 miles in extent, a belt of population with the same manners, habits, thought, tastes, actions, and interests; and, yes, the same religion—a flood of light, life, and liberty, which would spread over, enlighten, and enliven the heathenism of all Asia." If anything, the Reverend Colton is even more grandiloquent. It is true he evokes Berkeley and Malthus when he says that the commencement of the railroad "will be the commencement of a never ending and ever increasing tide of population, rolling onward in the western track of empire, wafting civilization on its bosom, to be stayed only by the waters of the Pacific." But even here he points to "an inexhaustible world of dormant wealth, which needs but the wand of this great scheme to wake it into activity and ceaseless energy." And his more general argument is that

> science, and art, and invention, allied to the provisions of nature, and coming to the aid of human enterprise, have multiplied and are multiplying the power of man for the accomplishment of his objects, in such amazing and amazingly increasing degrees, that science, and art, and invention themselves, in the utmost stretch of their combined force, would together halt, in any attempt to estimate the progress embodied in the results of their own energy in the hands of man. And what is the reason? I will tell you;—and I will explain it on principles of Christian philosophy: It is because the powers of God's providence, in the government of the world, employing men as instruments, are *cumulative*.

Harking back to Isaiah 66:8 ("Shall the earth be made to bring forth in one day? Or shall a nation be born at once?"), Colton is basically arguing that the Pacific railroad would help to bring forth the American nation while also creating the "intimate commercial contact" that would bring *all* nations into "amicable relations with each other." At the same time, and "by the same causes," he believes the railroad would "raise the lower conditions of human society, wherever found, to a level with the higher" and "impart a general impulse to the entire circle of humanity, to rise yet higher than the highest, and to move onward in the path of universal improvement." Condorcet couldn't have said it better himself.[110]

Delivered in 1850, Colton's "Lecture" suggests that the notion of Manifest Destiny had changed a great deal since John O'Sullivan's "Great Nation of Futurity" was published in 1839 while fundamentally affirming his prophetic vision. In the end, it was only as a matter of space that America could "manifest to mankind the excellence of divine principles." But once Whitney began to publicize his plan for a Pacific railroad, and even Whigs saw a way to consolidate the territory either annexed or won in the Mexican War, Manifest Destiny swept aside the barriers of party affiliation along with the barriers of space and time. Very swiftly it became a universal version of progress and perfectibility, confirming America's unique position in the world by turning the nation toward its interior and claiming, as Thomas Allen has put it, the future itself "as American territory."[111]

Although Manifest Destiny would temporarily founder among the sectional disputes that finally culminated in the Civil War, its principles of exceptionalism and expansionism would rarely waver after the war was over, sanctifying everything from the Union Pacific Railroad to the final removal of the Indians. The very indefiniteness of these principles — derived not only from a fungible view of liberty and "personal enfranchisement," but also from the "stupendous results of modern science," the "great projected lines of railroad communication," and the telegraph wires that "electrically united" the continent — insured that space itself remained open-ended and indefinite. In the end, enhancing the freedom to move simply advanced the clock of growth and development. We see this quite clearly in Palmer's *Across the Continent* and Gast's *American Progress*, each a kind of inventory of technology advancing to the horizon.

Simultaneously, of course, Manifest Destiny encouraged Americans to think of the *nation* as open-ended and indefinite, too — what Allen has called a "republic in time" as well as space — adding weight, though not finality, to Frémont's influence. More than fifty years after the *Report* appeared, the United States Postal Service thought enough of Frémont to issue a commemorative stamp that again showed him waving the national flag on the summit of the Wind River peak (fig. 28). This time, the image

FIG. 28. *Fremont on Rocky Mountains*, one of nine commemorative stamps issued by the U.S. Postal Service as part of the series Trans-Mississippi "Omaha" Exposition Stamps of 1898. Image courtesy of Bob Graham.

looks like a combination of the Bigelow illustration and Leutze's mural, with Frémont heroically holding the Stars and Stripes aloft, as in the original etching, but on a summit that is nearly identical to the rocky prominence in *Westward the Course of Empire Takes Its Way*. Though it was entitled *Frémont on Rocky Mountains* and was one of a set of nine meant to mark the Trans-Mississippi Exposition in Omaha, the stamp was issued in the middle of the Spanish-American War and was specifically created to raise money for the war. Certainly this celebrated image of a laudable, leveling, and centripetal moment in the republic's history was emblematic of a nation that would soon enhance its global axis by adding the territories of Puerto Rico, Guam, the Philippines, and the Caroline Islands. Indeed, the image could now be seen as an imperialist version of Isaiah's prophecy that "the mountain of the LORD's house shall be established in the top of the mountains," and "all nations shall flow into it." At the same time, it was even further proof that the fairly direct line of thought which connected the expansion and progress of the early 1840s to the even greater expansion of the late 1890s passed directly through Frémont's iconic description of the Continental Divide. For a nation so ready to see itself as the "historical centre" of the world — a nation destined to lead "a movement that shall draw the whole world around it and along with it in its gigantic march" — Frémont's *Report on an Exploration of the Country Lying between the Missouri River and the Rocky Mountains* could not have been more timely or shrewd. For it was in the *Report* that the geographical predestination of the United States, aligned once and for all with the Continental Divide, began to exceed the boundaries of the continent altogether.[112]

Afterword

NO ACCOUNT OF FRÉMONT'S ARDENT AND IMPRESSIVE *Report* can conclude without considering the issue of authorship. Calling something a work of art always makes this a crucial matter, and here it is almost imperative, since Jessie Frémont has long been suspected of writing all or part of the *Report*. The evidence for this claim is inconclusive, but so is the evidence that Frémont wrote it.

Ironically, it was Frémont himself who first opened this Pandora's box. In his *Memoirs*, published in 1886, he begins his account of the first *Report* with a peculiarly modern admission: "I write more easily by dictation. Writing myself I have too much time to think and dwell upon words as well as ideas." Many people dictate their memoirs these days or rely on voice-recognition technology, and forty years ago the "gonzo" journalist Hunter S. Thompson famously found that his IBM Selectric typewriter finally allowed him to type as fast as he thought. But in Frémont's case, it required a more human collaboration with his wife, Jessie. As he goes on to explain, he and Jessie developed a strict routine in which she joined him each morning "punctually at nine o'clock," and "from that hour until one the writing went on, with seldom anything to break the thread; the dictation sometimes continuing for hours, interrupted only when an occasional point of exceptional interest brought out inquiry or discussion." After "a light luncheon and then a walk to the river," they would "work again until dusk." Jessie became his ideal audience, his "second mind," whose "slight dissent" confirmed his own doubt and whose "pleased expression" embodied "the popular impression of a mind new to the subject." Eventually, they developed "a form of discussion impossible except with a mind and purpose in harmony with one's own and on the same level."[1]

Despite the harmonious give-and-take of this collaboration, Frémont flatly refers to Jessie's help as "the labor of amanuensis." He pointedly uses the word "dictation," and there is no indication she is putting any words in his mouth, no indication she is actually writing the *Report* itself. That this has not been taken at face value is largely the result of Allan Nevins's influential biography of Frémont—the first to include Jessie's comments from an unpublished memoir of her own. In those memoirs, Jessie writes: "The horseback life, the sleep in the open air, had unfitted Mr. Frémont for the indoor work of writing—and second lieutenants cannot indulge in secretaries. After a series of hemorrhages from the nose and head had convinced him he must give up trying to write his report, I was let to try, and thus slid into my most happy life-work." The memoirs also corroborate and add a little to Frémont's description of the daily routine: "I soon learned that I could not make a restless motion; it was hard, but that was lost in the great joy of being so useful to him, and so, swiftly, the report of the first expedition was written."[2]

Although Nevins himself judged the *Report* to be "nine-tenths" Frémont's," arguing that it was "close-packed with factual information which he alone could supply, and which determines its whole form and flavor," opinion still seems fairly evenly divided whether it is truly his or also hers. The lesser case for Jessie is that Frémont dictated the "factual information" while she added the poetic flourishes. The more significant claim is that Jessie turned what might have been an artless or merely scientific treatise into an adventure story. As Pamela Herr maintains in her biography of Jessie: "While John's observations and experiences formed its solid core, Jessie's hand can be seen in the graceful style, the skillful pacing, and the vivid scenes and vignettes that make it so readable." Like most of those who see Jessie's hand in the *Report*, Herr reads a great deal into the fact that Jessie went on to be a success-ful writer—at times, the family's sole source of income. Herr finds a "Victorian coyness" in Jessie's efforts to minimize her role and points to the greater truth revealed by her comment that she slid into her "most happy life-work" while writing the *Report*. If Herr does not extend this to a stylistic comparison of Frémont's and Jessie's writings, many others have—leading to the rather depressing spectacle of prejudice blithely masquerading as proof, with Jessie's fondness for quoting classical literature said to be too fancy for such a report and Frémont said to lack the skill for it. Some have even examined the original manuscript of the *Report*, looking to see whose handwriting it is in, only to find that the first nineteen sheets are in Jessie's hand, the rest in Frémont's, with corrections also in Jessie's. While the corrections might help to make the secondary case for Jessie, Stephen Fender has noted that they "seem neither frequent nor substantial, and serve to remove literary allusions and other sophisticated associations at least as often as to add them."[3]

So much of this is assumed or uncertain that it's hard to know where to stand. Perhaps the most fruitful approach, a close comparison of styles, turns out to be anything but conclusive. Unfortunately, the *Report* is the first document on record that either Frémont or Jessie might have written for publication—always a more rigorous and self-conscious process than writing letters or journals, even for someone like Thoreau, whose journal is sometimes taken to be his greatest work. We know from one of Frémont's early teachers that a Charleston newspaper probably published "some well-written verses" of his, inspired by Herodotus's *Histories* (though no one has unearthed them yet). We also know that Jessie was extremely well read, in exploration literature as well as the classics, and that she routinely helped to edit her father's speeches. What we do not know, as the two of them sat down to complete a report that had to meet the standards of the Army Corps of Topographical Engineers, is who may have influenced whom. Both seemed to be able writers, both seemed to be sensitive to language, both were familiar with the literature that helped to shape the *Report*. On the whole, their memoirs imply that it was Frémont's voice that prevailed, but Jessie's "Victorian coyness" casts doubt on this. And it's not a doubt dispelled by their other writings. Frémont's letters are generally less polished than hers, but Jessie almost always wrote from the comfort of home, while he usually wrote on the road; Frémont's *Memoirs* seem to be in the same style as the *Report*, but maybe she helped him with that, too; Jessie's own writings tend to be more high-toned than his, but something like *Far-West Sketches* is very much in the style of the *Report*. None of this is definitive.[4]

Comparing the two memoirs is even more frustrating, though Jessie's seems to be the more doubtful on this issue. It's true that "the horseback life" may have temporarily "unfitted" Frémont "for the indoor work of writing": anyone who's done rough labor for a while and then tried to draw or play the piano knows how coarse the fine motor skills can become. But he wasn't gone all that long, and the disturbing "hemorrhages from the nose and head" suspiciously echo the "flecks of blood from the throat" that Jessie says her father suffered from after speaking on the Senate floor — for which the literary precedent is that master of rhetoric, Pliny the Younger. Moreover, there's something very vulnerable about that "coyness" of hers, especially if we assume that her "most happy life-work" was not writing per se but the acknowledged *purpose* of that writing: furthering her husband's reputation and career. Obviously, vanity could have caused Frémont to diminish her contribution to the *Report*, but a desire to be useful and needed could have also driven her to inflate it. Among other things, Jessie was barely eighteen at the time, she had gone against her beloved father to marry Frémont, she had just given birth to a daughter instead of the son she had promised him (the "first hard blow" her pride had "ever sustained"), and she knew how much the *Report* would influence Frémont's future. What better way to compensate for her failings as a mother than to help her loving husband overcome his failings as a writer? Saying that she "was let to try" after the "hemorrhages" convinced Frémont to "give up trying to write his report" proves little more than a wish to support her husband. The nature and extent of that support remain unclear. After all, modesty can be as conspicuous and misleading as boastfulness.[5]

With nothing to settle it either way, Frémont's *Memoirs* seem to offer the most compelling evidence for how the *Report* was written. What we notice most about the *Memoirs* is Frémont's constant emphasis on firsthand observation; indeed, it is the possibility of "study without books — the learning at first hand from nature herself" — that ignites

Frémont's desire to be an explorer in the first place and remains "a source of never-ending delight" to him. But as he recounts the expeditions in which Joseph Nicollet and Louison Frenière taught him to survey and see the prairie, Frémont begins to clarify how this relates to writing expedition reports. Explaining why Nicollet's poor health has delayed the Coteau des Prairies report, Frémont remarks that "he was not in condition to reduce into shape the materials for his report, which were varied and interesting and embraced the labor of years of thought and study following upon years of travel." In an obvious justification for his own work, he goes on to say: "No second hand can do this like the first. The impressions made by the visible objects, the pleasure of the first experience and the anticipations of roused curiosity, the sense of danger threatened and met, the relief from obstacles overcome, cannot be transfused into a mind that is cold and unexcited." He concludes by saying that "to such physical description, the eye that has not seen cannot bring a mind to feel and comprehend."[6]

With the *Report* itself so clearly framed as a firsthand account — and its *authority* as a firsthand account so dependent on Frémont's credibility as an expert witness — the idea that he would have allowed someone else to write it seems far-fetched. It looks even more far-fetched if we accept that the way he conceives of firsthand knowledge resembles the philosophical distinction Bertrand Russell made between "knowledge by acquaintance" and "knowledge by description." And if we factor in Frémont's extraordinary ability to *compose* what he sees, even Nevins's apparently decisive link between the "factual information" of the *Report* and its "whole form and flavor" begins to look a little trivial or crude. Frémont brings a sophisticated topographic imagination to the *Report*, effortlessly shifting from foreground to background, territory to map, visible to not-yet-visible, while never losing sight of the landscape before him, and it is this, more than anything else, that gives the *Report* its true "form and flavor." Only someone who had traveled the ground of the *Report* could have created the self-similar landscape it depicts; only someone who had seen the ground whole could have fragmented or interrupted it the way he does. While this was not a guarantee of accuracy or truth, merely of the way in which the landscape was structured and described, in fact many of Frémont's descriptions are good enough to be recognized more than 150 years later. The landscape of the *Report* is always real and rhetorical at the same time.

That it *is* a landscape substantially weakens the claim that Jessie's "sharp eye for a good story" turned "the expedition into a splendid adventure." Like Herr, most of those who make this claim point to the descriptions of Kit Carson ("one of the finest pictures of a horseman I have ever seen"), the buffalo hunts ("singling out a cow, I gave her my fire, but struck too high"), and the various engagements with Indians ("a charge from three hundred naked savages is a circumstance not well calculated to promote a cool exercise of judgment") as the crucial elements of that "splendid adventure." Yet the most lengthy and exciting episodes in the *Report* are the ascent of the Wind River Range and the trip down the rapids of the upper Platte. Frémont outfitted the expedition with these adventures in mind, recklessly refusing to give up the boat trip, even after he saw the river's speed and the shoreless gorge it passed through, and the *Report* is completely shaped by the two incidents, both as a narrative and as an account of physical geography. Even the Indians and the buffalo hunts are eventually incorporated into this aesthetic scheme. While there is every reason to call the *Report* an adventure, it is essentially a topographic adventure, an encounter with the landscape. From the most direct and detailed examination of the terrain to the most elevated and indirect rhetoric of Manifest Destiny, it is the landscape that counts. Only Frémont had seen that landscape firsthand, and only he was in a position to make another mind "feel and comprehend" it.[7]

And so we return to Nevins's "nine-tenths" Frémont's. Although he placed too much emphasis on Frémont's science and too little on his art, Nevins's conclusion seems about right. In her role as amanuensis and ideal audience, Jessie's greatest contribution may have been to help Frémont create an informal, accelerated style, matching the restless pace of the expedition itself. The *Report* undoubtedly includes some of the most astute and influential descriptions of landscape ever written, and it often reads as if Frémont were simply translating the movements of his eye into words. This might have been harder or less successful if he had not been dictating these words. A case could also be made that the interruptions and discussions that occurred as he was dictating influenced both the more reflective elements of the *Report* and its elusive yet rigorous composition. What we're left with, though, is a document Jessie may indeed have helped to elicit or edit but that is almost surely Frémont's from beginning to end.

Notes

INTRODUCTION

1. Robert Smithson, *The Writings of Robert Smithson*, ed. Nancy Holt (New York: New York University Press, 1979), 179.

2. Smith quoted in Rick Van Noy, *Surveying the Interior: Literary Cartographers and the Sense of Place* (Reno: University of Nevada Press, 2003), 14.

3. Anonymous quoted in Peter Benes, *New England Prospect: Maps, Place Names, and the Historical Landscape* (Boston: Boston University Press, 1980), 14; Denton quoted in Wayne Franklin, *Discoverers, Explorers, Settlers: The Diligent Writers of Early America* (Chicago: University of Chicago Press, 1979), 77.

4. See Albert K. Weinberg, *Manifest Destiny: A Study of National Expansionism in American History* (Chicago: Quadrangle Books, 1963), 43–71; Thomas Morton, *New English Canaan of Thomas Morton* (New York: B. Franklin, 1967), 115, 120–21; Texas traveler quoted in Robin W. Doughty, *At Home in Texas: Early Views of the Land* (College Station: Texas A&M University Press, 1987), 79.

5. Surveyor general quoted in Martin Brückner, *The Geographic Revolution in Early America: Maps, Literacy, and National Identity* (Chapel Hill: Published for the Omohundro Institute of Early American History and Culture by the University of North Carolina Press, 2006), 239; Gertrude Stein, *The Geographical History of America; or, The Relation of Human Nature to the Human Mind* (New York: Random House, 1936), 72; James Fenimore Cooper, *The Pioneers* (New York: New American Library, 1964), 174. See Bill Hubbard Jr., *American Boundaries: The Nation, the State, the Rectangular Survey* (Chicago: University of Chicago Press, 2009).

6. Quoted in Brückner, *Geographic Revolution*, 100; Jefferson to Chastellux, September 2, 1785, and Jefferson to William Short, August 4, 1820, both in *Writings: Autobiography; A Summary View of the Rights of British America; Notes on the State of Virginia; Public Papers; Addresses, Messages and Replies; Miscellany; Letters* by Thomas Jefferson (New York: Literary Classics of the United States, 1984), 827, 1434.

7. For multiple references to these two metaphors, see, for instance, Perry Miller, *Errand into the Wilderness* (Cambridge MA: Belknap Press of Harvard University Press, 1956); Roderick Nash, *Wilderness and the American Mind* (New Haven CT: Yale University Press, 1967); and Sacvan Bercovitch, *The American Jeremiad* (Madison:

University of Wisconsin Press, 1978). Thomas Hobbes, *Leviathan; or, The Matter, Forme, & Power of a Common-wealth Ecclesiasticall and Civill* (New York: Barnes & Noble Books, 2004), 91–92; Timothy Flint, *Recollections of the Last Ten Years in the Valley of the Mississippi* (Carbondale: Southern Illinois University Press, 1968), 124.

8. John Filson, "Appendix: The Adventures of Col. Daniel Boon; Containing a Narrative of the Wars of Kentucke," in *The Discovery, Settlement, and the Present State of Kentucke* (Fairfield WA: Ye Galleon Press, 2001), 51, 52, 55, 58; Jefferson, *Writings*, 142–44.

9. Burnet quoted in Marjorie Hope Nicolson, *Mountain Gloom and Mountain Glory: The Development of the Aesthetics of the Infinite* (Ithaca NY: Cornell University Press, 1959), 210, 213; Thomas Cole, "Essay on American Scenery," in *American Art, 1700–1960: Sources and Documents*, ed. John W. McCoubrey (Englewood Cliffs NJ: Prentice-Hall, 1965), 101; Jefferson to Maria Cosway, October 12, 1786, in Jefferson, *Writings*, 870. The classic treatise on aesthetic categories is Edmund Burke's *A Philosophical Enquiry into the Origins of our Ideas of the Sublime and the Beautiful* (1757). Burke argued that the sublime derived from vastness, uniformity, magnificence, terror, and awe and the beautiful from smallness, smoothness, sweetness, and grace. Toward the end of the eighteenth century, prompted by the landscape designs of "Capability" Brown, Humphry Repton, and William Shenstone, not to mention an emerging tourist industry in England that often included visits to the country estates they had designed, theorists such as William Gilpin, Uvedale Price, and Richard Payne Knight began to posit the picturesque as an unstable middle term — indicating that a scene was "like a picture," or worthy of being pictured, but also that it possessed elements of novelty, irregularity, abruptness, or extreme variation.

10. Nathaniel P. Willis, *American Scenery; or, Land, Lake, and River: Illustrations of Transatlantic Nature* (London: George Virtue, 1840), 2.

11. "Manifest Destiny" has long been a contested term as to both meaning and origin. Traditionally, the term itself has been attributed to O'Sullivan. However, Linda S. Hudson has challenged this view in *Mistress of Manifest Destiny: A Biography of Jane McManus Storm Cazneau, 1807–1878* (Austin: Texas State Historical Association, 2001), 45–47, 60–62, arguing that the author of the phrase was really Cazneau. Since Hudson's most compelling piece of evidence is a controversial, computer-generated comparison of O'Sullivan's and Cazneau's grammar, while the rest of her argument is either iffy or circumstantial or cuts both ways, most historians have taken a wait-and-see approach, sticking with O'Sullivan for the time being.

12. Benton quoted in Jessie Benton Frémont, "Biographical Sketch of Senator Benton, in Connection with Western Expansion," in *Memoirs of My Life* by John Charles Frémont (New York: Cooper Square Press, 2001), 1.

13. Anders Stephanson, *Manifest Destiny: American Expansionism and the Empire of Right* (New York: Hill and Wang, 1995), xiii; John O'Sullivan, "The Great Nation of Futurity," *United States Magazine and Democratic Review* 6, no. 23 (November 1839): 426–30.

14. John O'Sullivan, "Annexation," *United States Magazine and Democratic Review* 17, no. 85 (July/August 1845): 5–10; John O'Sullivan, "The True Title," *New York Morning News*, December 27, 1845.

15. "Frémont's Expeditions," *United States Magazine and Democratic Review* 17, no. 85 (July/August 1845): 68. For a succinct yet inclusive outline of Frémont's army expeditions, see Vincent Ponko Jr., "The Military Explorers of the American West, 1838–1860," in *A Continent Comprehended*, vol. 3, *North American Exploration*, ed. John Logan Allen (Lincoln: University of Nebraska Press, 1997), 332–68; of course, the classics are still William H. Goetzmann's *Army Exploration in the American West* (New Haven CT: Yale University Press, 1959) and *Exploration and Empire: The Explorer and the Scientist in the Winning of the American West* (New York: Alfred A. Knopf, 1966).

16. Young quoted in Frémont, *Memoirs*, 415; "California," *United States Magazine and Democratic Review* 20, no. 108 (June 1847): 558.

17. Though he pays Benton little attention for some reason, see Walter Nugent, *Habits of Empire: A History of American Expansion* (New York: Alfred A. Knopf, 2008), 157–86, for a concise summary of the dispute over Oregon Territory.

18. Frémont, "Biographical Sketch," 10–11.

19. Thomas Hart Benton, "On the Physical Geography of the Country between Missouri and California, with a View to Show its Adaptation to Settlement, and the Construction of a Railroad," in *Discourse of Mr. Benton, of Missouri, before the Maryland Institute* (Washington DC: J. T. and L. Towers, 1854), 1–16.

20. Flint, *Recollections*, 131. Except where noted, these and all other biographical details have been taken from Tom Chaffin, *Pathfinder: John Charles Frémont and the Course of American Empire* (New York: Hill and Wang, 2002); Ferol Egan, *Frémont: Explorer for a Restless Nation* (Garden City NY: Doubleday, 1977); and Allan Nevins, *Frémont: Pathmarker of the West* (Lincoln: University of Nebraska Press, 1992).

21. Frémont, *Memoirs*, 59, 64–65, 69.

22. Historians have generally followed Nevins's lead in referring to the report Frémont wrote after his 1842 expedition as "the first report" and the one written after his 1843–44 expedition as "the second report." What makes things confusing is that the first report was issued separately in 1843, while the second was almost immediately bound together with the first and issued as a single volume in 1845.

To simplify matters, then, the report of 1843 will always be called "the *Report*," the later report will be called "the second report," and occasionally it will make sense to refer to "the combined report." A modern reprint of the combined report has been published as John C. Frémont, *The Exploring Expedition to the Rocky Mountains* (Washington DC: Smithsonian Institution Press, 1988). Since the *Report* itself is only seventy-one pages long and is quoted so extensively, no attempt will be made to cite page numbers.

23. James P. Ronda, *Finding the West: Explorations with Lewis and Clark* (Albuquerque: University of New Mexico Press, 2001), 66; Martha A. Sandweiss, *Print the Legend: Photography and the American West* (New Haven CT: Yale University Press, 2002), 204. Obviously, the removal of a Native presence in the West, so intrinsic to the expansion that took place after 1830 or so, is a crucial element of American history. But like the new kinds of domesticity that began to develop along the overland trails and the effort to exclude even free blacks from Oregon Territory, it is mostly peripheral to this study of Frémont's *Report* and will only be referred to in passing.

PART I. PICTURESQUE AMERICA

1. Anthony Vidler, *Warped Space: Art, Architecture, and Anxiety in Modern Culture* (Cambridge MA: MIT Press, 2000), 19.

2. Flint, *Recollections*, 66, 64.

3. Flint, *Recollections*, 66; Josiah Gregg, *Commerce of the Prairies* (Norman: University of Oklahoma Press, 1954), 9–12.

4. Report quoted in Roy M. Robbins, *Our Landed Heritage: The Public Domain, 1776–1970* (Lincoln: University of Nebraska Press, 1976), 226; Francis Parkman Jr., *The Oregon Trail* (New York: Oxford University Press, 1996), 23; Flint, *Recollections*, 130.

5. Ross quoted in Weinberg, *Manifest Destiny*, 30.

6. All quoted in Weinberg, *Manifest Destiny*, 48, 51, 58.

7. Ralph Waldo Emerson, "The Young American," in *Nature: Addresses and Lectures* by Ralph Waldo Emerson (New York: AMS Press, 1968), 369; Hector St. John de Crèvecoeur, *Letters from an American Farmer* (London: J. M. Dent & Sons, Ltd.; New York: E. P. Dutton & Company, 1912), 69; Jefferson, *Writings*, 290; Paul W. Gates, *History of Public Land Law Development* (Washington DC: Written for the Public Land Law Review Commission, 1968), 64.

8. Zebulon Montgomery Pike, *The Expeditions of Zebulon Montgomery Pike, to Headwaters of the Mississippi River, through Louisiana Territory, and in New Spain, during the Years 1805–6–7*, 3 vols., ed. Elliott Coues (New York: Francis P. Harper, 1895), 2:396, 397, 428, 435, 523.

9. Smithson, *Writings*, 54. See Benoît Mandelbrot, *The Fractal Geometry of Nature* (San Francisco: W. H. Freeman, 1982).

10. Martyn J. Bowden, "The Great American Desert and the American Frontier, 1800–1882: Popular Images of the Plains," in *Anonymous Americans: Explorations in Nineteenth-Century Social History*, ed. Tamara K. Hareven (Englewood Cliffs NJ: Prentice-Hall, 1971), 52–53.

11. Edwin James, *Account of an Expedition from Pittsburgh to the Rocky Mountains, Performed in the Years 1819, 1820; by Order of the Hon. J. C. Calhoun, under the Command of Maj. S. H. Long, of the U.S. Top. Engineers*, 3 vols. (London: Longman, Hurst, Rees, Orme and Brown, 1823), 2:147, 3:223, 2:148. Note that while this report was ably written by James, who served as the expedition's biologist and geologist, all quotes will be attributed to Long, since that is how the expedition is generally identified. Also note that the "Great Desert" was often referred to at the time as the "Great American Desert." In keeping with Long's map designation and Frémont's low-key terminology, however, the less inflammatory term will be used throughout.

12. James Fenimore Cooper, *The Prairie*, ed. James P. Elliott (Albany: State University of New York Press, 1985), 13.

13. Thomas Cole, *Annual II: Studies on Thomas Cole, an American Romanticist*, ed. Howard S. Merritt (Baltimore MD: Museum of Art, 1967), 47, 50.

14. Flint, *Recollections*, 11; Long quoted in Kris Fresonke, *West of Emerson: The Design of Manifest Destiny* (Berkeley: University of California Press, 2003), 72; George Catlin, *Letters and Notes on the Manners, Customs, and Conditions of North American Indians*, 2 vols. (New York: Dover Publications, 1973), 1:218.

15. Edward W. Said, *Orientalism* (New York: Pantheon Books, 1978), 92. Obviously, Said was referring to the body of writing about the Orient, not the Great Desert, but the examples are equivalent. Gregg, *Commerce*, 355; Parkman, *Oregon Trail*, 154; Washington Irving, *Three Western Narratives: A Tour on the Prairies; Astoria; The Adventures of Captain Bonneville* (New York: Literary Classics of the United States, 2004), 359. For a complementary analysis of Irving, see Stephanie LeMenager, *Manifest and Other Destinies: Territorial Fictions of the Nineteenth-Century United States* (Lincoln: University of Nebraska Press, 2004), which argues that many of those who wrote about the West before 1840 — Irving and Cooper, in particular — were willing to see it as part of the world but not part of the nation.

16. Linn quoted in Thomas Hart Benton, *Thirty Years' View; or, A History of the Working of the American Government for Thirty Years, from 1820 to 1850*, 2 vols. (New York: D. Appleton and Company), 2:469.

17. James Fenimore Cooper, "American and European Scenery Compared," in *The Home Book of the Picturesque; or, American Scenery, Art, and Literature, Comprising a Series of Essays by Washington Irving, W. C. Bryant, Fenimore Cooper, and*

Others (Gainesville FL: Scholars' Facsimiles & Reprints, 1967), 51; Ralph Waldo Emerson, "Self-Reliance," in *The Selected Writings of Ralph Waldo Emerson*, ed. Brooks Atkinson (New York: Modern Library, 1992), 149. Not that even the most nationalistic Americans stopped working with a European audience in mind; see Lawrence Buell, "Postcolonial Anxiety in Classic U.S. Literature," in *Postcolonial Theory and the United States: Race, Ethnicity, and Literature*, ed. Amritjit Singh and Peter Schmidt (Jackson: University Press of Mississippi, 2000), 196–218.

18. Henry T. Tuckerman, "The Philosophy of Travel," *United States Magazine and Democratic Review* 14, no. 67 (May 1844): 537; "Development of Nationality in American Art," *Bulletin of the American Art Union* 9 (December 1851): 137–39.

19. Willis, *American Scenery*: this and all subsequent quotes are from the preface, iii–iv, and the introduction, 1–3.

20. William Gilpin, *Observations on the River Wye, and Several Parts of South Wales, &c.: Relative Chiefly to Picturesque Beauty: Made in the Summer of 1770* (London: Printed by A. Strahan for T. Cadell Junior and W. Davies, 1800), 81; Gilpin quoted in Christopher Hussey, *The Picturesque: Studies in a Point of View* (London: Cass, 1983), 115; Benedict Anderson, *Imagined Communities: Reflections on the Origin and Spread of Nationalism* (London: Verso, 1991), 21–23; Susan Shelby Magoffin, *Down the Santa Fe Trail and into Mexico: The Diary of Susan Shelby Magoffin 1846–1847* (Lincoln: University of Nebraska Press, 1982), 83.

21. Sidney K. Robinson, *Inquiry into the Picturesque* (Chicago: University of Chicago Press, 1991), 8. And see W. H. Bartlett, *Bartlett's Classic Illustrations of America: All 121 Engravings from "American Scenery," 1840* (Mineola: Dover Publications, 2000). This dynamic of recalibrating the picturesque to make it "American" can be seen as just one element of the transnationalism analyzed at length by Leonard Tennenhouse in *The Importance of Feeling English: American Literature and the British Diaspora, 1750–1850* (Princeton NJ: Princeton University Press, 2007). "Only by reproducing the terms of their own domination," Tennenhouse explains, "can new groups introduce the differences that may, at some point, add up to their cultural emergence."

22. Catlin, *Letters and Notes*, 1:18–19; Uvedale Price, *Essays on the Picturesque, as Compared with the Sublime and the Beautiful, and, on the Use of Studying Pictures for the Purpose of Improving Real Landscape*, 3 vols. (London: Printed for J. Mawman, 1810), 1:68; Magoffin, *Down the Santa Fe Trail*, 81; Robinson, *Inquiry into the Picturesque*, 8. For Lewis's description of the falls, see Gary E. Moulton, ed., *The Journals of the Lewis and Clark Expedition* (Lincoln: University of Nebraska Press, 1983–2001), June 13–14, 1805. The entire text of this edition is available online at http://lewisandclarkjournals.unl.edu/.

23. Seward quoted in Richard H. Immerman, *Empire for Liberty: A History of American Imperialism from Benjamin Franklin to Paul Wolfowitz* (Princeton NJ: Princeton University Press, 2010), 101.

24. Beth L. Lueck, *American Writers and the Picturesque Tour: The Search for National Identity, 1790–1860* (New York: Garland Publishing, 1997), 16–18, has shown how advances in transportation actually altered the preferred routes and destinations for tourists every year or two, though few traveled beyond the Northeast until the 1840s or so.

25. For a study of how the Northeast, New England in particular, temporarily reemerged as the model for a national landscape during the 1890s, see Julia B. Rosenbaum, *Visions of Belonging: New England Art and the Making of American Identity* (Ithaca NY: Cornell University Press, 2006). Significantly, Rosenbaum focuses on the World's Columbian Exposition, which is where Frederick Jackson Turner first enunciated his famous frontier thesis. And this, in the words of David W. Noble, *Death of a Nation: American Culture and the End of Exceptionalism* (Minneapolis: University of Minnesota Press, 2002), 12, "moved New England out of an irrelevant colonial past to become the source of the intellectual and artistic vitality of Lincoln's nation."

26. The term "topographic geology" has been taken from Edward Hitchcock, *Report on the Geology, Mineralogy, Botany, and Zoology of Massachusetts* (Amherst MA: Press of J. S. and C. Adams, 1833), where there is a brief introduction to part 2, which states that "the connection between the aspect of the earth's surface and the nature of the rocks beneath, is so obvious, that I have thought it would not be a misnomer to denominate an account of the natural scenery, Topographical Geology. In the following sketch of the scenery of Massachusetts, my principal object will be to direct the attention of the man of taste to those places in the State, where he will find natural objects particularly calculated to gratify his love of novelty, beauty and sublimity." Both quoted in Rebecca Bedell, *The Anatomy of Nature: Geology and American Landscape Painting, 1825–1875* (Princeton NJ: Princeton University Press, 2001), 3; Emerson, "The Poet," in Atkinson, *Selected Writings*, 296; Henry David Thoreau, *A Week on the Concord and Merrimack Rivers; Walden: or, Life in the Woods; The Maine Woods; Cape Cod* (New York: Literary Classics of the United States, 1985), 104.

27. Bedell, *Anatomy of Nature*, 20; Willis, *American Scenery*, 9, 11.

28. Cole quoted in Bedell, *Anatomy of Nature*, 19.

29. Charles Preuss, *Exploring with Frémont: The Private Diaries of Charles Preuss, Cartographer for John C. Frémont on His First, Second, and Fourth Expeditions to the Far West*, trans. Erwin G. and Elisabeth K. Gudde (Norman: University of

Oklahoma Press, 1958), 5, 18, 14, 20. For a discussion which claims that Frémont understood "he was seeing a new world" but lacked "the cultural preparation to express it," see Anne Farrar Hyde, *An American Vision: Far Western Landscape and National Culture, 1820–1920* (New York: New York University Press, 1990), 1–11. For a discussion of how confusing Lewis and Clark had found the West forty years earlier, see Frank Bergeron, "Wilderness Aesthetics," *American Literary History* 9, no. 1 (Spring 1997): 128–61.

30. Frémont, *Memoirs*, 21; Benton, *Thirty Years' View*, 2:580.

31. Frémont, *Memoirs*, 24, 602.

32. Joseph N. Nicollet, *Joseph N. Nicollet on the Plains and Prairies: The Expeditions of 1838–39 with Journals, Letters, and Notes on the Dakota Indians*, ed. Edmund C. Bray and Martha Coleman Bray (Saint Paul: Minnesota Historical Society Press, 1976), 2.

33. Donald Jackson and Mary Lee Spence, eds., *The Expeditions of John Charles Frémont*, 3 vols. (Urbana: University of Illinois Press, 1977), 1:12.

34. Nicolet, *On the Plains and Prairies*, 15, 75.

35. Nicollet, *On the Plains and Prairies*, 22, 36, 54.

36. Frémont, *Memoirs*, 44.

37. For a contrasting view of Frémont's style, see Stephen Fender, *Plotting the Golden West: American Literature and the Rhetoric of the California Trail* (Cambridge: Cambridge University Press, 1981), 37–50. Fender claims that Frémont "felt uncertain as to what stylistic grid to impose on his material" and therefore vacillated, not oscillated, between scenery and science until he reached the summit — at which point "Frémont the frontier dreamer awoke into Frémont the patriotic surveyor" and settled on a rhetoric of science alone. Bergeron, "Wilderness Aesthetics," 143–53, adopts Fender's notion of a vacillating style to describe the journals of Lewis and Clark. More generally, there is a well-developed sphere of aesthetic criticism devoted to the relation between art and science, some of which is relevant to the following analysis of the *Report*. See, for instance, Holmes Rolston III, *Environmental Ethics: Duties to and Values in the Natural World* (Philadelphia: Temple University Press, 1988); Yuriko Saito, "The Aesthetics of Unscenic Nature," *Journal of Aesthetics and Art Criticism* 56, no. 2 (Spring 1998): 101–11; Robert S. Fudge, "Imagination and the Science-Based Aesthetic Appreciation of Unscenic Nature," *Journal of Aesthetics and Art Criticism* 59, no. 3 (Summer 2001): 275–85; and Allen Carlson and Arnold Berleant, eds., *The Aesthetics of Natural Environments* (Peterborough ON: Broadview Press, 2004).

38. To see just how radical this approach was, compare the discussion of landmarks and fixed points in D. Graham Burnett, *Masters of All They Surveyed: Exploration,*

Geography, and a British El Dorado (Chicago: University of Chicago Press, 2000), 14–16, 119–98. The essential difference is that during the great era of European discovery, explorers usually sought to locate and map unknown territory, while Frémont sought to *dis*locate and map a territory already known as the Great Desert.

39. Steven Shapin, *The Scientific Revolution* (Chicago: University of Chicago Press, 1996), 108. And see Nathaniel Lewis, *Unsettling the Literary West: Authenticity and Authorship* (Lincoln: University of Nebraska Press, 2003), 19–47. Although the focus in what follows is on science and art, while Lewis is concerned with authorship, it is clear that Frémont's obsession with verification and truth was shared by almost everyone writing about the West at the time—as was his emphasis on the landscape.

40. Flint quoted in Cooper, *Prairie*, xxix.

41. Irving, *Three Western Narratives*, 82.

42. For a contrary opinion of Frémont's approach to landscape, see Patricia Nelson Limerick, *Desert Passages: Encounters with the American Deserts* (Niwot: University Press of Colorado, 1989), 25–44, which argues that "Frémont denied complexity or ambiguity in nature."

43. Brückner, *Geographic Revolution*, 51–97, including all quotes.

44. Bradford Terry and Francis H. Allen, eds., *The Journal of Henry D. Thoreau* (New York: Dover Publications, 1962), February 14, 1840 (1:119); Cole, "Essay," 101, 102, 108, 103. For an informative, if limited, study of Cole and the picturesque, see Earl A. Powell, *Thomas Cole* (New York: Harry N. Abrams, 1990), 20–47.

45. "A Report of an Exploration of the Country Lying between the Missouri River and Rocky Mountains," *Athenæum*, March 16, 1844, 237–38; "Frémont's Expeditions," 77. And again see Lewis, *Unsettling the Literary West*, 19–47, for the way in which this was typical of western writing in general.

46. Geneva M. Gano, "At the Frontier of Precision and Persuasion: The Convergence of Natural Philosophy and National Philosophy in John C. Fremont's *1842, 1843–44 Report and Map*," *American Transcendental Quarterly* 18, no. 3 (September 2004): 131–54. Note that Gano traces Frémont's apparent objectivity to the picturesque itself, which she characterizes as "the *lingua franca* of scientific exploration." And since she cites Fresonke's *West of Emerson* in support of this idea, it should also be noted that Fresonke makes three significant points: (1) that both the Pike and Long reports embody a version of the picturesque; (2) that the metaphor of the Great Desert resulted from a blindness inherent to the picturesque; and (3) that the picturesque was more or less opposed to the ambitions of the Jacksonian era and therefore reached its aesthetic limits around the time of Emerson and Thoreau. Obviously, all of this is at odds with what is being said here.

47. Bacon quoted in Margarita Bowen, *Empiricism and Geographical Thought: From Francis Bacon to Alexander von Humboldt* (Cambridge: Cambridge University Press, 1981), 45; Tuckerman, "Philosophy of Travel," 529.

48. John Conron, *American Picturesque* (University Park: Pennsylvania State University Press, 2000), 3–8; James, *Account of an Expedition*, 2:172–73.

49. Martin J. S. Rudwick, "A Visual Language for Geology," *History of Science* 14 (pt. 3), no. 25 (September 1976): 177; J. B. Krygier, "Envisioning the American West: Maps, the Representational Barrage of 19th Century Expedition Reports, and the Production of Scientific Knowledge," *Cartography and Geographic Information Systems* 24, no. 1 (January 1997): 27–50.

50. Bertrand Russell, "Knowledge by Acquaintance and Knowledge by Description," *Proceedings of the Aristotelian Society* n.s. 11 (1910–11): 108–28. Again, this is not to deny the many parallels to Said's notion of Orientalism, in that the Great Desert is clearly a text, not a territory, and Frémont's *Report* is no less a representation than Pike's or Long's. In this context it may be worth repeating a quote that appears in Bill Ashcroft, Gareth Griffiths, and Helen Tiffin, *The Empire Writes Back: Theory and Practice in Post-Colonial Literatures* (London: Routledge, 1989), 141. Speaking of how difficult it was to separate himself from English and American culture while still writing in English, a Canadian writer recently said: "At one time I considered it to be the task of the Canadian writer to give names to his experience, to be the namer. I now suspect, that, on the contrary, it is his task to un-name." An impasse of this sort is precisely what provoked Frémont's notion of the double negative—and what made it such a compelling re-presentation of the West. For the double negative itself began as a process of unnaming.

51. See Frémont, *Memoirs*, 603–4, for a summary of the descriptive approach he began to develop in the *Report*. And for a hint of how dubious the sublime had become as a mode of scientific description by the 1870s—even in the eyes of those who adopted it—see John P. Herron's discussion of Clarence King in *Science and the Social Good: Nature, Culture, and Community, 1865–1965* (New York: Oxford University Press, 2010), 60, 66.

52. "Expeditions to Santa Fé," *North American Review* 60, no. 126 (January 1845): 198; "California," *United States Magazine and Democratic Review* 23, no. 122 (August 1848): 169.

53. For a contrary analysis, emphasizing Frémont's "data points" rather than his composition, see Michael A. Bryson, *Visions of the Land: Science, Literature and the American Environment from the Era of Exploration to the Age of Ecology* (Charlottesville: University Press of Virginia, 2002), 9.

54. James Turner, *The Politics of Landscape: Rural Scenery and Society in English Poetry 1630–1660* (Cambridge MA: Harvard University Press, 1979), 15.

55. Walter Benjamin, *The Arcades Project* (Cambridge MA: Harvard University Press, 1999), 476.

56. "Subvoucher, New York, 6 May 1842 U.S. to James R. Chilton," in Jackson and Spence, *Expeditions of John Charles Frémont*, 1:145; Preuss, *Exploring with Frémont*, 32. Frémont would be plagued with disaster in his efforts to photograph the West: see Ava F. Kahn's introduction to Solomon Nunes Carvalho, *Incidents of Travel and Adventure in the Far West with Colonel Frémont's Last Expedition* (Lincoln: University of Nebraska Press, 2004).

57. Willis, *American Scenery*, iv.

58. Washington Irving, "Traits of Indian Character," in *The Sketch Book of Geoffrey Crayon, Gent.* by Washington Irving (London: John Murray, 1820), 215, 235. Lee Clark Mitchell's *Witnesses to a Vanishing America: The Nineteenth-Century Response* (Princeton NJ: Princeton University Press, 1981) is still the best account of this peculiarly American nostalgia.

59. Catlin, *Letters and Notes*, 2:223, 1:206, 2:231; Thoreau, *Maine Woods*, 722.

60. Again, it is Frémont's need to redefine a region already defined negatively that separates the *Report* from many of the narratives written during the era of European exploration that also sought to reduce a peopled land to landscape alone. See, for instance, Mary Louise Pratt, *Imperial Eyes: Travel Writing and Transculturation* (London: Routledge, 2008), 50, 60, 132.

61. Irving, *Three Western Narratives*, 653–54.

62. Thoreau, *Walden*, 400.

63. There has long been a need to modify the view, first expressed by Henry Nash Smith in *Virgin Land: The American West as Symbol and Myth* (Cambridge MA: Harvard University Press, 1950), 121–260, that the West became a popular place in the American imagination only as it morphed into "the garden of the world." We have already noted that the figure of a well-watered and fertile country to the west had been a given of almost every atlas before 1810 or so. But this prospect of agrarian bliss had been routed so decisively by the rhetoric of the Great Desert that the West of the late 1830s and early 1840s had come to be seen as the *antithesis* of a garden paradise. If people were again willing to view the region as attractive, it was mainly, or at least initially, because Frémont's aesthetic *transcended* agrarianism altogether. Moreover, it also transcended what LeMenager, *Manifest and Other Destinies*, 1–103, has called the "maritime" narratives of Cooper and Irving. It is worth noting that Nash refers to Frémont only in passing and always as an acolyte or instrument of Benton, while LeMenager disdainfully dismisses his achievements

in a single sentence. But for statistical proof of Frémont's influence, see Bowden, "The Great American Desert," 55–59, which shows how decisively the image of the Great Desert began to disappear from atlases after 1844. That this was specifically the result of Frémont's reports, and not just the effect of a more approving view of expansion, is suggested by Bowden's analysis of several Vermont newspapers printed from 1849 to 1851. There he found that "the words 'desert' and 'arid plains' were used five times to describe portions of the West, in each case in reference to the Great Basin Country of the Far West." It was not until Frémont surveyed and named the Great Basin that people began using this phrase and distinguishing the actual deserts of Utah and Nevada from the so-called Great Desert east of the Rockies.

64. Edwin Bryant, *What I Saw in California* (Lincoln: University of Nebraska Press, 1985), 183.

65. Bryant, *What I Saw*, 22.

66. Bryant, *What I Saw*, 22, 24, 26, 25, 58, 61, 67.

67. Bryant, *What I Saw*, 175, 182–83, 187; Mark Twain, *Roughing It* (Berkeley: University of California Press, 1995), 124; Emerson, *Nature*, 38.

68. Bryant, *What I Saw*, 27, 32–33, 71.

69. Bryant, *What I Saw*, 82, 92, 117.

70. Brigitte Bailey, "Gender, Nation, and the Tourist Gaze in the European 'Year of Revolutions': Kirkland's *Holidays*," *American Literary History* 14, no. 1 (Spring 2002): 60.

71. Bryant, *What I Saw*, 99–101.

72. Wadsworth quoted in Merrill J. Mattes, *The Great Platte River Road: The Covered Wagon Mainline via Fort Kearny to Fort Laramie* (Lincoln: Nebraska State Historical Society, 1969), 353–54.

73. Bryant, *What I Saw*, 101–2.

74. Bryant, *What I Saw*, 216–18.

75. Anderson, *Imagined Communities*, 44; Jefferson to William Buchanan and James Hay, January 26, 1786, and Jefferson to Major L'Enfant, April 10, 1791, both in Jefferson, *Writings*, 845, 976; Henry Adams, *The Education of Henry Adams* (New York: Penguin Books, 1995), 99.

76. Henry David Thoreau, "Autumnal Tints," in *Collected Essays and Poems*, ed. Elizabeth Hall Witherall (New York: Literary Classics of the United States, 2001), 393.

77. Goetzmann, *Exploration and Empire*, 489–529. The theory of uniformitarianism assumed that the forces which had formed the earth to begin with were still shaping it today; a competing theory, catastrophism, assumed that the earth had remained largely the same after being deluged and convulsed by a series of events long in the past. For a general survey of earth science during this period, see Mott

T. Greene, *Geology in the Nineteenth Century: Changing Views of a Changing World* (Ithaca NY: Cornell University Press, 1984).

78. John McPhee, *Basin and Range* (New York: Farrar, Straus and Giroux, 1980), 127–28, is the first to use the term "deep time."

79. Goetzmann, *Exploration and Empire*, 320.

80. Hyde, *An American Vision*, 201.

81. See Aubrey L. Haines, *Yellowstone National Park: Its Exploration and Establishment* (Washington DC: U.S. National Park Service, 1974), 85–128.

82. All quotes taken from Haines, *Yellowstone National Park*, 115, 98, 120, 126.

83. See Thurman Wilkins, *Thomas Moran: Artist of the Mountains* (Norman: University of Oklahoma Press, 1966), 5; also Joni Louise Kinsey, *Thomas Moran and the Surveying of the American West* (Washington DC: Smithsonian Institution Press, 1992), 64.

84. Scott Herring, *Lines on the Land: Writers, Art, and the National Parks* (Charlotte: University of Virginia Press, 2004), 10. For all the etchings, see Nathaniel P. Langford, "The Wonders of the Yellowstone," *Scribner's Monthly* 2, nos. 1 and 2 (May 1871): 1–17, (June 1871): 113–28, available online at http://cdl.library.cornell.edu/moa/browse.journals/scmo.html.

85. President, Northern Pacific, quoted in Haines, *Yellowstone National Park*, 101. Diary available at http://www.nps.gov/yell/historyculture/thomasmoransdiary.htm.

86. For the way Moran and Jackson collaborated, see Mary Panzer, "Great Pictures of the 1871 Expedition: Thomas Moran, William Henry Jackson, and *The Grand Canyon of the Yellowstone*," in *Splendors of the American West: Thomas Moran's Art of the Grand Canyon and Yellowstone*, ed. Anne Morand (Birmingham AL: Birmingham Museum of Art; Seattle: Distributed by the University of Washington Press, 1990), 43–58; on the way viewing public parks has been influenced by the conventions of art, photography, and museum exhibitions, see Thomas Patin, "Exhibitions and Empire: National Parks and the Performance of Manifest Destiny," *Journal of American Culture* 22, no. 1 (Spring 1999): 41–59; and Lucy R. Lippard, *On the Beaten Track: Tourism, Art and Place* (New York: New Press, 1999), 135–52. Henry T. Tuckerman, *Book of the Artists* (New York: G. P. Putnam and Son, 1867), 371.

87. Moran quoted in George W. Sheldon, *American Painters* (New York: Benjamin Blom, 1972), 124, 125–26.

88. Brett quoted in Barbara Novak, *Nature and Culture: American Landscape and Painting, 1825–1875* (New York: Oxford University Press, 1980), 254.

89. For the Borghese attribution, see Herring, *Lines on the Land*, 27.

90. Jackson quoted in Wilkins, *Thomas Moran*, 52.

91. Another, far darker reason Congress might have acted with such eagerness is that the *Grand Canyon* is not a "pure landscape" at all but a painting that documents the *transformation* of the West into pure landscape. Although it is so concealed in the woods of the left foreground as to be invisible in most reproductions, Moran has actually included the figure of an Indian with a slain deer; while farther away, in silhouette, are two figures usually taken to be Hayden and Moran himself gazing out at the scene before them. Deliberately or not, this juxtaposition represents the arc of history in which Indians were gradually erased from the wilderness to preserve it as scenery. See, for instance, Mark David Spence, *Dispossessing the Wilderness: Indian Removal and the Making of the National Parks* (New York: Oxford University Press, 1999).

92. *New York Herald* quoted in Haines, *Yellowstone National Park*, 128.

93. Flint, *Recollections*, 79.

94. William Cullen Bryant, ed., *Picturesque America: or, The Land We Live In* (New York: D. Appleton and Company, 1872–74), all quotes from the preface.

95. Twain, *Roughing It*, 130.

PART 2. WESTWARD THE COURSE OF EMPIRE

1. Henry David Thoreau, "Walking," in Witherall, *Collected Essays and Poems*, 231, 229, 233–34 (emphasis added).

2. William Cullen Bryant, "Thanatopsis," in *The Poetical Works of William Cullen Bryant*, ed. Henry C. Sturges (New York: D. Appleton and Company, 1929), 22; Jonathan Carver, *Three Years Travels throughout the Interior Parts of North America* (Charlestown: Printed by Samuel Ethridge for West and Greenleaf, 1802), 8, 46. For the general background to this history, see Ronda, *Finding the West*, 1–37; James P. Ronda, "Passion and Imagination in the Exploration of the American West," in *A Companion to the American West*, ed. William Deverell (Malden MA: Blackwell, 2004), 53–76; Charles A. Miller, *Jefferson and Nature: An Interpretation* (Baltimore MD: Johns Hopkins University Press, 1988), 235–36; and Alan Taylor, "Securing America: Jefferson's Fluid Plans for the Western Perimeter," in *Across the Continent: Jefferson, Lewis and Clark, and the Making of America*, ed. Douglas Seefeldt, Jeffrey L. Hantman, and Peter S. Onuf (Charlottesville: University of Virginia Press, 2005), 45–83.

3. See Thomas R. Hietala, *Manifest Design: American Exceptionalism and Empire* (Ithaca NY: Cornell University Press, 2003), 10–54, 71–83, 230–39.

4. Benton, "Occupation of the Mouth of the Oregon," in *Register of Debates in Congress*, 18th Cong., 2nd sess., March 1, 1825, 709–13.

5. Charles de Secondat, baron de Montesquieu, *The Spirit of the Laws*, ed. and trans. Anne M. Cohler, Basia Carolyn Miller, and Harold Samuel Stone (Cambridge: Cambridge University Press, 2004), 124, 283; Charles de Secondat, baron de Montesquieu, *Considerations on the Causes of the Greatness of the Romans and Their Decline*, trans. David Lowenthal (New York: Free Press, 1965), 94–95.

6. General Court and Mather quoted in Peter N. Carroll, *Puritanism and the Wilderness: The Intellectual Significance of the New England Frontier, 1629–1700* (New York: Columbia University Press, 1969), 217, 216.

7. Jefferson to John C. Breckinridge, August 12, 1803, Jefferson to John Taylor, May 28, 1816, Jefferson to P. S. Dupont de Nemours, April 24, 1816, and Jefferson to François de Marbois, June 14, 1817, all in Jefferson, *Writings*, 1138, 1392–93, 1387, 1410.

8. James, *Account of an Expedition*, 3:237.

9. Robert A. Caro, *The Power Broker: Robert Moses and the Fall of New York* (New York: Vintage Books, 1975), 218.

10. Turgot quoted in Emma Rothschild, *Economic Sentiments: Adam Smith, Condorcet, and the Enlightenment* (Cambridge MA: Harvard University Press, 2001), 74.

11. For two especially fine studies of the revolutionary period and its aftermath, see Drew R. McCoy, *The Elusive Republic: Political Economy in Jeffersonian America* (Chapel Hill: University of North Carolina Press, 1980) and Michael Lienesch *New Order of the Ages: Time, the Constitution, and the Making of Modern American Political Thought* (Princeton NJ: Princeton University Press, 1988).

12. C. P. Courtney, "Montesquieu and Natural Law," in *Montesquieu's Science of Politics: Essays on "The Spirit of the Laws,"* ed. David W. Carrithers, Michael A. Mosher, and Paul A. Rahe (Lanham MD: Rowman & Littlefield Publishers, 2001), 54.

13. Smith quoted in McCoy, *Elusive Republic*, 19; Rothschild, *Economic Sentiments*, 236, 238; Kames and Smith quoted in McCoy, *Elusive Republic*, 36–37, 38; Thoreau, *Walden*, 352.

14. McCoy, *Elusive Republic*, 20.

15. Montesquieu, *Considerations*, 39; Montesquieu, *Spirit of the Laws*, 47.

16. Mellen quoted in Bercovitch, *American Jeremiad*, 114.

17. George Berkeley, "On the Prospect of Planting Arts and Learning in America," in *The English Literatures of America: 1500–1800*, ed. Myra Jehlen and Michael Warner (New York: Routledge, 1997), 1060–61; Crèvecoeur, *Letters from an American Farmer*, 43–44.

18. Quoted in Bercovitch, *American Jeremiad*, 111. See the introduction to Iain McLean and Fiona Hewitt, eds., *Condorcet: Foundations of Social Choice and Political Theory* (Aldershot, Eng.: Edward Elgar, 1994), 3–82. Malthus quoted in John

Avery, *Progress, Poverty and Population: Re-reading Condorcet, Godwin and Malthus* (Portland OR: Frank Cass, 1997), 73.

19. John Locke, *An Essay Concerning Human Understanding* (New York: Dover Publications, 1959), 3.1.1–5, 3.6.37, 2.28.10. Obviously this was also the nominalism that Russell addressed in "Knowledge by Acquaintance and Knowledge by Description." And see Neal Wood, "*Tabula Rasa*, Social Environmentalism, and the 'English Paradigm,'" *Journal of the History of Ideas* 53 (October–December 1992): 647–68.

20. Smith quoted in Rothschild, *Economic Sentiments*, 227, 225; Antoine-Nicolas de Condorcet, *Sketch for a Historical Picture of the Progress of the Human Mind*, trans. June Barraclough (London: Weidenfeld and Nicolson, 1955), 134, 142.

21. Condorcet, *Sketch*, 4, 173, 176, 186, 181, 188, 193; Rothschild, *Economic Sentiments*, 191.

22. Rothschild, *Economic Sentiments*, 212; Jefferson to William Green Munford, June 18, 1799, and Jefferson to Jean Baptiste Say, February 1, 1804, both in Jefferson, *Writings*, 1064–66, 1144. As Rothschild notes, it was also in 1799 that Jefferson put together yet another of the many reading lists he composed over the years — a list that, in this case, included Locke's *Essay*, Smith's *Wealth of Nations*, and Condorcet's *Sketch*.

23. Benton, "Occupation," 712.

24. Major L. Wilson, "The Concept of Time and the Political Dialogue in the United States, 1828–48," *American Quarterly* 19, no. 4 (Winter 1967): 619–44, later incorporated into *Space, Time, and Freedom: The Quest for Nationality and Irrepressible Conflict 1815–1861* (Westport CT: Greenwood Press, 1974). Wilson's analysis of the dialectic between space and time has cast a long shadow. Aside from McCoy's *Elusive Republic* and Lienesch's *New Order of the Ages*, its influence can be seen in such works as Myra Jehlen, *American Incarnation: The Individual, the Nation, and the Continent* (Cambridge MA: Harvard University Press, 1986); David W. Noble, *Death of a Nation: American Culture and the End of Exceptionalism* (Minneapolis: University of Minnesota Press, 2002); and Thomas M. Allen, *A Republic in Time: Temporality and Social Imagination in Nineteenth-Century America* (Chapel Hill: University of North Carolina Press, 2008).

25. Adams, *Education of Henry Adams*, 49; Webster quoted in Wilson, "Concept of Time," 625.

26. Jackson quoted in Wilson, "Concept of Time," 632.

27. "Legislative Embodyment of Public Opinion," *United States Magazine and Democratic Review* 19, no. 98 (August 1846): 85–86; "The Whigs and the War," *American Review* 6, no. 4 (October 1847): 331, 346.

28. Hawthorne quoted in Yonatan Eyal, *The Young America Movement and the Transformation of the Democratic Party, 1828–1861* (Cambridge: Cambridge University Press, 2007), 223.

29. Jackson and Spence, *Expeditions of John Charles Frémont*, 1:121–22.

30. Benton, *Thirty Years' View*, 2:478.

31. Vernon Volpe, "The Origins of the Frémont Expeditions: John J. Abert and the Scientific Exploration of the Trans-Mississippi West," *Historian* 62, no. 2 (2000): 245–63, Poinsett and Abert quoted on 249, 250–51.

32. Irving, *Three Western Narratives*, 792.

33. Preuss, *Exploring with Frémont*, 38.

34. Howard Mumford Jones, *O Strange New World; American Culture: The Formative Years* (New York: Viking Press, 1964), 363–64.

35. Frémont, *Memoirs*, 30; Henry David Thoreau, "A Walk to Wachusett," in Witherall, *Collected Essays and Poems*, 49, 53; Elias L. Magoon, "Scenery and Mind," in *Home Book of the Picturesque*, 26.

36. William Bradford, *Of Plymouth Plantation, 1620–1647*, notes and introduction by Samuel Eliot Morison (New York: Alfred A. Knopf, 1952), 62; Elias L. Magoon, *Westward Empire: or, The Great Drama of Human Progress* (New York: Harper & Brothers, 1856), 413.

37. LeMenager, *Manifest and Other Destinies*, 12.

38. The consensus is that Frémont did, indeed, climb the peak now named for him. See the online site, http://www.longcamp.com/bob_fpk.html, which makes an especially detailed and convincing case for Frémont Peak. Indeed, www.longcamp .com is easily the best online resource for accurate and updated information about Frémont, and its author, Bob Graham, has been a helpful correspondent as well as the source of many illustrations in the book.

39. Bacon quoted in Bowen, *Empiricism and Geographical Thought*, 39, 38; Thoreau, *A Week on the Concord and Merrimack Rivers*, 295.

40. *Pinta* captain quoted in Susan Scott Parrish, *American Curiosity: Cultures of Natural History in the Colonial British Atlantic World* (Chapel Hill: University of North Carolina Press, 2006), 25, see also 41, 57, 59, 22.

41. Jefferson, "Instructions to Captain Lewis," in Jefferson, *Writings*, 1126–32.

42. See David Roberts, *A Newer World: Kit Carson, John C. Frémont, and the Claiming of the American West* (New York: Simon & Schuster, 2000), 23–49, where the entire trip to the summit is recounted as a kind of farce. It is also parodied in the "I Conquer the Gorner Grat" chapter of Mark Twain's *A Tramp Abroad* (1880), a reference again courtesy of Bob Graham.

43. See http://www.longcamp.com/bob_fpk.html.

44. "Frémont's Expeditions," 76–77.

45. Moulton, *Journals of the Lewis and Clark Expedition*, August 13, 1805.

46. Arthur M. Schlesinger, *The Age of Jackson* (Boston: Little, Brown, 1945), 291. Aside from the Harrison campaign, there is another, slightly earlier precedent for Frémont's decision to include a flag: see Nicollet, *On the Plains and Prairies*, 79, for an account of a July Fourth celebration in which Frémont was delegated to raise the flag on a freestanding bit of rock. And for an analysis of how Jessie Benton Frémont became a political symbol during Frémont's own campaign for president, see David Grant, "'Our Nation's Hope Is She': The Cult of Jessie Frémont in the Republican Campaign Poetry of 1856," *Journal of American Studies* 43, no. 2 (2008): 187–213.

47. Bercovitch, *American Jeremiad*, 124, Sherwood quoted on 125.

48. Patricia Cline Cohen, *A Calculating People: The Spread of Numeracy in Early America* (New York: Routledge, 1999), 155, 169, 173; O'Sullivan quoted in Edward L. Widmer, *Young America: The Flowering of Democracy in New York City* (New York: Oxford University Press, 1999), 51. It is now apparent that "more" was an especially fungible notion. Hietala, *Manifest Design*, 27–29, 110–11, notes that after the 1840 census proved the population was doubling every twenty-three years or so, the mantra of "more people" morphed into an almost frenzied campaign for more land. For a splendid analysis of the nexus between population and expansion, see Nugent, *Habits of Empire*. Seybert quoted in Cohen, *A Calculating People*, 168.

49. Lienesch, *New Order of the Ages*, 202; Stephanson, *Manifest Destiny*, 12, 19; Cooper quoted in Weinberg, *Manifest Destiny*, 18–19; Parker quoted in Stephanson, *Manifest Destiny*, 54; Gardiner quoted in Lienesch, *New Order of the Ages*, 21. It is here, in the claims of Cooper, Parker, and Gardiner (not to mention Jefferson's republicanism founded "not on conquest, but in principles of compact and equality"), that we see how much Frémont's nexus of science and expansionism added to the way colonial Americans had, in the words of Tennenhouse, *The Importance of Feeling English*, 17, "shifted the source of imperial authority from political policy, or *translatio imperii*, to education — the domain of *translatio studii*" (a shift he also identifies with the way in which Americans chose to interpret Berkeley's "westward the course of empire takes its way").

50. Eyal, *Young America Movement*, 34 (emphasis added), 166.

51. George S. Burleigh, *Signal Fires on the Trail of the Pathfinder* (New York: Dayton and Burdick, 1856), 51–53; Joaquin Miller, *Overland in a Covered Wagon*, ed. Sidney Firman (New York: D. Appleton and Company, 1930), 42–43.

52. John Bigelow, *Memoir of the Life and Public Services of John Charles Frémont* (New York: Derby and Jackson, 1856), 54–55.

53. Even if Frémont did make the incident up, there's an intriguing possibility it was still inspired by real events. See Frémont, *Memoirs*, 58–59, where he describes an episode in which he and Nicollet carry out a series of night observations on a hill overlooking the Potomac.

54. John Cotton, "Gods Promise to His Plantations," in *Old South Leaflets* 3, no. 53 (Boston, [1896]), 8; Cooper, *Prairie*, 65; Flint, *Recollections*, 140–41.

55. James, *Account of an Expedition*, 3:12. Chaffin, *Pathfinder*, 144–45, makes much the same point; but, like Bigelow, he conflates the conflicting images of the bee, which are discussed below, into a single image of "the bee-as-advance scout."

56. Cooper, *Prairie*, 65, 101, 376. It is more than possible that Cooper was inspired to write his account of bee hunting by recalling a similar account in Crèvecoeur's *Letters from an American Farmer*. If so, it would be yet another reminder of the way prairies differed from forests.

57. Bryant, "The Prairies," in Sturges, *Poetical Works*, 130–33.

58. Irving, *Three Western Narratives*, 40–43.

59. For a somewhat contrary view of this episode, see Peter Antelyes, *Tales of Adventurous Enterprise: Washington Irving and the Poetics of Western Expansion* (New York: Columbia University Press, 1990), 124–27.

60. Magoon, "Scenery and Mind," 5; Browne quoted in Ernst Robert Curtius, *European Literature and the Latin Middle Ages*, trans. Willard R. Trask (Princeton NJ: Princeton University Press, 1953), 323.

61. See Arthur O. Lovejoy, *The Great Chain of Being: A Study of the History of an Idea* (Cambridge MA: Harvard University Press, 1964); Locke, *Essay*, 3.6.12.

62. John O'Sullivan, introduction to *United States Magazine and Democratic Review* 1, no. 1 (October 1837): 1–15, and quoted in Widmer, *Young America*, 39–40; quoted in Richard V. Francaviglia and Jimmy L. Bryan Jr., "'Are We Chimerical in This Opinion?': Visions of a Pacific Railroad and Westward Expansion before 1845," *Pacific Historical Review* 71, no. 2 (May 2002): 187, 185–86; Ruggles, Webster, and Stevenson quoted in Wilson, *Space, Time and Freedom*, 56, 96, 67.

63. For a sense of how this reenacts narratives of "anti-conquest," see Pratt, *Imperial Eyes*, 37–83. It is telling that Frémont resorts to the apparent innocence and passivity of specimen collection precisely at the point he wishes to rebut Irving's tale of aggressive expansion gone awry.

64. Henry Tuckerman, "Over the Mountains, Or the Western Pioneer," in *Home Book of the Picturesque*, 115. Stephan Oettermann, *The Panorama: History of a Mass Medium* (New York: Zone Books, 1997), 322, has looked to this "immensity" to explain why Americans preferred the scrolling panorama to the fixed, circular model popular in Europe. "For Europeans," he writes, a "360-degree vista" represented "an

enormous expansion of perspective. Americans on the other hand, were dealing with dimensions" that "could not be grasped or conquered simply by climbing to an elevated point of view and surveying the horizon."

65. Irving, *Three Western Narratives*, 790–92.

66. Denis Cosgrove, *Apollo's Eye: A Cartographic Genealogy of the Earth in the Western Imagination* (Baltimore MD: Johns Hopkins University Press, 2001), x, 2.

67. J. L. Allen, "Division of the Waters: Changing Concepts of the Continental Divide, 1804–44," *Journal of Historical Geography* 4, no. 4 (1978): 370; Daniel J. Boorstin, *Cleopatra's Nose: Essays on the Unexpected*, ed. Ruth F. Boorstin (New York: Random House, 1994), 3–17. Chaffin, *Pathfinder*, 140–42, also includes a discussion of Frémont's achievement but without relating it to either Jefferson's *Notes* or Irving's *Bonneville*.

68. Benton quoted in Smith, *Virgin Land*, 25; Horace Bushnell, "The Day of Roads," in *Work and Play* (New York: Charles Scribner's Sons, 1910), 429–30.

69. Cosgrove, *Apollo's Eye*, 11.

70. For a comparison to the way summit views usually emphasized the visual, see Albert Boime, *The Magisterial Gaze: Manifest Destiny and American Landscape Painting, c. 1830–1865* (Washington DC: Smithsonian Institution Press, 1991); also see Pratt, *Imperial Eyes*, 200–204.

71. Cosgrove, *Apollo's Eye*, 27.

72. Magoon, "Scenery and Mind," 2. Magoon uses this word while affirming a theory of knowledge taken directly from Locke's *Essay*: "The diversified landscapes of our country exert no slight influence in creating our character as individuals, and in confirming our destiny as a nation" (3).

73. Ellen Churchill Semple, *American History and Its Geographical Condition* (Boston: Houghton Mifflin Company, 1903), 232; Bruce A. Harvey, *American Geographics: U.S. National Narratives and the Representation of the Non-European World, 1830–1865* (Stanford CA: Stanford University Press, 2001), 21; Brückner, *Geographic Revolution*, 101–7.

74. Harvey, *American Geographics*, 28, Mitchell and Savage quoted on 36.

75. Denis Wood and John Fels, *The Natures of Maps: Cartographic Constructions of the Natural World* (Chicago: University of Chicago Press, 2008), xvi, 7. There is an often-quoted passage in Frémont, *Memoirs*, 64, which implies that he would never tolerate an incomplete cartography. Describing the hydrographical map being compiled after the second Nicollet expedition, Frémont writes: "The making of such a map is an interesting process. It must be exact. First the foundations must be laid in observations made in the field; then the reduction of these observations to latitude and longitude; afterward the projection of the map, and the laying down upon it of

positions fixed by the observations; then the tracing from the sketch-books of the lines of the rivers, the forms of the lakes, the contours of the hills." But the *Report* occupies a special place in the history of the nation, and it seems clear that Frémont was temporarily willing to forgo specificity if it allowed him to create a projection that mapped a new nation onto a partially explored continent.

76. Weinberg, *Manifest Destiny*, 50. To understand the map Frémont had in mind all along, see Frémont, *Exploring Expedition*, 3–4.

77. George Kateb, "Aestheticism and Morality: Their Cooperation and Hostility," *Political Theory* 28, no. 1 (February 2000): 5–35; Walter Benjamin, "The Work of Art in the Age of Mechanical Reproduction," in *Illuminations*, ed. Hannah Arendt (New York: Schocken, 1969), 242.

78. Rothschild, *Economic Sentiments*, 137, and see 228–36; Rufus Wilmot Griswold, *The Prose Writers of America* (Philadelphia: Carey & Hart, 1847), 52.

79. Melish quoted in Brückner, *Geographic Revolution*, 258, 259, *North American Review* essay quotes from 239, 263.

80. Burnett, *Masters of All They Surveyed*, 65; resolution quoted in Walter W. Ristow, "Simeon De Witt, Pioneer American Cartographer," in *Kartengeschichte und Kartenbearbeitung*, ed. Karl-Heinz Meine (Bad Godesburg: Kirschbaum Verlag, 1968), 107; Caroline Kirkland, *A New Home, Who'll Follow? or Glimpses of Western Life*, ed. Sandra A. Zagarell (New Brunswick NJ: Rutgers University Press, 1990), 12, 30–31.

81. Thoreau, *Walden*, 549–55. Laura Dassow Walls, *Seeing New Worlds: Henry David Thoreau and Nineteenth-Century Science* (Madison: University of Wisconsin Press, 1995), 110–11, has suggested that the *Report* either influenced or provoked Thoreau's measurement of Walden Pond. More recently, Anne Baker, *Heartless Immensity: Literature, Culture, and Geography in Antebellum America* (Ann Arbor: University of Michigan Press, 2006), 44–63, has more specifically linked Thoreau's measurement to Frémont's survey of the Great Salt Lake.

82. William Gilpin, *Mission of the North American People: Geographical, Social, and Political* (New York: Da Capo Press, 1974), 124.

83. Bercovitch, *American Jeremiad*, 23.

84. Leonard Lutwack, *The Role of Place in Literature* (Syracuse NY: Syracuse University Press, 1984), 43, has noted that "one of the most satisfying narrative motifs is the journey of the hero from a central place to a number of outlying places and from them back to the starting point." The *Report* relies on this pleasure to some extent but also undercuts its unity and wholeness by treating the mouth of the Kansas — a site central to the continent but peripheral to the nation — as Frémont's point of departure and return. In effect, the *Report* displaces the existing center by creating a new center — which must, however, still be realized.

85. Linn quoted in Frémont, *Memoirs*, 164; *Niles National Register* quoted in Chaffin, *Pathfinder*, 146. Chaffin is one of many to point out that the *Report* exerted an influence that quickly exceeded the thousand extra copies printed for Congress, mostly because it was so quickly excerpted in newspapers and magazines whose circulation made it available to millions of Americans. Its greatest effect may have been to set in motion an entirely new pattern of emigration. A fairly recent study—Robert E. Lang, Deborah Epstein Popper, and Frank J. Popper, "'Progress of the Nation': The Settlement History of the Enduring American Frontier," *Western Historical Quarterly* 26, no. 3 (Autumn 1995): 292—cites the 1890 census to show that after 1840 or so, the nation began to relinquish its habit of *gradually* occupying the frontier in favor of a more "western style" of emigration where "Americans leapfrogged to particular, limited locations, creating more remote nodes and scattered corridors of population."

86. Benton quoted in Frémont, "Biographical Sketch," 16.

87. Young quoted in Frémont, *Memoirs*, 415; Jessie Benton Frémont quoted in Jackson and Spence, *Expeditions of John Charles Frémont*, 1:xxi.

88. Nevins, *Frémont*, 621.

89. Emerson, "The Young American," 395; Widmer, *Young America*, 6; O'Sullivan, introduction, also quoted in Widmer, *Young America*, 42, Field quoted on 22.

90. Widmer, *Young America*, 12; Emerson, "The Young American," 370, 364, 363, 370–71.

91. It may be impossible to know when Emerson first read Frémont. There is a reference to Frémont in a journal entry from 1846, and elsewhere Emerson notes that he purchased the combined report in May 1846. But with all the coverage it received at the time, he had to have been aware of the *Report*, if only in the form of a review. Moreover, the *Report* focused almost exclusively on the kind of topographic geology that would encourage someone to call the region "the nervous, rocky West." See Ralph Waldo Emerson, *The Journals and Miscellaneous Notebooks of Ralph Waldo Emerson*, vol. 8 (1841–43), ed. Ralph Orth and Alfred R. Ferguson, vol. 9 (1843–47), ed. William H. Gilman and J. E. Parsons (Cambridge MA: Harvard University Press, 1970, 1971).

92. Recently, Mark Rifkin, *Manifesting America: The Imperial Construction of U.S. National Space* (New York: Oxford University Press, 2009), has argued that the inherent contradictions of a nation annexing territory it supposedly had a right to as a matter of propinquity and the "excellence of divine principles" led to a legal justification for removing both Indians and Mexicans which stressed that they had voluntarily "acquiesced" to their removal in the name of universal freedom. O'Sullivan's "great nation of futurity" seems to share this illusion of peaceful expansion.

93. O'Sullivan quoted in Widmer, *Young America*, 45; Eyal, *Young America Movement*, 65–66, 71, 69.

94. Francaviglia and Bryan, "'Are We Chimerical,'" 181.

95. "Railroads," *United States Magazine and Democratic Review* 21, no. 112 (October 1847): 342.

96. Jefferson, "Instructions to Captain Lewis," in Jefferson, *Writings*, 1127; Flint, *Recollections*, 79.

97. Asa Whitney, *A Project for a Railroad to the Pacific* (New York: George W. Wood, 1849), 5, 7, 33; Breese quoted in Whitney, *Project for a Railroad*, 45.

98. Harvey, *American Geographics*, 28; Whitney quoted in David Haward Bain, *Empire Express: Building the First Transcontinental Railroad* (New York: Viking, 1999), 29; Mills quoted in Francaviglia and Bryan, "'Are We Chimerical,'" 195–96.

99. Gunther S. Stent, "Meaning in Art and Science," in *The Origin of Creativity*, ed. Karl H. Pfenninger, Valerie R. Shubik, and Bruce Adolphe (New York: Oxford University Press, 2001), 31–42.

100. Rev. Calvin Colton, *A Lecture on the Railroad to the Pacific. Delivered, August 12, 1850, at the Smithsonian Institute, Washington. At the Request of Numerous Members of Both House of Congress* (New York: A. S. Barnes & Company, 1850), 14, 9.

101. "Pacific Rail-road," *United States Magazine and Democratic Review* 27, no. 150 (December 1850): 537; "California," *American Review*, 332.

102. "Railroad to the Pacific," *United States Magazine and Democratic Review* 25, no. 135 (September 1849): 243; "California," *American Review*, 332–33; Madison quoted in Hietala, *Manifest Design*, 183.

103. Gilpin, *Mission of the North American People*, 34, 49, 55, 64, 67, 68–69, 104, 183.

104. Jefferson to William Ludlow, September 6, 1824, in Jefferson, *Writings*, 1496–97. For a discussion of panoramas and progress, see Baker, *Heartless Immensity*, 69–76.

105. "Emanuel Leutze's notes describing *Westward the Course of Empire Takes Its Way* (c. 1862)," available at http://www.fandm.edu/x10244.xml.

106. Whitney, *Project for a Railroad*, 13, 39; Thoreau, *Walden*, 416. As Anderson, *Imagined Communities*, 191, has cogently pointed out, Americans generally sought to demolish the British Empire by "rearranging its internal distribution of power, *reversing* the previous relationship of subjection," so that the center of power was transferred "from a European to an American site." For example, Walter A. McDougall, *Promised Land, Crusader State: The American Encounter with the World since 1776* (Boston: Mariner Books, 1997), 98, recounts a popular joke of the time in which three Americans abroad toast their native land. The first says, "Here's to the United States—bounded on the north by British America, on the south by the Gulf

of Mexico, on the east by the Atlantic, and on the west by the Pacific Ocean." The second counters, "Here's to the United States—bounded on the north by the North Pole, on the south by the South Pole, on the east by the rising, and on the west by the setting sun." The third concludes, "I give you the United States—bounded on the north by the Aurora Borealis, on the south by the precession of the equinoxes, on the east by the primeval chaos, and on the west by the Day of Judgment!"

107. "Pacific Rail-road," 540; Walt Whitman, *Specimen Days*, and "Pioneers! O Pioneers!," both in *The Portable Walt Whitman*, ed. Mark Van Doren (New York: Penguin Books, 1977), 576, 211; Whitman quoted in Perry Miller, *Nature's Nation* (Cambridge M A: Harvard University Press, 1967), 2.

108. "Railroads," 342; "California," *American Review*, 331.

109. Eugene Lies, "Westward, Ho!," *United States Magazine and Democratic Review* 24, no. 127 (January 1849): 43.

110. Whitney, *Project for a Railroad*, 39; Colton, *Lecture on the Railroad*, 14, 15, 3, 15.

111. Allen, *Republic in Time*, 32.

112. For another instance of a western icon morphing into an image of outright imperialism, see Richard Slotkin, "Buffalo Bill's 'Wild West' and the Mythologization of the American Empire," in *Cultures of United States Imperialism*, ed. Amy Kaplan and Donald E. Pease (Durham N C: Duke University Press, 1993), 164–81, which relates how "Custer's Last Fight," traditionally the final episode in Cody's reenactment of western history, was replaced in 1899 by the "Battle of San Juan Hill."

AFTERWORD

1. Frémont, *Memoirs*, 163, 414.

2. Frémont, *Memoirs*, 163; Jessie Benton Frémont quoted in Nevins, *Frémont*, 118–19.

3. Nevins, *Frémont*, 118; Pamela Herr, *Jessie Benton Frémont: A Biography* (New York: Franklin Watts, 1987), 82; Fender, *Plotting the Golden West*, 45.

4. Bigelow, *Memoir*, 25.

5. Frémont, "Biographical Sketch," 6; quoted in Catherine Coffin Phillips, *Jessie Benton Frémont: A Woman Who Made History* (1935; Lincoln: University of Nebraska Press, 1995), 68.

6. Frémont, *Memoirs*, 66.

7. Herr, *Jessie Benton Frémont*, 82, 81.

Index

Cooper, James Fenimore, xiii, xxi, 17, 18, 24, 25, 60, 87, 116, 162; *The Prairie*, 11–12, 17, 35, 83, 150, 151, 152
Courthouse Rock, xxvii, 42, 71–73, 77
Crèvecoeur, Hector St. John de, 7, 116, 207

Davis, Jefferson, xiv, xv
Democratic Party, xix, 103, 122–23, 146–47, 152, 185–86, 190, 197, 205, 206, 207
Devil's Gate, xxvii, 42, 55, 58, *59*, 92, *94*
Devil's Slide, 83, *84*, 92, *93*
double negative, 41–43, 47, 68, 70–71, 91, 172, 230n50

Emerson, Ralph Waldo, 7, 18, 21, 25, 27, 46, 47, 48, 68, 171, 185–86, 242n91
emigrants, xii, xxi, xxvii, xxviii, 52, 56, 62, 64, 72, 75, 97, 125, 126, 178, 188, 203
emigration, xxvi, 34, 103, 125, 149, 178, 184, 186, 197, 242n85
empiricism, 34–35, 44, 117, 134–41, 143, 144

Filson, John, xv–xviii, 22, 33
Flint, Timothy, xv, xvii, xxiv–xxv, 3–5, 12–13, 35, 91, 138, 150, 192
Fort Laramie, xxvi, xxvii, 39, 56, 58, 63, 70, 143
Frémont, Jessie Benton, xxii, 184, 213–19
Frémont, John Charles: aesthetic cravings and, xxix, 158–73, 174, 175, 176, 177–78; Apollonian or geographic gaze of, 160, 165, 166, 167, 169, 194; Asa Whitney and, 191–95; authorship of *Report* and, 213–19; barometer and, 31, 36, 38, 51, 56–57, 126–28, 131, 132, 134–40, 144, 164, 165; bee and, 131–32, 134, 147–58, 239n53; California and, xxi–xxii, 178, 179–80, 183, 187; Continental Divide and,

xxi, xxix, 55, 56, 97, 159–62, 163, 165, 168–69, 183, 195, 197, 204, 211; credibility of, 34–35, 134–35, 138, 148, 192, 217; defining the *Report*, xxi, xxvi–xxix, 223–24n22; double negative of, 41–43, 46, 47, 172, 230n50; early life of, xxv, 29–30, 215; on eastern Kansas, 35–41, 42, 43, 52–53, 54, 55, 87, 91, 168; empiricism of, 34–35, 44–46, 47, 49, 50, 135–41, 144; flag and, 131, 134, 141–44, 147, 160, 164, *180*, *181*, *182*, 188, 209, 238n46; geography and, xxvi, xxvii–xxix, 42–43, 45–46, 96–97, 126–28, 145, 160–62, 163, 166, 167, 169, 175, 177, 195, 199, 218; geometric imagination of, 26, 34, 56, 168; Great Desert and, xxix, 14–15, 26, 42, 46, 47–50, 62, 64, 96–97, 130, 134, 166, 167, 169, 174, 179, 231–32n63; John O'Sullivan and, 184–85, 187, 188–90; Joseph N. Nicollet and, xxv, xxvi, 30, 31, 32–33, 38, 217, 239n53; Manifest Destiny and, xxix, 160, 169, 172, 177, 178, 179, 180, 184–85, 205–11; maps and, xxi, xxv, xxvi, xxvii, xxix, 29–30, 33, 34, 38, 42, 65, 140, 144, 159, 162, 163–69, 173–76, 179, 184, 189, 191–92, 194–95, 217, 228–29n38, 240–41n75, 241n76; Oregon and, xxi, xxii, xxvi, xxvii, 14, 56, 57, 97, 103, 108, 125–26, 140, 178, 179, 183, 188; photography of, 57–58; picturesque of, xxix, 15, 26–28, 33, 34, 44, 45, 63–64, 95, 135, 195, 205; progress and, 123, 141, 143–44, 146–47, 149, 154, 157, 168, 176, 177–78, 180, 183, 210–11; river navigation and, 102, 125, 127, 176–77, 192, 218; second and third expeditions of, xxi–xxii, 14, 74, 91, 162, 179, 187, 191, 199, 223–24n22; South Pass and, xxvi, xxvii, 27, 39, 55–57, 58, 63, 71, 72, 97, 104, 125–27, 142, 157, 168, 191,

193; Stephen Long and, 14, 15, 32, 35, 38, 44, 45, 46, 47, 49, 50, 51, 76, 130, 132, 134, 139, 142, 160, 161, 194; style of, 14–15, 33–34, 38–57, 72–73, 195, 214–19, 227–28n29, 228n37, 229n39, 229n42, 230n51; Thomas Hart Benton and, xxii, xiv–xxvi, 30, 31, 125–26, 127, 142, 180; topographic geology of, 27–28, 51, 57, 58, 64, 130, 134, 163, 188, 242n91; transcontinental railroad and, xxix, 180, 184, 185, 192–93, 194–95, 196–98, 203; Washington Irving and, 61, 62–63, 127–28, 130, 139, 154, 157–58, 159–62, 164, 165; Wind River summit and, xxi, xxvi, xxvii, 26–27, 57, 58, 97, 126–27, 130, 131–34, 142, 146, 147, 158, 159–60, 168, 176, 180–83, 201–3, 237n38; Zebulon Pike and, 14, 15, 32, 35, 38, 40, 44, 46, 49, 50, 76, 96, 130, 134, 146, 151, 194

Frenière, Louison, 33, 217

Gadsden Purchase, xix, 41, 179

geography, 30, 31, 41, 46, 101, 102, 125, 126, 145, 162, 164, 166, 167, 193–94, 218; defining U.S. as national entity, xi–xv, xviii, xxiii–xxiv, 5–7, 104–9, 120–23, 160, 173–75, 200; defining U.S.'s continental center, 185, 190, 194–95, 198, 200–205, 241n84, 243n106; and garden of the world, 10, 138, 231–32n63; geographical predestination and, xxiii, xxix, 7, 8, 97, 211; golden meane and, xxii, xxiv, 193, 199; John Frémont and, xxvi, xxvii–xxix, 42–43, 45–46, 96–97, 126–28, 145, 160–62, 163, 166, 167, 169, 175, 177, 195, 199, 218; latitude and longitude and, xi–xv, xxi, xxiii–xxiv, 6, 30, 68, 92, 96, 141, 144, 163, 174, 180, 191, 194, 199, 205; lay of the land and, xxix, 6–8, 56, 63, 96, 130, 195; maps

and, xi–xii, xiii, xxii, xxiv, 4, 11, 13, 31, 47, 91, 102, 128, 162, 163, 166–67, 173–75, 179, 188, 194, 198; national grid and, xi, xiii, 79, 105, 106, 107, 114–15, 174; propinquity and, 5, 8, 15, 76, 87, 96, 169, 189, 242n92; westward course of empire and, xix, 115–17, 123, 130, 151–52, 194, 200–205, 207, 210, 238n49; "Zona temperata" and, xii, xxiv, 111

geology, xvi–xvii, 31, 39, 47, 75–77, 79, 232n77; art and, 27–28, 69–70, 88; history and, 64, 77

Gilpin, William (clergyman/aesthetician), 20, 23, 222n9

Gilpin, William (in Frémont's second expedition), 176, 199–200

"Gods Promise to His Plantations" (Cotton), 129, 149, 177

gold rush, xxii, 65, 71, 179

Goshen's Hole, xxvii, 62–63, 72, 77

Great Basin, 140, 162, 231–32n63

great chain of being, 156–57

Great Desert, xxix, 12–13, 32, 47, 50, 62, 64, 89, 95, 96, 97, 138, 166, 167, 179, 184, 199, 225n11, 225n15, 228–29n38, 230n50, 231–32n63; as barrier to the nation, 7–11, 13–14, 15, 42, 97, 130, 134, 160, 169, 174, 189, 197; John Frémont and, xxix, 14–15, 26, 42, 46, 47–50, 62, 64, 96–97, 130, 134, 166, 167, 169, 174, 179, 231–32n63; self-similarity and, 9–10, 26–27; sublime and, 12–13, 67–68

Green River near Flaming Gorge (O'Sullivan), 79, *80*

Gregg, Josiah, 4, 13, 40, 50, 51, 138

Hakluyt, Richard, xii–xiii, xxii, xxvi, 192, 199

Hayden, Ferdinand V., 76, 79–81, 85

Hitchcock, Edward, 25, 227n26